GNOSTICISM

The Doctrinal Foundation Of the New Bible Versions

2 Thessalonians 2:7

"For the mystery of iniquity doth already work: he who now letteth will let, until he be taken out of the way."

By Mrs. Janet Moser
28819 West Kalong Circle
Southfield, Michigan 48034

Put in digital format
By Pastor Miguel Maciel
Sent By Col. Pedro Almeida
Of Brazil, July, 2013

The digital format corrected for scanning misprints
By Pastor D. A. Waite, Th.D., Ph.D.
900 Park Avenue, Collingswood, New Jersey 08108 USA
Completed And Published, February, 2014

Published by

THE BIBLE FOR TODAY PRESS

900 Park Avenue
Collingswood, New Jersey 08108
U.S.A.

Pastor D. A. Waite, Th.D., Ph.D.

Bible For Today Baptist Church

Church Phone: 856-854-4747

BFT Phone: 856-854-4452

Orders: 1-800-John 10:9

e-mail: BFT@BibleForToday.org

Website: www.BibleForToday.org

Fax: 856-854-2464

We Use and Defend

The King James Bible

March, 2014

BFT 4088

Copyright, 2014
All Rights Reserved

ISBN #978-1-56848-099-2

Cover Design and Publishing facilitated by:
The Old Paths Publications, Inc.
www.theoldpathspublications.com
706-865-0153

PUBLISHER/EDITOR'S FOREWORD

December 29, 1996

This study was made by Mrs. Janet Moser who lived in Southfield, Michigan, who has passed on to her reward in Heaven. She was first introduced to the truths about the superiority of the King James Bible and the Masoretic Hebrew, Aramaic, and Greek Textus Receptus that underlies it by listening to this writer on a radio broadcast. The program was hosted by Miss Barbara Egan. It is called "LET'S GO VISITING." Barbara interviewed me on that broadcast about my book, *DEFENDING THE KING JAMES BIBLE*. Upon hearing the broadcast, Mrs. Moser contacted me. Later on, she came for a visit with her husband and another couple to the home of Mrs. Waite and me. They purchased many books and materials from our BIBLE FOR TODAY and returned to their home in Michigan.

When she began looking into the heresies of Westcott and Hort, she became interested in some of their views relating to Gnosticism. From this interest, she began a search which has resulted in this study. I persuaded her to let us have it as it is, so that others might begin to see what she had found out through her intensive study. Because Mrs. Moser suffered from a severe allergic condition, she remained in a sympathetic environment such as her home. Her home was her best place to be. This allowed her the time to do research, to study, and to write. We admire such a person who filled her time with important spiritual pursuits.

I have added page numbers to her study and made a TABLE OF CONTENTS so that it might be easier to see all that is contained within it. I have also added an exhaustive INDEX OF WORDS, PHRASES, AND SCRIPTURES which will enable the reader easily to look up the many details about Gnosticism that are found in this research book.

The author, Mrs. Janet Moser, is now with the Lord. I appreciate all the good research she has done in this book. It is hoped that many will profit greatly by it.

Sincerely for God's Words,

D. A. Waite

DAW/w
1 Corinthians 15:58

Pastor D. A. Waite, Th.D., Ph.D., Director
The Bible For Today, Incorporated
900 Park Avenue, Collingswood, New Jersey 08108, USA
Phone: 856-854-4727; Fax: 856-854-2464
E-Mail: BFT@BibleForToday.org
Websites: www.BibleForToday.org and
www.BibleForTodayBaptistChurch.org

ACKNOWLEDGMENTS

I wish to acknowledge and thank the following people for their assistance in this book:

- **Mrs. Janet Moser**–the original author, who spent many hours in doing this research on Gnosticism in order to warn every Bible-believing Christian of the dangers of the new versions who have founded their translations on the Gnostic Critical Greek Texts. I put her copy that she sent me into print several years ago and have distributed it widely. In this present format, her work has now been placed in a digital format so it can be more easily distributed.

- **Pastor Miguel Maciel**–from Brazil, who received Mrs. Moser's book and wanted to translate it into Portuguese. He first scanned the book into English and sent me a copy of his scanned English copy which I have used. I have cleared up any imperfections that were found in the scanned copy that he sent to me.

- **Col. Pedro Almeida**–also from Brazil, who is one of our Dean Burgon Society Executive Committee members and a friend of mine for many years. He told me about Pastor Miguel's work and sent the digital English files to me little by little as he scanned the original English document. Col. Almeida is helping Pastor Maciel with his Portuguese translation.

- **Yvonne Sanborn Waite**–my wife, for allowing me to take so many hours at my desk, away from her, in order to get this book into proper digital format and as free from mistakes as possible.

- **Anne Marie Noyle**–from Canada, who is a member of our 𝕭𝖎𝖇𝖑𝖊 𝖋𝖔𝖗 𝕿𝖔𝖉𝖆𝖞 𝕭𝖆𝖕𝖙𝖎𝖘𝖙 𝕮𝖍𝖚𝖗𝖈𝖍. She has volunteered scores of hours to go through the scanned digital copy several times and to make important suggestions in order to correct any imperfections that were found in Pastor Miguel's scanned copy. I have taken her recommendations and have made the needed corrections for entry into this present edition of *GNOSTICISM: THE DOCTRINAL FOUNDATION OF THE NEW BIBLE VERSIONS*.

- **Dr. Kirk DiVietro**–Vice President of the Dean Burgon Society, and longtime friend, who took the three pictures, scanned by Mrs. Noyle, (Figures 4, 4.1, and 5) and skillfully placed them into the digital text of the book.

- **The Lord Jesus Christ**–Who has saved those of us who have genuinely trusted in Him for salvation. He Who is "*the Way, the Truth, and the Life*" has put within our hearts to spread the truths that are in this book to the ends of the earth. May the Lord Jesus Christ use our labors for His glory!

TABLE OF CONTENTS

GNOSTICISM: THE MYSTERY OF INIQUITY

2 Thessalonians 2:7

"For the mystery of iniquity doth already work: only He who now letteth will let until He be taken out of the way."

This study is dedicated to our Lord Jesus Christ, the One who has hindered the heresies of Gnosticism through the preserved Traditional Hebrew, Aramaic, and Greek Words underlying the King James Bible which that Bible has faithfully translated into English. The King James Bible, because of its clear teachings, is the foremost foe of the philosophy and theology of Gnosticism anywhere to be found.

Irenaeus (130-202 A.D.) as a Roman Catholic theologian had many heresies of his own. Because of this, we cannot support him for the most part. I am glad, however, for at least two things about his positions and we are able to support: (1) He used, approved of and supported the Traditional Greek New Testament Textus Receptus in most of his quotations; and (2) He was also a strong opponent of Gnosticism. (See Dr. Jack Moorman's book, *Early Manuscripts, Church Father, and the Authorized Version*, page 348. It is available as **BFT #3230 @ $20.00 + $8.00 S&H**.) Because of his opposition to Gnosticism (and only for that purpose), we are quoting some of Irenaeus' statements.

These quotes are found in Book #33, pp. 315-316, 358:

> *"Inasmuch as certain men have set the truth aside, and bring in lying words . . . I have felt constrained, my dear friend, to compose the following treatise in order to expose and counteract their machinations. **THESE MEN FALSIFY THE ORACLES OF GOD**, and prove themselves evil interpreters of the good word of revelation. They also overthrow the faith of many, by drawing them away, under a pretense of superior knowledge, from Him Who founded and adorned the universe; as if, forsooth, they had something more excellent and sublime to reveal. . . by means of specious and plausible words, they cunningly allure the simple minded to inquire into their system; but they nevertheless clumsily destroy them, while they initiate them into their blasphemous and impious opinions . . . and these simple ones are unable, even in such a matter, to distinguish falsehood from truth.*
> *   **ERROR, INDEED, IS NEVER SET FORTH IN ITS NAKED DEFORMITY**, lest being thus exposed, it should at once be detected. But **IT IS CRAFTILY DECKED OUT IN AN ATTRACTIVE DRESS, SO AS**, by its outward form, **TO MAKE IT APPEAR TO THE INEXPERIENCED** (ridiculous as the expression may seem) **MORE TRUE THAN THE TRUTH ITSELF**. Lest, therefore, through my neglect, some should be carried off, even as sheep are by wolves, while **THEY PERCEIVE NOT THE TRUE CHARACTER OF THESE MEN**, because they outwardly are covered with sheep's clothing (against whom the Lord has enjoined us to be on our guard) and because their language resembles ours, while their sentiments are very different, **I HAVE DEEMED IT MY DUTY (AFTER READING SOME OF THE COMMENTARIES** . . . and after making **MYSELF ACQUAINTED WITH THEIR TENETS** . . .) **TO UNFOLD TO THEE, MY FRIEND, THESE PORTENTOUS AND PROFOUND MYSTERIES . . . I DO THIS, IN ORDER THAT THOU**, obtaining an acquaintance with these things, **MAYEST IN TURN***

EXPLAIN THEM TO ALL THOSE WITH WHOM THOU ART CONNECTED, AND EXHORT THEM TO AVOID SUCH AN ABYSS OF MADNESS AND OF BLASPHEMY AGAINST CHRIST. I INTEND, THEN, TO THE BEST OF MY ABILITY, WITH BREVITY AND CLEARNESS TO SET FORTH THE OPINIONS OF THOSE WHO ARE NOW PROMULGATING HERESY . . . *I shall also endeavor, according to my moderate ability, to furnish the means of overthrowing them, by showing how absurd and inconsistent with the truth are their statements. Not that I am practiced either in composition or eloquence; but MY feeling of affection prompts me to make known to thee, and all thy companions, those doctrines which have been kept in concealment until now, but which are at last, through the goodness of God, brought to light.*
'For there is nothing covered, that shall not be revealed; and hid, that shall not be known' (Matthew 10:26b KJB).

Thou wilt not expect from me. . . any display of rhetoric, which I have never learned, or any excellence of composition, which I have never practiced, or any beauty and persuasiveness of style, to which I make no pretensions. But thou wilt accept in a kindly spirit what I in a like spirit write to thee simply, truthfully, in my own homely way; whilst ***THOU THYSELF*** *(as being more capable than I am)* ***WILT EXPAND THOSE IDEAS OF WHICH I SEND THEE***.

. . . *For there will not now be need of many words to overturn their system of doctrine, when it has been made manifest to all. So, in our case, since we have brought their* ***HIDDEN MYSTERIES***, *which they keep in silence among themselves,* ***TO THE LIGHT***, *it will not now be necessary to use many words in destroying their system of opinions.* ***FOR IT IS NOW IN THY POWER, AND IN THE POWER OF ALL THY ASSOCIATES TO FAMILIARIZE YOURSELVES WITH WHAT HAS BEEN SAID, TO OVERTHROW THEIR WICKED AND UNDIGESTED DOCTRINES***, *and to set forth doctrines agreeable to the truth.* ***I SHALL FURNISH MEANS FOR OVERTHROWING THEM THAT I MAY NOT ONLY EXPOSE THE WILD BEAST TO VIEW, BUT MAY INFLICT WOUNDS UPON IT FROM EVERY SIDE***."

PRINCIPLES AND PURPOSE FOR GNOSTIC DOCTRINAL STUDY

1. The principles behind this study

a. Evil men can ONLY produce evil works/words

Matthew 7:15-20-- "*Beware of false prophets, which come to you in sheep's clothing, but inwardly they are ravening wolves. Ye shall know them by their fruits. Do men gather grapes of thorns, or figs of thistles? Even so every good tree bringeth forth good fruit; but* ***A CORRUPT TREE BRINGETH FORTH EVIL FRUIT***. *A good tree cannot bring forth evil fruit.* ***NEITHER CAN A CORRUPT TREE BRING FORTH GOOD FRUIT***. *Every tree that bringeth not forth good fruit is hewn down, and cast into the fire. Wherefore by their fruits ye shall know them.*"

Matthew 12:33-- "***EITHER MAKE THE TREE GOOD, AND HIS FRUIT GOOD; OR ELSE MAKE THE TREE CORRUPT, AND HIS FRUIT CORRUPT***: *for the tree is known by his fruit.*"

Z

CORRUPT TREE/ROOT	CORRUPT FRUIT
(Gnostic root)	(Gnostic fruit)
Alexandrian Gnostics	GNOSTIC SCRIPTURES
	BSA (Greek N.T. MSS)
V	V
Clement and Origen	Commentaries using BSA AND
V	GNOSTIC SCRIPTURES
	V
Westcott and Hort	Greek N.T. (Using BSA)
V	English Revised Version
Philip Schaff	American Standard Version
	V
	Nestle/Aland Greek N.T.
	Revised Standard Version
	Berkley Bible
	Amplified Bible
V	Jerusalem Bible
	New English Bible
	New American Standard Version
	Living Bible
	Today's English Version
	New International Version
	New King James Version
	English Standard Version
V	V
Jesus Seminar	Scholars Version
	(Combination of BSA
	PLUS GNOSTIC SCRIPTURES)

b. Man condemns himself as a heretic by his own words (in commentaries, etc)

Matthew 12:34-37-- "*O generation of vipers, HOW CAN YE, BEING EVIL, SPEAK GOOD THINGS? for out of the abundance of the heart the mouth speaketh. A good man out of the good treasure of the heart bringeth forth good things: and AN EVIL MAN OUT OF THE EVIL TREASURE BRINGETH FORTH EVIL THINGS. But I say unto YOU, that every idle word that men shall speak they shall give account thereof in the day of judgment. FOR BY THY WORDS THOU SHALT BE JUSTIFIED, AND BY THY WORDS THOU SHALL BE CONDEMNED.*"

c. Small corruptions introduced into Scripture contaminates it all due to the process of determining doctrine

Isaiah 28:9-10-- "*Whom shall he teach knowledge? and whom shall he make to understand DOCTRINE? them that are weaned from the milk, and drawn from the breasts. FOR PRECEPT MUST BE UPON PRECEPT, PRECEPT UPON PRECEPT; LINE UPON*

LINE, LINE UPON LINE; HERE A LITTLE, AND THERE A LITTLE."

Galatians 5:9-- "*A little leaven leaveneth the whole lump.*"

d. Corrupted Scripture and doctrine produces a corrupted faith

I1 Corinthians 2:17-- "*For we are not as many, which* ***CORRUPT THE WORD OF GOD.***"

I Peter 1:23, 25-- "***BEING BORN AGAIN, NOT OF CORRUPTIBLE SEED, BUT OF INCORRUPTIBLE,*** *by the word of God which liveth and abideth forever.* ***BUT THE WORD OF THE LORD ENDURETH FOR EVER. AND THIS IS THE WORD WHICH BY THE GOSPEL IS PREACHED UNTO YOU.***"

Romans 10:17-- "*So then faith cometh by hearing, and hearing by the* ***WORD OF GOD.***"

2. The purpose of this study

a. To prove that Origen and Clement were heretical Gnostics.

b. To prove that Westcott and Hort were Gnostics who were disciples of Origen and thereby had a purpose for creating a different Greek New Testament and Revised English Version based on the Gnostic Alexandrian Greek Texts.

c. To prove that the Greek variants found in the Alexandrian Greek Manuscripts (S, B, A) were not mistakes, but were intentionally changed to conform the Bible to Gnostic doctrine, due to the fact that Alexandria was the home of Gnosticism, and the major Gnostic teachers such as CLEMENT, ORIGEN, Basilides, Capocrates, Valentinus, and Apelles.

d. To prove that all the English versions that have come out after the King James Version have corrupted verses that allow for Gnostic doctrinal interpretation, because they have as their foundation the corrupted Alexandrian Greek Manuscripts.

SECTION I: INTRODUCTION

SUMMARY OF STUDY

Jeremiah 33:3-- "*Call unto me, and I will answer thee, and shew thee great and mighty things, which thou knowest not.*"

John 16:13-- "*howbeit when he, the Spirit of truth, is come, he will guide you into all truth:*"

I John 2:27-- "*But the anointing which ye have received of him abideth in you, and ye need not that any man teach you: but as the same anointing teacheth you of all things, and is truth, and is no lie, and even as it hath taught you, ye shall abide in him.*"

1 Corinthians 2:13--"... *the Holy Ghost teacheth; comparing spiritual things with spiritual.*"

My research into historical Gnosticism and the application of Gnosticism to this present time was a result of seeking an answer from the Lord concerning a question that I had about Bible versions: **WHAT IS THE REASON BEHIND THE DIFFERENCES IN THE CRITICAL GREEK TEXTS THAT ARE THE BASIS FOR THE NEW BIBLE VERSIONS AND THE TRADITIONAL GREEK TEXT THAT IS THE BASIS FOR THE KING JAMES VERSION? IS THERE A COMMON PURPOSE BEHIND THESE DIFFERENCES?**

In my search for the answer, the Lord led me into studying II Thessalonians 2 (which reveals man's 'falling away' into Gnostic mysteries in the last days of the church) as well as many different subjects. I have sought to systematically outline the significant quotes about Gnosticism that I have found through researching these various subjects--both its historical facts and its future purpose. I have sought to keep my own observations to a minimum in the main outline points, and use Bible verses, books, and article quotes as the proof texts, allowing you to form your own judgment based on the words of men as opposed to the Words of the Lord Jesus Christ (John12:48; Matthew 12:3-37).

I feel strongly that Christians are being deliberately misled concerning the following facts about the new versions, and this deception has caused many believers to turn away from using the King James Version and adopt the new versions.
>   1) The new versions are merely revisions of the King James Version
>   2) The changes found in the new versions do not affect any doctrine
>   3) The Greek texts upon which the new versions are based are the "oldest and best," with the King James being based on inferior later texts

The truth of the matter is that the Greek manuscripts (Antiochian MSS.) behind the King James Version are the foundation of Christian **FUNDAMENTALISM**, while the Greek manuscripts (Alexandrian MSS.) behind the new versions are part of the foundation of Christian **GNOSTICISM** (the Nag Hammadi Library, part of the Dead Sea Scrolls, and the N.T. Apocrypha being the rest of the foundation).

There is a movement within the Church, particularly in Bible Colleges and Seminaries to completely reject the King James Version and adopt the new versions ONLY. In Gordon Fee's book, *HOW TO READ THE BIBLE FOR ALL IT'S WORTH,* he suggests that when studying the Bible "you should use almost any modern translation rather than the KJV" (p. 34). This is an important book because it is used at Cedarville College and other colleges as required reading early in the College years. He also endorses the book "*APOSTOLIC FATHERS*" by Lightfoot and in particular the new introduction in the book where it is stated that:
>   "*Lightfoot was convinced of the necessity of dealing with the New Testament, not in isolation as was the usual practice, but in relation to the **ENTIRE CORPUS OF EARLY CHRISTIAN WRITINGS**.*"

We find that what is being referred to as "*early Christian writings*" includes "*the apostolic fathers as well as Gnostic and apocryphal documents*" p. 14-15. So we see that he feels that one can best understand the New Testament only if he uses Gnostic documents to give him added insight, along with using the new versions.

In addition, Robert Gromacki, chairman of the Biblical Education Department at Cedarville College, adds in His pamphlet *TRANSLATIONS ON TRIAL--Is Your Bible the Word of God?* on page 59, concerning textual variants that:

> *"No basic evangelical doctrine is damaged or weakened by these omissions . . . **IT IS BEST NEITHER TO PROVE NOR DISPROVE ANY DOCTRINAL POSITION USING PASSAGES WITH DISPUTED VARIANT READINGS**. Serious Bible students should use passages where there are no disputed textual variations for presenting or negating a view."*

He is saying that we cannot defend the Christian faith (Biblical fundamentalism) using any of the passages that contain changed readings--presumably using any Bible version. That adds up to over 8,000 word changes in the New Testament alone. That is a lot of verses that are now "out of bounds" for defending the faith. A question comes to mind concerning these two statements: if no doctrine is damaged or weakened, then why can't we use the changed verses? **OBVIOUSLY, BECAUSE DOCTRINE HAS BEEN CHANGED**!

Upon your investigation of Section II "DOCTRINES OF DEVILS," you will see that **THESE CHANGES DO AFFECT DOCTRINE** by allowing for a Gnostic doctrinal interpretation. The Lord Himself has prophesied that in the last days Christian doctrine would be affected by demonic doctrine--I Timothy 4:1, and that men would reject Christian doctrine, and be turned to Gnostic doctrines and fables (II Timothy 4:3-4).

Once the Church has adopted the new versions containing the leaven of Gnostic doctrine, the next step will be to change the Canon of Scripture by merging portions of Gnostic writings ("scriptures") with portions of our Bible. We see the beginning of this process happening through the work of the Jesus Seminars on *"THE FIVE GOSPELS."* In this book, they have discarded most of Words of the Lord Jesus Christ in the Canonical Gospels, as Words that the Lord Jesus Christ did not say. They have also added the Gnostic Gospel of Thomas, declaring that it *"represents an early stage in Christian gospel writing,"* and that *"the Fellows of the Jesus Seminar found them to be EARLIER VERSIONS OF CANONICAL SAYINGS AND PARABLES,"* p. 501. As one compares similar texts found in both the Canonical texts and the book of Thomas (i.e. Luke12:49), preference is shown for the Thomas reading, an action which declares Thomas to be *"the oldest and best"* manuscript.

The final step will be to remove selected verses from our Bible. The Gnostic writings, and all the corrupt documents from the Ancient mystery religions, will be used to create a World Bible as the basis for the One World religion and the One World government which will be ruled over by the Antichrist during the Great Tribulation period.

For proof of the final step, please consider what the following New Agers have stated in their respective books:

1) Miriam Starhawk: *YOGA JOURNAL*, May/June 1986, p. 56

> Article "Witchcraft and the Religion of the Great Goddess" *"We need to create a **RELIGION OF HERETICS** who refuse to toe any ideological lines or give their allegiance to any **DOCTRINES OF EXCLUSIVITY**"* (Fundamental Christianity).

2) Vera Alder, *WHEN HUMANITY COMES OF AGE*, p. 31

"*The __ANCIENT WISDOM__, as it existed in all old civilizations, will be sifted, pieced together, correlated and synthesized with the finding of modern scientists and the developments in religious fields.*"

3) Lola Davis, *TOWARD A WORLD RELIGION FOR THE NEW AGE*, pp. 187-188:
  "*Religious data previously unavailable has been found or released. Among these are the __DEAD SEA SCROLLS__; the vast treasures of religious writings found in the Potola in Tibet; __CHRISTIAN WRITINGS DELETED FROM THE BIBLE DURING THE 4TH CENTURY__ (Gnostic); writings of Teilhard de Chardin; and previously carefully guarded knowledge of the __ANCIENT WISDOM__, including the writings of the Tibetan in the Alice Bailey books; writings of mystics from various religions; the materials offered by the Rosicrucians; and many books on Buddhism and Hindu philosophies and practices . . . Probably much of this knowledge could be advantageously used in __SYNTHESIZING THE MAJOR RELIGIONS WITH A WORLD RELIGION FOR THE NEW AGE__.*"

4) Peter De Coppens, Forward, in F. Aster Barnwell, __THE MEANING OF CHRIST FOR OUR AGE__:
  "*If the final planetary synthesis of the Eastern and Western spiritual traditions is to be realized, __EASTERN MYSTICISM__ must be __INCORPORATED INTO TRADITIONAL CHRISTIANITY__.*"

5) William Thompson, in David Spangler, *REVELATION: THE BIRTH OF A NEW AGE*, Introduction:
  "*The new spirituality does not reject the earlier patterns of the great universal religions. Priest and church will not disappear; they will not be forced out of existence in the New Age; they will be __ABSORBED INTO THE EXISTENCE OF THE NEW AGE__.*"

6) PERMANENT INSTRUCTION--drawn up by Italian Freemasons (exposed by Malachi Martin: *THE KEYS OF THIS BLOOD*, Touchstone, 1990:
  "*. . . we must turn our attention to an ideal that has always been of concern to men aspiring to the regeneration of all mankind . . . the liberation of the entire world and the establishment of the republic of brotherhood and world peace . . . Among the many remedies, there is one which we must never forget: . . . __THE TOTAL ANNIHILATION OF CATHOLICISM AND EVEN OF CHRISTIANITY__.*"

The above statements from New Agers who want to create a world Bible that is **FREE FROM DOCTRINAL EXCLUSIVITY**, sounds very similar to a statement written by Dr. John Davis, "*THE NEW INTERNATIONAL VERSION*--Why another English translation of the Bible?" appearing in Spire, Vol. 12, Book #2, p. 7--Fall, 1983 (a quarterly from Grace Theological Seminary):
  "*The answer to that question was that prior to the NIV most English translations suffered from archaic style, __THEOLOGICAL BIAS__ or inadequate translation skill to be __ACCEPTED INTERNATIONALLY AS A STANDARD BIBLE__. . . . In an effort to __PREVENT THE INTRODUCTION OF DENOMINATIONAL DISTINCTIVES OR THEOLOGICAL IDIOSYNCRASIES INTO THE TRANSLATION PROCESS__ . . . a five-step process was established for the translation.*"

You will also discover in Section I, "PROPAGATORS OF GNOSTICISM," that Westcott and Hort (the two men who were responsible for the Critical Greek text and the Revised English version in 1881) were themselves heretics that embraced the Gnostic doctrines of Origen, and therefore had a hidden motive for creating a new Bible version. Philip Schaff (the man responsible for the American Standard Version of 1901) also was a heretic and was the father of the Ecumenical Movement. His purpose was to create a Bible version that would further the merger of all religions and nations into a New World Order. George Schriver, in his biography, *PHILIP SCHAFF, CHRISTIAN SCHOLAR AND ECUMENICAL PROPHET* says:

> "*he was convinced that such an **ECUMENICAL REVISION** (of the Bible) would foster the bond of **INTERDENOMINATIONAL AND INTERNATIONAL UNION**"* (p. 71-73).

Finally, proof that Gnosticism is the religion behind the New Age Movement is found in a book by Peter Jones, *THE GNOSTIC EMPIRE STRIKES BACK*, p. 16:

> "*The new spirituality of the West is, according to Theodore Roszak, a New Age spokesman, THE RECLAMATION AND RENEWAL OF THE OLD GNOSIS*" (that is, pre-Christian Gnosis).

The purpose of this study is to prove that the new versions **ALLOW FOR THE TEACHING OF GNOSTIC DOCTRINE AND CONCEPTS**, because their chief architects were themselves Gnostics. It is my hope that you will see that this is so, as you seek the Lord's guidance through your own personal investigation of the following study. It is also my hope as you finish this study, that you will be moved to reject these new versions, and "*earnestly contend for the faith which was once delivered unto the saints*" (Jude 3)--that faith which is consistent with Fundamental Christianity, the Traditional (Antiochian) Greek manuscripts, and the King James Version.

Jude 3-- "*Beloved . . . it was needful for me to write unto you, and exhort you that ye should earnestly contend for the faith which was once delivered unto the saints.*"

I Thessalonians 5:6-- "*Therefore let us not sleep as do others; but let us watch and be sober.*"

II Timothy 4:3-- "*For the time will come that they will not endure sound doctrine. . . and they shall turn away their ears from the truth, and shall be turned unto fables.*"

Romans 13:11-- "*And that, knowing the time, that now it is high time to awake out of sleep: for now is our salvation nearer than when we believed.*"

IDENTIFYING "*THE MYSTERY OF INIQUITY*" AS GNOSTICISM
II Thessalonians 2:7

1. Gnostic terminology and concept

II Thessalonians 2:7-- "*the **MYSTERY** of iniquity*"

> Gnosticism is a Mystery Religion that sought to identify with Christianity in order to make disciples of Christians. It uses the term "mystery" concerning its secret Scriptures and doctrines.

2. Gnostic historical roots

II Thessalonians 2:7- *"the mystery of iniquity . . . doth already work: . . ."*

Gnosticism is the embodiment of the ancient Mystery Religions and was being practiced as Philosophy, Cabalism, and Essenism before the Lord Jesus Christ's first advent. It continued through the Apostolic period and then became known as Gnosticism, and later emerged as the Knights Templars, Jesuits, Freemasonry, Rosicrucians, and the New Age Movement.

3. Gnostic letters

II Thessalonians 2:2-- *"That ye be not soon shaken in mind, or be troubled, neither by spirit, nor by word, nor by **LETTER AS FROM US**, as that the day of Christ is at hand."*

Gnosticism relies on extra-Canonical "apostolic" letters for its doctrines as Found in "The Nag Hammadi Library" and the Dead Sea Scrolls

> The Prayer of the Apostle Paul
> The Apocryphon of James
> The Apocryphon of John
> The Gospel of Thomas
> The Gospel of Philip
> The Book of Thomas the Contender
> The (First) Apocalypse of James
> The (Second) Apocalypse of James
> The Acts of Peter and the Twelve Apostles
> The Apocalypse of Peter
> The Letter of Peter to Philip
> The Act of Peter
> The Secret Gospel of Mark

4. Gnostic doctrine

II Thessalonians 2:4– *". . . so that he as God sitteth in the temple of God, shewing himself that HE IS GOD."*

Gnosticism's main doctrine and final goal is that **man will become God** (see Genesis 3:5).

5. Gnostic propagation/Method of operation

II Thessalonians 2:3-- *"Let no man **DECEIVE YOU** by any means . . ."*

II Thessalonians 2:2-- *"Be not soon shaken in mind, or be troubled, neither **BY SPIRIT**, nor **BY WORD**, nor by letters **AS FROM US** . . ."*

II Thessalonians 2:9-- *"Even him, whose coming is after the working of Satan with all **POWER AND SIGNS AND LYING WONDERS**,"*

Gnosticism's main methods of operation is through deception and magic.

It seeks to deceive its own disciples concerning who they really worship (Satan), referring to him as the God of forces and Lucifer, the angel of light, and exalting him as the God of Wisdom (Gnosis).

It seeks to influence the Church by secretly introducing Gnostic doctrines through changing the Words in the true Canon of the Bible (see I1 Peter 2:1, Jude 4).

It seeks to deceive mankind through the use of **SPIRIT GUIDES** (prophetic mediums), and through **SIGNS AND WONDERS** (Hermetic magic) which they refer to as a New Pentecost.

6. Gnostic influence

II Thessalonians 2:3-- "*Let no man deceive you by any means: for that day shall not come, except there come A FALLING AWAY FIRST, . . .*"

The "*falling away*" as seen in its context of verse 2 would have to refer to the **FALLING AWAY FROM CHRISTIANITY INTO GNOSTICISM**, which we see happening in the world today.

7. Gnostic purpose

II Thessalonians 2:4– "*Who OPPOSETH AND EXALTETH HIMSELF above all that is called God or that is worshipped; so that he AS GOD SITTETH IN THE TEMPLE OF GOD, shewing himself that he is God.*"

Gnosticism's main purpose has been to:

1. Overthrow and destroy the God of the Bible (which they view as the evil Creator (see Psalm 2).

2. Rebuild the temple in Jerusalem and to place one of its own upon God's throne in the temple, thereby becoming the Messianic ruler of the world, the one which we know as the Antichrist.

IDENTIFYING THE 7-HEADED DRAGON AS GNOSTICISM

1. The dragon is Satan, and the dragon with 7 heads is a Gnostic symbol of spiritual resurrection power.

Revelation 12:9--"*And the great dragon was cast out, that old SERPENT, CALLED THE DEVIL, AND SATAN, which deceiveth the whole world . . .*"

Revelation 12:3– "*And there appeared another wonder in heaven; and behold a great red DRAGON, HAVING SEVEN HEADS and ten horns, and seven crowns upon his heads.*"

Revelation 13:1-2-- "*And I stood upon the sand of the sea, and saw a beast rise up out of the sea, HAVING SEVEN HEADS and 10 horns, and upon his horns ten crowns, and upon his heads THE NAME OF BLASPHEMY . . . and the dragon gave him his power, and his seat, and great authority.*"

2. The 7th head that is wounded to death represents the Gnostic dead Christ that supposedly resides within every man and must be resurrected through the initiation process, and is also known as the 'Higher Self'.

> Revelation 13:3– *"I saw **ONE OF HIS HEADS AS IT WERE WOUNDED TO DEATH; AND HIS DEADLY WOUND WAS HEALED**: and all the world wondered after the beast."*

(**FIGURE 4**)

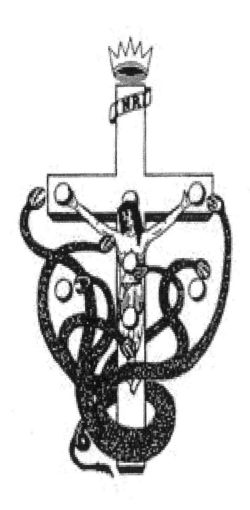

This diagram appears on the lid of Christian Rosenkreutz's symbolic tomb in the Vault of the Adepti. It shows the candidate's ego submitting to the Higher Self (also known as the True Will or the Holy Guardian Angel), where it is freed from the corruption of the personal complexes. The candidate is symbolically bound to the Cross of the Elements; from this process the Rose blooms forth.

3. The 10 horns represent the kingdom of earth divided into 10 regions and reigned over by 10 Gnostic kings (reduced to 7 after the rise of the Antichrist) See following map of 10 world regions which was put out by the Club of Rome, high level occultic group, and is a Global blueprint for the New World Order (*Mankind at the Turning Point, The Second Report to the Club of Rome*, by Mihajlo Mesarovic and Edward Pestel, p. 38)

> Daniel 7:7-8-- *"After this I saw. . . a fourth beast. . . and it was diverse from all the beasts that were before it; and it had **TEN HORNS**. I considered the horns, and, behold, there came up*

among them another little horn, before whom there were three of the first horns plucked up by the roots. . . ."

Daniel 7:24-- *"And the ten horns out of **THIS KINGDOM** are **TEN KINGS** that shall arise: and another shall rise after them; and he shall be diverse from the first, and he shall subdue three kings."*

Revelation I7:12-13– *"And the ten horns which thou sawest are ten kings, which have received no kingdom as yet; but receive power as kings one hour with the beast. These have one mind, and shall give their power and strength unto the beast."*

(FIGURE 4.1--Regionalization of the World System)

4. The 7th head (resurrected Christ within) is symbolized by the 7th point of light within the Star of David which is occultic version of Revelation 22:16.

Revelation 22:16-- *"I Jesus have sent mine angel to testify unto you these things in the churches.*

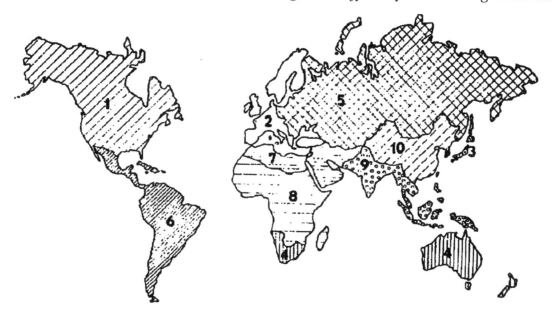

*I am the root and the offspring of David, and the bright an morning **STAR**."*

5. The 6 points of the occultic Star of David represents the outer man with the 7th point in the center representing the resurrected Christ within, and will probably become the mark of the beast, a mark **ALREADY BEING TATTOOED** on occultic Gnostic initiates (Hermetic Order of the Golden Dawn's Aleister Crowley loved to call himself the "Beast" and said his number was 666. Also Christian Rosenkreutz, the supposed leader of the Rosicrucians, used this Gnostic mark.) Please note in the picture below that the Star of David is placed at the right hand of the Gnostic initiate.

Revelation 13:16-18–"*And he causeth all . . . to receive a* __MARK IN THEIR RIGHT HAND__*, or in their foreheads: And that no man might buy or sell, save he that had the mark, or the name of the beast, or the number of his name. Here is wisdom. Let him that hath understanding count* __THE NUMBER OF THE BEAST__*; for* __IT IS THE NUMBER OF A MAN__*; and his number is Six hundred threescore and six (666).*"

(FIGURE 5--Fall 1995/Gnosis Magazine 41)

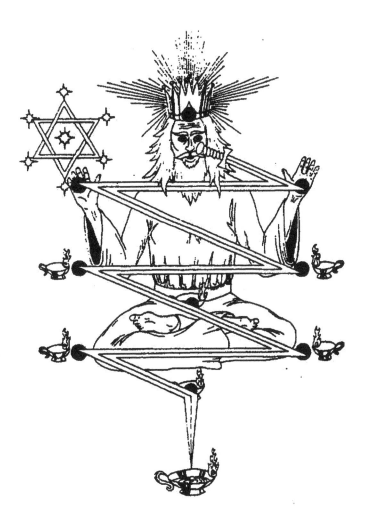

This dragon, also from the lid of Christian Rosenkreutz's tomb, depicts the Higher Self enthroned in the candidate's psyche. The lightning bolt represents the influx of divine guidance and energy passing through the Tree of Life from on high. The cups at the lower stations hold this energy as it descends.

This dragon has a long history. It is found as early as the Paleolithic period in the form of the serpent associated with the consort of the Great Mother Goddesses as well as with her Tree of Life. This same serpent appears later in the Egyptian myths of Ra's struggles with the serpent-fiend Apep. In this same negative light, it is encountered yet again in the New Testament book of Revelation.

Nonetheless, the serpent remains an important symbol of resurrection and the renewal of life, since it sheds its skin on a regular basis. When interpreted psychologically, this serpentine dragon represents what Jung calls the complexes of the personal unconscious.

The unfolding initiatic process inevitably leads to the situation represented by the diagram entitled "The Garden of Eden after the Fall" (figure 3. Page 39). This diagram is shown to the candidate during initiation into the 4-7 Grade of Philosophus. Here, the heads of the dragon arise into consciousness; as shown in the diagram.

THE PROPAGATORS OF GNOSTIC DOCTRINE

(Specific doctrinal views of these men will be covered in Section II DOCTRINES OF DEVILS)

1. **CLEMENT** (Teacher at Alexandrian School)

The Stromata. Miscellanies, of S. Clement are our source of information about the Mysteries in his time. He himself speaks of these writings as a "miscellany of **GNOSTIC NOTES**, according to the true philosophy," and also describes them as memoranda of the teachings he had himself received from Pantaenus . . .

> *"The Lord . . . allowed us to communicate of those divine **MYSTERIES**, and of that holy light, to those who are able to receive them. He did not certainly disclose to the many what did not belong to the many; but to the few to whom He knew that they belonged, who were capable of receiving and being molded according to them. But **SECRET THINGS** are entrusted to speech, not to writing, as is the case with God. And if one say that it is written, 'There is nothing secret which shall not be revealed, nor hidden which shall not be disclosed,' let him also hear from us, that to him who hears **SECRETLY**, even what is **SECRET** shall be manifested. This is what was predicted by this oracle. And to him who is able **SECRETLY** to observe what is delivered to him, that which is **VEILED** shall be disclosed as truth; and what is **HIDDEN** to the many shall appear manifest to the few. . . . The **MYSTERIES** are delivered **MYSTICALLY**, that what is spoken may be in the mouth of the speaker; rather not in his voice, but in his understanding. . . The writing of these memoranda of mine, I well know, is weak when compared with that spirit . . . which I was privileged to hear. But it will be an image to recall the archetype to him who was struck with the Thyrsus.*

(The Thyrsus, we may here interject, was the wand borne by Initiates, and candidates were touched with it during the ceremony of Initiation. It had a mystic significance symbolizing the spinal cord and the pineal gland in the Lesser Mysteries, and a Rod, known to Occultists, in the Greater. To say therefore "*to him who was struck with the Thyrsus*" was exactly the same as to say, "*to him who was initiated into the Mysteries.*")

> *"We profess not to explain **SECRET THINGS** sufficiently--far from it--but only to recall them to memory, whether we have forgot aught, or whether for the purpose of not forgetting. Many things, I well know, have escaped us through length of time, that have dropped away unwritten . . . There are then some things of which we have no recollection; for the power that was in the blessed men was great . . . There are also some things which remained unnoted long . . . **THESE I REVIVE IN MY COMMENTARIES**. Some things **I PURPOSELY OMIT**, in the exercise of a wise selection, **AFRAID TO WRITE WHAT I GUARDED AGAINST SPEAKING**; not grudging . . . but fearing for my readers, lest they should stumble by taking them in a wrong sense; and, as the proverb says, we should be found 'reaching a sword to a child.' For it is impossible that what has been written should not escape (become known) although remaining unpublished by me . . . Some things my treatise will hint; on some it will linger; some it will merely mention. **IT WILL TRY TO SPEAK IMPERCEPTIBLY, TO EXHIBIT SECRETLY, AND TO DEMONSTRATE SILENTLY.**"*

This passage, if it stood alone, would suffice to establish the existence of a secret teaching in the Early

Church. But it stands by no means alone. In chapter xii of this same book #I, headed, "The Mysteries of the Faith **NOT TO BE DIVULGED TO ALL**," Clement declares that, since others than the wise may see his work,

> "It is requisite, therefore, to **HIDE IN A MYSTERY THE WISDOM SPOKEN**, which the Son of God taught. . . ."

After much examination of Greek writers, and an investigation into philosophy, S. Clement declares that:

> "the **GNOSIS** imparted and revealed by the Son of God, is wisdom . . . And the **GNOSIS** itself is that which has descended by transmission to a few, having been imported **UNWRITTEN BY THE APOSTLES**."

A very long exposition of the life of the Gnostic, the Initiate, is given, and S. Clement concludes it by saying:

> "Let the specimen suffice to those who have ears. For it is not required to unfold the mystery, but only to indicate what is sufficient for those who are partakers in knowledge to bring it to mind." (Book #1, p. 55-62 Annie Besant, an occultist)

2. **ORIGEN** (Disciple of Clement, and teacher at Alexandrian school)

Harnack says of Origen's Christology:

> "**ALL IMAGINABLE HERESIES** have here been touched upon." (Book #70 p. 90)

Written by George Scholarius, the Byzantine philosopher and theologian:

> "Our Asian divines say on the one hand that 'Origen is the whetstone of us all,' but on the other hand, that '**HE IS THE FOUNT OF FOUL DOCTRINES** . . . he was also the father of Arianism, and worst of all, said that hellfire would not last for ever' . . . It has been disputed whether Origen could be saved . . . No discussion can proceed far without coming back to the perennial problem of his orthodoxy . . . The main contemporary gravamen against him was . . . on account of his **DOCTRINE**, in particular his eschatology." (Book #8, p. 95-98)

Writing in 374-75, Epiphanius concludes his immense attack on Origen's **HERESY** with the summary charge that Origen was "blinded by Greek culture." (Book #8, p. 100)

> "To Origen there flocked 'countless heretics' (EH 6.18.2) as well as orthodox, in order to be instructed by him in all areas of learning." (Book #35, p. 59)

> "We have . . . seen that Origen, one of the sanest of men and **VERSED IN OCCULT KNOWLEDGE**, teaches that the Scriptures are threefold . . ." (Book #1, p. 275-276)

3. **HORT** (Greek New Testament 1881, Revised English Version, 1881)

> "She (Hort's mother) was unable to enter into **HIS THEOLOGICAL VIEWS**, which to her school and generation **SEEMED A DESERTION OF THE ANCIENT WAYS**." (Book #10, Vol.1, p. 7-8, written by Hort's son)

> "**WESTCOTT . . . AND I HAVE STARTED A SOCIETY FOR THE INVESTIGATION OF GHOSTS AND ALL SUPERNATURAL APPEARANCES AND EFFECTS** . . . our own temporary name is the **GHOSTLY GUILD**" (Book #10, Vol.1, p. 211)

> "I long to be rid of dear, good, prosy Justin Martyr, and in the midst of Tertullian and

ORIGEN . . ." (Book #10, Vol., p. 215)

"_The positive_ **_DOCTRINES EVEN OF THE EVANGELICALS SEEM TO ME PERVERTED RATHER THAN UNTRUE_**." (Book #10, Vol.1, p. 400)

"_Also--but this may--I have a sort of craving that our text should be cast upon the world before we deal with_ **_MATTERS LIKELY TO BRAND US WITH SUSPICION_**. _I mean, a text issued by_ **_MEN ALREADY KNOWN FOR WHAT WILL UNDOUBTEDLY BE TREATED AS DANGEROUS HERESY_**, _will have great difficulties in finding its way to regions which it might otherwise hope to reach, and whence it would not be easily banished by subsequent alarms._" (Book #10, Vol.1, p. 445, written to Westcott concerning their soon to be published Greek text–the basis for the Revised Version of 1881)

"_There is the strangest blindness about the_ **_UNITARIAN POSITION_**. _It is_ . . . _difficult to measure the weight of acceptance won beforehand for the Revision by the single fact of_ **_OUR WELCOMING A UNITARIAN_** . . ." (Book #10, Vol.2, p. 400--concerning having a Unitarian on the Revision committee of the Revised Version of 1881)

"_. . . I have become Harold Browne's Examining Chaplain_ . . . _I wrote to warn him that_ **_I WAS NOT SAFE OR TRADITIONAL IN MY THEOLOGY, AND THAT I COULD NOT GIVE UP ASSOCIATION WITH HERETICS AND SUCH LIKE_**; _but after a single question he made no difficulty._" (Book #10. Vol.2, p. 165)

4. **WESTCOTT** (Greek New Testament 1881, Revised English Version 1881)
"_He took a strange interest_ . . . **_IN MORMONISM_** . . . _I recollect his procuring and studying the Book of Mormon about 1840._" (Book #23, Vol .1, p. 19-20, written by Westcott's son)

"_Stanley's sermon on St. John, which I extremely admire, and yet it is called_ '**_HERESY_**' _at Oxford._" (Book #23, Vol.1, p. 53)

"_I can never look back on my Cambridge life with sufficient thankfulness. Above all, those hours which were spent over_ **_PLATO_** _and Aristotle have wrought that in me which I pray may never be done away._" (Book #23, Vol.1, p. 175-176)

"_But from Cambridge days, I have read the writings of many who are called_ **_MYSTICS WITH MUCH PROFIT_**." (Book #23, Vol .1, p. 231)

"_I feel most keenly the disgrace of circulating what I feel to be_ **_FALSIFIED COPIES OF HOLY SCRIPTURES_**." (Book #23, Vol.1, p. 228-229, concerning the Traditional Received Text basis of the King James Version)

"_My father's orthodoxy was AGAIN called in question two years later. In 1867 he wrote a tract entitled 'The Resurrection as a Fact and a Revelation'_ . . . _and was already in type, when one of the Society's episcopal referees detected_ **_HERESY_** _in it. The writer was unable to omit the suspected passage, as he held it to be essential to his argument._" (Book #23, Vol.1, p. 25.6, written by Westcott's son)

*"The Churchmen, I see, praises the book on the Canon as a necessary article in a clergyman's library. It is strange, but **ALL THE QUESTIONABLE DOCTRINES WHICH I HAVE EVER MAINTAINED ARE IN IT**."* (Book #23, Vol.1, p. 290)

*"My father's promised contributions, however, were . . . his articles on the **ALEXANDRIAN DIVINES, INCLUDING CLEMENT AND GREATEST OF ALL, ORIGEN. FOR TWENTY YEARS THE WORKS OF ORIGEN WERE CLOSE TO HIS HAND, AND HE CONTINUALLY TURNED TO THEM AT EVERY OPPORTUNITY."* (Book #23, Vol.1, p. 319--written by Westcott's son)

5. **PHILIP SCHAFF** (American Standard Version, 1901)

*"It would be considered **HERESY** for any historian . . . to suggest that an appreciative study of the history of Catholicism had any value or relevance whatsoever for Protestants . . . This mind set could never entertain the idea that the ancient and medieval Catholic church played the major role in the organic development of Christianity from the days of Jesus to the days of Luther and Calvin . . . Schaff's approach to Christian history was bound to suffer misunderstanding and opposition in this context."* (Book #11, p. 18)

*"This meant, in part, that **PROTESTANTISM WAS NEITHER A REVOLUTION NOR A RESTORATION**; It organically evolved out of **MEDIEVAL CATHOLICISM, WHICH IN ITS OWN WAY HAD BEEN THE BEARER OF CHRISTIANITY IN THE MEDIEVAL PERIOD** . . . He valued the empirical church and yet hoped for some union or age of **EVANGELICAL CATHOLICISM** in the future when the best of Protestant and Catholic **TRADITIONS MIGHT ORGANICALLY EVOLVE INTO THE HIGHER AGE**."* Book #11. p. 22)

(Schaff's **HERESY TRIAL** begins in which he is exonerated of all charges in 1845. Book #11, p. 24)

*"(He) was invited to chair the committee whose main responsibility was a revision of the English Bible . . . It was one of his most **ECUMENICAL EFFORTS** bringing together many of the finest scholars from the leading Protestant denominations of Great Britain and the United States . . . Schaff was deeply committed to the project, for he was convinced that such an **ECUMENICAL REVISION** would foster the bond of INTERDENOMINATIONAL AND INTERNATIONAL UNION . . . ."* (Book #11, p. 71-73)

*"**THE CHANGES** thus far are in the right direction and should **CONTAIN THE GERMS OF A NEW THEOLOGY**. Every age must produce its own theology. Such a theology will prepare the way for the reunion of Christendom."* (Book #34, p. 142, quoted from 'THE LIFE OF PHILIP SHAFF.')

*"Schaff's remaining energies were reserved for a major task that had been assigned to him--the presentation of a paper at the unprecedented World Parliament of Religions, to be held in Chicago . . . From the early stages of planning Schaff had supported the concept of a gathering of representatives from **ALL THE MAJOR RELIGIONS OF THE**

WORLD. He believed that it would offer the 'broadest platform for the broadest study of comparative religion.' **HE NEVER BELIEVED THAT HE WAS COMPROMISING ANY OF HIS CHRISTIAN PRINCIPLES BY PARTICIPATING IN DIALOGUE WITH OTHER RELIGIONS. HE COULD EASILY SIT ON A PLATFORM ALONG WITH MOSLEMS, HINDUS, AND BUDDHISTS WITH NO EMBARRASSMENT OR QUALMS OF CONSCIENCE**." (Book #11, p. 102-103)

"Even in the wake of the First Vatican Council of 1870, he insisted that the future would bring a changed atmosphere within the Roman Catholic church that would lend itself to union efforts . . . Schaff was convinced that any future organic union must be preceded by a spiritual union. . . . The 20th century ecumenical movement committed itself early to this ideal . . . . This insight also appropriated the **BASIC TRUTH OF THE PRIORITY OF CHRISTIAN COMMUNITY OVER 'PURE DOCTRINE.'**" (Book #11, p. 110)

"He insisted that each section of Christendom must come to the realization that its tradition does not possess the whole truth nor the fullness of catholicity." (Book #11, p. 112)

"Schaff admitted that the orthodox system of Christianity is 'a human system which requires **CONSTANT REFORMATION.'** *Opposed to all 'blind* **TRADITIONALISTS'**, *he declared it to be the great mission of German theology* **'TO RESTORE THE OLD FAITH** *(Gnosticism), but in a new form, which shall make real progress toward the ultimate reconciliation and free, intelligent agreement of the human mind with divine truth."* (Book #19, p. 187)

"So there is a **BELIEVING AND CHRISTIAN GNOSTICISM** *as well as an unbelieving and anti-(or pseudo-) Christian Gnosticism."* (Book #19, p. 207)

SECTION II: DOCTRINES OF DEVILS (I Timothy 4:1)

A. Satan's lies concerning Scripture changes of Greek, Hebrew, English

II Thessalonians 2:11–*"And for this cause God shall send them strong delusion, that they should believe A* **LIE**."

John 8:44–*"Ye are of your father the devil, and the lusts of your father ye will do. He was a murderer from the beginning,* **AND ABODE NOT IN THE TRUTH, BECAUSE THERE IS NO TRUTH IN HIM. WHEN HE SPEAKETH A LIE, HE SPEAKETH OF HIS OWN: FOR HE IS A LIAR, AND THE FATHER OF IT**."

I Timothy 4:1-2--*"Now the Spirit speaketh expressly, that in the latter times some shall depart from the faith, giving heed to seducing spirits, and doctrines of devils;* **SPEAKING LIES** *in hypocrisy; having their conscience seared with a hot iron;"*

Romans 1:25–*"Who* **CHANGED THE TRUTH OF GOD INTO A LIE**, *and worshipped and served the creature more than the Creator, . . ."*

1. The basic lie concerning textual changes (They do not affect doctrine)

*"People usually say, 'The Westcott and Hort text has a few omissions **BUT NO MAJOR DOCTRINES ARE INVOLVED.' WELL, MAJOR DOCTRINES ARE INVOLVED**. Secondly they say, 'If they take a doctrine out here, it is found somewhere else in the New Testament.' Well, I don't care if they leave it in 100 other places; if they take it out any place, it is a defective, deficient Greek version and a defective, deficient English version based upon it. You know why the heretics took out some things but not all of them? **THEY WANTED THE BIBLE TO AGREE WITH THEM**. The heretics who flourished in the first hundred years after the Bible was written did not have every New Testament book in their possession, so they couldn't rip out, change, recopy, or forge various verses throughout the New Testament. **THEY COULD ONLY DO SUCH THINGS WITH THE BOOKS THEY HAD IN THEIR HANDS . . . HOW MANY WORDS OF GOD HAVE TO BE LEFT OUT OF YOUR BIBLE BEFORE IT IS NO LONGER 100% GOD'S WORD**? Just one? That would be enough for me. But when you have over 5,600 changes involving almost 10,000 words, you have serious trouble."* (Book #5, p. 44)

2. Examples of the lie concerning scripture changes

*"The main differences between the KJV-NKJV and the NASB-NIV can be seen in the **OMISSION OF . . . VERSES, PARTS OF VERSES, AND SHORT PASSAGES. . . . NO BASIC EVANGELICAL DOCTRINE IS DAMAGED OR WEAKENED BY THESE OMISSIONS**."* (Book #4, p. 59 - Robert Gromacki, Pres. Cedarville College)

*"Only about 400 affect the sense; and of these 400 only about 50 are of real significance for one reason or another, and **NOT ONE OF THESE 50 AFFECT AN ARTICLE OF FAITH OR A PRECEPT OF DUTY** which is not abundantly sustained by other and undoubted passages, or by the whole tenor of Scripture teaching"* (Book #5, p. 133, quoting Philip Schaff, who also stated *"The changes thus far . . . should contain the germs of a **NEW THEOLOGY**"*--a statement concerning his changing of the "Creed."

*". . . **NOT ONE** (doubtful disputed rendering) **AFFECTS A SINGLE VITAL DOCTRINE OF THE WORD OF GOD**"* (Book #5, p. 134, quoting Dr. Arthur T. Pierson)

*"The differences in the translations are so minor, so insignificant, that we can be sure **NOT A SINGLE DOCTRINE, NOT A SINGLE STATEMENT OF FACT, NOT A SINGLE COMMAND OR EXHORTATION HAS BEEN MISSED** in our translations."* (Book #5, p. 134, quoting Dr. John R. Rice)

3. Promotion of the lie concerning textual changes--(They will need to change verses that would convict of sin against the word of God.)

(John 3:19-20–*"And this is the condemnation, that light is come into the world, and men loved darkness rather than light, because their deeds were evil. For every one that doeth evil hateth the light, neither cometh to the light, **LEST HIS DEEDS SHOULD BE REPROVED**."*

Romans 13:9--(Example of key Greek textual change)
BYZ S >KJV -- "**THOU SHALT NOT BEAR FALSE WITNESS**."
BYZ BA > WH NU >NASV NIV ESV -- **omit**

4. Purpose of the lie concerning textual changes

a. To make man the final authority concerning Scripture rather than God thereby validating textual criticism

Romans 1:25–"*Who changed the truth of God into a lie, **AND WORSHIPPED AND SERVED THE CREATURE MORE THAN THE CREATOR . . .***"

b. To render changed passages 'out of bounds' as doctrinal proof texts

II Timothy 3:16–"**ALL SCRIPTURE** is given by inspiration of God and is profitable for **DOCTRINE**, for reproof, for correction, for instruction in righteousness:"

"*It is best neither to **PROVE NOR DISPROVE ANY DOCTRINAL POSITION USING PASSAGES WITH DISPUTED VARIANT READINGS**. Serious Bible students should **USE PASSAGES WHERE THERE ARE NO DISPUTED TEXTUAL VARIATIONS FOR PRESENTING OR NEGATING A VIEW**.*" (Book #4. p. 59)

5. Exposing the lie concerning- (Compare Gnostic doctrines with changes in the Critical Greek/English versions)

1 Corinthians 2:13–". . . *the Holy Ghost teacheth; **COMPARING SPIRITUAL THINGS WITH SPIRITUAL**.*"

B. Satan's lies concerning doctrine

I Timothy 4:1–"Now the Spirit speaketh expressly, that in the latter times some shall depart from the faith, giving heed to seducing sprits, and **DOCTRINES OF DEVILS**;"

II Timothy 4:3-4--"*For the time will come when **THEY WILL NOT ENDURE SOUND DOCTRINE;** but after their own lusts shall they heap to themselves teachers, having itching ears; and they shall turn away their ears from the truth, and shall be turned unto fables.*"

Matthew 16:12–"*Then understood they how that He bade them not beware of the leaven of bread, but of the **DOCTRINE OF THE PHARISEES AND OF THE SADDUCEES**.*"

Revelation 2:15–"*So hast thou also them that hold the **DOCTRINE OF THE Nicolaitans** which thing I hate.*"

Revelation 2:14–"*But I have a few things against thee, because thou hast there them that hold **THE DOCTRINE OF BALAAM**, who taught Balac to cast a stumbling-block before* *the children of Israel, to eat things sacrificed unto idols, and to commit fornication.”*

Revelation 2:24–*“But unto you I say, and unto the rest of Thyatira, as many as do not have **THIS DOCTRINE, AND WHICH HAVE NOT KNOWN THE DEPTHS OF SATAN**, as they speak; . . .”*

1. Ecumenical unity is more important than pure Biblical doctrine

II John 9-10–*“Whosoever transgresseth, and abideth not in the **DOCTRINE** of Christ, hath not God. He that abideth in the **DOCTRINE** of Christ, he hath both the Father and the Son. If there come any unto you, and bring not this **DOCTRINE**, receive him not into your house, neither bid him God speed:”*

*“The union of Christ with his church, Schaff considered a divine gift. The 20th century ecumenical movement committed itself early to this ideal of the necessity of the recognition of the prior koinonia as a preface to anything else. This initial realization and experience would provide the right atmosphere for formal ecumenical efforts. **THIS INSIGHT ALSO APPROPRIATED THE BASIC TRUTH OF THE PRIORITY OF CHRISTIAN COMMUNITY OVER 'PURE DOCTRINE.'**”* (Book #11, p. 110)

2. Gnostic doctrine is the true doctrine

Genesis 3:5–*“For God doth know that in the day ye eat thereof, then your eyes shall be opened, and **YE SHALL BE AS GODS**, knowing good and evil.”*

*“. . . Gnosticism produced real thinkers who unfolded the contents of the secret 'knowledge' in elaborate **DOCTRINAL SYSTEMS** . . .”* (Book #20, p. 35)

*“Emanation from the Deity of **ALL** spiritual beings, progressive degeneration of these beings from emanation to emanation, redemption and return of **ALL** to the purity of the Creator; and, after the re-establishment of the primitive harmony of **ALL**, a fortunate and truly **DIVINE CONDITION OF ALL**, in the bosom of God; **SUCH WERE THE FUNDAMENTAL TEACHINGS OF GNOSTICISM**.”* (Book #6, p. 248)

KEY TO DOCTRINAL STUDY OUTLINE

a) Rejected truth

These are verses that both refute Gnostic doctrine and are verses which the Gnostics disregard when coming up with their doctrine.

b) Gnostic doctrine

These references are either from Gnostics themselves (past and present) or are about the beliefs of Gnostics such as from the writings of Irenaeus.

c) Gnostic Scriptures

These are references from Gnostic writings that are part of the Nag Hammadi Library, or the Dead Sea Scrolls.

d) Greek textual changes

1. Early "Church" (Gnostic) Fathers

Clement
Origen
Marcion

2. Greek Manuscripts

BYZ = Byzantine (a.k.a. Antiochian, Textus Receptus, Traditional)

Alexandrian texts
S = Sinaiticus
B = Vaticanus
A = Alexandrinus
C

Present Greek texts used
WH = Westcott and Hort, 1881
NU = Nestle/Aland - United Bible Society, 26th Edition

3. English versions
KJV = King James Version
NASV = New American Standard Version
NIV = New International Version
ESV = English Standard Version (added to the original book)

4. English text wording is slightly different from the English versions represented above because it follows word for word from the Greek/English Interlinear New Testament by Thomas Newberry (Book #24)

DOCTRINES OF DEVILS - I Timothy 4:1

1. Bibilology (Scriptures)

a. Revelation

1) God reveals truth both to writers of Scripture and **PHILOSOPHERS**.
2) The Bible is **NOT** God's **PRIMARY REVELATION** to man.
3) Occult Gnostic revelations form the basis for the Bible and are **SUPERIOR** to the Bible which is incomplete.

4) Jesus revealed Gnostic scriptures **IN SECRET** to the apostles after he died.
5) Purpose of revelation is to reveal man's deepest self (**GOD WITHIN**).
6) Present new revelations are given by '**SPIRIT GUIDES**' and are **SUPERIOR** to the written word of God.

b. Inspiration

1) God did not superintend **EVERY** word of Scripture.
2) Jesus **DID NOT SAY EVERYTHING** attributed to him in the Gospels.
3) God's word is **FULL OF ERRORS**.

c. Preservation

1) The Apostolic Bible As only a **TEMPORARY SUBSTITUTE** until the real one is revealed to future generations.

d. Authority

1) Only Gnostic scriptures are **AUTHORITATIVE**.

e. Propagation

1) The true word of God is **KEPT SECRET** through an **ORAL TRADITION**.

f. Interpretation

1) The Bible can only be understood in the light of **OTHER DOCUMENTS**.
2) The Bible is to be **INTERPRETED ALLEGORICALLY**.
3) Only the spiritually mature can understand **HIDDEN MEANING**

2. Theology (God)

a. Person of God

1) There is an **UNKNOWN GOD** who is not the Creator.
2) God is a **MONAD** existing in **THREE FORMS**--Father, Mother, and Son.
3) God has a **FALLEN NATURE** and only the father is good.
4) God is **ANDROGYNOUS**.
5) The term Lord refers to the Father, and **NOT TO JESUS**.
6) The son is **NOT EQUAL** to the Father.
7) The son is **WISER** than the Father.
8) The third person of Gnostic trinity is the **GREAT MOTHER** who is the personification of wisdom (**SOPHIA**) and the holy spirit.
9) God is the **UNIVERSAL FATHER** of all mankind.

b. Works of God

1) An **EVIL GOD** or 7 powers **CREATED** the world which is also evil.

c. Worship of God

1) Serpents are worshipped as representing God.

d. Abiding place of God

1) Androgynous God and his spirit is **WITHIN EVERY MAN**.

3. Christology (Christ)

a. The pre—existence of Christ

1) The Christ was a **CREATED BEING** and therefore had a beginning in time.
2) The Logos is the angel of the Lord (Demiurge) **BEFORE HIS REBELLION**.
3) The Logos was **DEFECTIVE** before he was illuminated.
4) The living word is the **SON OF CHRIST**.
5) The **PRIMAL MAN** revealed himself in Christ.
6) The Primal Man is **ANDROGYNOUS** (bisexual).
7) The **SERPENT** in the garden with the **LUMINOUS JESUS**.

b. The Incarnation and birth of Christ

1) Jesus was **NOT GOD INCARNATE** and did not have all of God's **ATTRIBUTES**.
2) The Savior became manifest in an **INVOLUNTARY SUFFERING**.
3) **JOSEPH**, not God, **WAS FATHER** of Jesus.
4) Incarnation of Christ is **CONTINUING PROCESS**, not historical event.
5) Jesus was begotten by the Logos, and is **NOT THE LOGOS**.

c. The life and person of Jesus

1) Jesus is **NOT** the "**LORD GOD ALMIGHTY**."
2) The **SON OF MAN IS SEPARATE** from Jesus Christ.
3) Jesus had a **SIN NATURE** like every other man.
4) The **CHRIST IS SEPARATE** from Jesus.
5) The Christ came upon Jesus at his **BAPTISM** in order to **ENLIGHTEN AND PERFECT** him.
6) Jesus was **DEIFIED IN STAGES** by the Logos and **DID NOT HAVE A SPIRIT** until later in life (at baptism or death).

d. The Words of Jesus Christ

1) The Words of Jesus do not cause man to have **ETERNAL LIFE**.

e. The work of Christ

1) The savior came to **DESTROY BAD PEOPLE AND SAVE GOOD PEOPLE**.

2) Jesus **DOES NOT CALL** people to enter the heavenly kingdom.

f. The miracles of Christ

1) Jesus performed natural **MAGICAL ACTS** that **APPEARED** as miracles.

g. The suffering and death of Christ

1) The Primal Man is slain for man's redemption at the **BEGINNING OF CREATION** and **CONTINUES TO DIE DAILY**.
2) Jesus **DID NOT FULFILL O.T. MESSIANIC SUFFERINGS** because **HE IS NOT THE ONLY CHRIST**.
3) The savior **DID NOT DIE** on the cross, but rather another Jesus who was a demoniac.

h. The resurrection of Christ

1) The resurrection of Christ was **SPIRITUAL, NOT BODILY**.
2) The resurrection of Jesus happened **BEFORE HE DIED**.
3) The resurrected Christ meets with his disciples through **DIVINATION** in order to reveal to them his **SECRET PLAN**.

i. The return of Jesus Christ

1) Second coming of Christ is **NOT LITERAL**, but figurative and refers to the spiritual coming of Christ into the life of the believer.

4. Pneumatology (Holy Spirit)

a. Person of the Holy Spirit

1) **SOPHIA** is the Holy Spirit.
2) The Sophia spirit reveals **HERSELF** as a saint and as a **WHORE**.

b. Works of the Holy Spirit
1) The Sophia spirit **CREATED** the world.
2) The spirit is the source of **DIRECT REVELATION**.

c. Indwelling of the spirit

1) The Sophia spirit is **INCARNATED AND REINCARNATED** in human bodies.

5. Anthropology (Man)

a. The creation of man

1) Man was created by the **ANGELS**.

b. The person of man

1) Man was **PRE-EXISTENT** before he was born and was **ONE WITH GOD**.
2) Man **SINNED IN HIS PRE-EXISTENT STATE** and became a soul before he was born.
3) The **DIVINE SPARK** (Christ) **IS WITHIN ALL MANKIND**, and all have potential to **BECOME CHRISTS, DIVINE, AND GOD**.
4) Man has a spiritual 'twin' which is his transcendental, higher self.
5) Man becomes **PERFECTED** through a series of **REINCARNATIONS** or **EVOLUTIONARY PROCESSES**.
6) Some races of man are **INFERIOR TO OTHER RACES** due to evolution.
7) Perfect man is **BISEXUAL** (androgynous).
8) Perfected man **STOPS BEING A SOUL** and becomes spirit.

c. The person of Mary

1) Mary is **THE LOGOS, THE WORLD MOTHER**.

d. The propagation of man

1) Marriage and sexual propagation is **EVIL**.

6. Angelology (Angels, Satan)

a. Lucifer, Satan, Serpent, Devil

1) The Devil is an **INSTRUMENT OF GOD** and will ultimately **BE PARDONED**.
2) Lucifer is **CHRIST** and the **GOD OF TRUTH**.
3) Satan is **NOT A PERSON**, but rather an evil **FORCE**.

b. Angels

1) Angel of the Lord was **DEMIURGE** who had not yet rebelled against God.
2) Man's is his **TRANSCENDENTAL SELF**.
3) Man can SEE his guardian angel.
4) The guardian angel is our **SPIRIT GUIDE**.

7. Hamartiology (Sin)

a. The causes of sin, evil

1) **EROS** (sex) is the **ORIGIN OF DEATH**.
2) **UNCONSCIOUSNESS** (lack of gnosis) and not sin is the **CAUSE OF EVIL**.

b. Freedom from the law

1) The <u>**LAW**</u> is to be <u>**REJECTED**</u>.

c. Sinful acts

1) Idolatry is <u>**NOT EVIL**</u>.
2) Marriage and sexual propagation <u>**IS EVIL**</u>.
3) Prostitution is <u>**NOT EVIL**</u>.
4) Homosexuality/bisexuality is <u>**NOT EVIL**</u>, but is sign of perfection.
5) Eating meat <u>**IS EVIL**</u>.
6) Drinking alcohol <u>**IS EVIL**</u>.
7) Killing people is sometimes <u>**NECESSARY**</u>.
8) Pride is <u>**NOT EVIL**</u>, but is the means of salvation.

8. Soteriology (Salvation)

a. Saviour of salvation

1) <u>**LUCIFER**</u> is the Savior.
2) <u>**APOSTLES**</u> will help save the world.
3) <u>**SOPHIA**</u> is the redeemer.
4) The <u>**SOTER**</u> (heavenly savior) saves the Gnostics, while the earthly Jesus saves the Psychics.

b. Means of salvation

1) Man is saved through <u>**GNOSIS**</u>.
2) Man is saved by the <u>**SYMBOLIC DEATH**</u> of Christ <u>**WITHIN MAN, NOT BY THE BLOOD**</u> of Christ.
3) Man is saved/perfected through <u>**ASCETICISM**</u> (extreme self-denial).
4) Man is <u>**NOT**</u> saved just <u>**BY WORDS**</u>.
5) Man is saved by <u>**FOLLOWING THE EXAMPLE OF THE REDEEMER**</u> in obedience.
6) Man is saved through <u>**SACRAMENTS**</u>.
7) Man is saved through <u>**SACRED FORMULAS AND NAMES**</u>.
8) Man is saved by <u>**INITIATION RITES**</u> (baptism, bridal chamber).
9) Man is saved through <u>**FAITH IN HIMSELF**</u> and his own good works rather than the person and work of Jesus Christ.
10) Man is saved (born again) when he <u>**RECOGNIZES**</u> that he has the <u>**MYSTICAL CHRIST IN HIM**</u> and is therefore divine or God ("<u>**I AM**</u>").
11) Man is saved through <u>**SECRET SYMBOLS**</u>.
12) Man must be <u>**BORN AGAIN TWICE**</u>.

c. Objects of salvation

1) Redemption includes the <u>**ANGELS**</u>, even <u>**SATAN**</u>.
2) Redemption includes <u>**JESUS CHRIST**</u> (the Primal Man).
3) The <u>**WHOLE WORLD**</u> has been redeemed (<u>**UNIVERSAL SALVATION**</u>).
4) Only <u>**THE GOOD**</u> are saved.
5) Souls of men are saved, <u>**NOT THEIR BODIES (NO BODILY RESURRECTION)**</u>.

d. Process of salvation

1) Man is saved/perfected **IN STAGES**.

e. Event of salvation

1) Salvation is a **MYTH** and **NOT AN HISTORICAL EVENT**.

f. Proofs of salvation

1) The saved person will **SHINE (BE LUMINOUS)**.
2) He will enter the kingdom **LAUGHING**.
3) He will have **VISIONS** of God and the Savior.
4) He will speak in **TONGUES**.
5) He will **LIFT UP HIS HANDS** in praise.
6) He will have **OUT-OF-BODY EXPERIENCES**.
7) He will experience **DIRECT NEW REVELATIONS** from God.

g. Meaning of redemption

1) Is the returning of man to his pre-existent **STATE OF DUTY** before his fall in eternity past.

h. Purpose and results of salvation

1) To know that **MAN** himself **IS THE SON OF MAN**.
2) To **UNITE** the Gnostic with the Savior, not with God.
3) To be **WEDDED TO THE ANGELS**.
4) To experience **SINLESS PERFECTION** while on earth.
5) To attain **CHRISTHOOD AND BECOME DIVINE** through Gnosis.
6) To become **ABSORBED BACK INTO THE GODHEAD (BECOME GOD**.)

9. Ecclesiology (Church)

a. Organization of the church

1) There is an **UPPER CLASS** of the elect.

b. Works of the church

1) Don't pray, fast, or give alms.
2) Don't witness to unbelievers or large crowds.

c. Members of the Church

1) The church consists of **MANY** pre-existent souls.

d. Worship of the church

1) **SABBATH OBSERVANCE** is necessary to see God.

e. Ordinances of the church

1) The Eucharist **IS JESUS**.

f. Place and headquarters of the true church and God's temple

1) Is in **ALEXANDRIA, EGYPT**.

10. Eschatology (Future things)

a. Resurrection/rapture

1) There is **NO BODILY RESURRECTION** or rapture.

b. Second coming of Christ

1) Is **FIGURATIVE AND PRESENT**, not literal and future.

c. Heaven

1) Is **NOT LITERAL PLACE**, but is figurative.

d. Hell

1) Is **NOT LITERAL PLACE**, but figurative, and is a type of **PURGATORY**.
2) Is **NOT** the place of **EVERLASTING JUDGMENT**.

e. New heavens and earth

1) Will come about when a portion of mankind has **REDEEMED ITSELF**.
2) There will be a **GODLESS** and classless **SOCIETY** (Man will be god).

1. BIBLIOLOGY (Scripture)

a. Revelation

1) God reveals truth BOTH to writers of Scripture and Philosophers

a) Rejected truth.

Colossians 2:8–"*Beware lest any man spoil you through **PHILOSOPHY** and vain deceit after the **TRADITIONS OF MEN**, after the rudiments of the world, and not after Christ.*"

b) Gnostic doctrine

MASONIC-- "*THE GNOSTICS DERIVED THEIR LEADING DOCTRINES AND IDEAS FROM PLATO AND PHILO*, *the Zend-avesta and the Kabalah, and the Sacred books of India and Egypt; and thus introduced into the bosom of Christianity the cosmological and theosophical speculations, which had formed the larger portion of the ancient religions of the Orient, joined to those of the Egyptian, Greek, and Jewish doctrines, which the neo-Platonists had equally adopted in the Occident . . . **THE DOMINANT DOCTRINES OF PLATONISM WERE FOUND in GNOSTICISM**.*" (Book #4, p. 248-249)

"*It (Masonry) is **PHILOSOPHICAL**, because, it . . . revives the Academy of Plato, and the wise teachings of Socrates. It reiterates the maxims of Pythagoras, Confucius, and Zoroaster and reverentially enforces the sublime lessons of Him who died. upon the Cross.*" (Book #6, p. 221)

SCHAFF--"***THERE IS NO NECESSARY CONFLICT*** *between faith and criticism any more than between revelation and reason or **BETWEEN FAITH AND PHILOSOPHY. GOD IS THE AUTHOR OF BOTH**, and he cannot contradict himself.*"   (Book #19, p. 205)

c) Gnostic scriptures,

d) Greek textual changes

Acts 17:18 (Critical text does not reveal that Paul preached the gospel to the philosophers)
BYZ > KJV-- because he preached **UNTO THEM** Jesus and the resurrection
SB > WH NU > NASV NIV ESV   - **omits "unto them"**

II Peter 1:21
BYZ > KJV - . . . **HOLY** men of God spake as they were moved by the Holy Ghost
B > WH NU > NASV NIV ESV- omits "**holy**"

Revelation 22:6
BYZ (pt) >   -the Lord God of the **HOLY** prophets
BYZ (pt) SA > WH NU > NASV NIV ESV - omits "**holy**"

2) The Bible is not God's primary revelation to man (comp. Psalm 138:2)

a) Rejected truth

Psalm 138:2–". . . *for Thou hast magnified Thy word above all Thy name.*"

Romans 10:17–"*Faith cometh by hearing . . . the word of God*"

b) Gnostic doctrine

ORIGEN–"*According to him,* **THE COSMOS, GOD'S FIRST REVELATION** *is threefold: spiritual, psychic, and material. In the same way* **THE SCRIPTURES, WHICH CONSTITUTE GOD'S SECOND REVELATION**, *are threefold.*" (Book #71 p. 86)

HORT--from commentary on I Peter
I Peter 1:23 "*It (that is, the word translated* **WORD***) is God's whole utterance of Himself in His incarnate Son, the* **WRITTEN OR SPOKEN RECORD OF THIS UTTERANCE**, *or of any part of it,* **BEING A WORD ONLY IN A SECONDARY SENSE**." (Book #14, p. 6)

c) Gnostic scriptures.

d) Greek changes

Luke 22:61
BYZ A > KJV NASV? "*Peter remembered* **the WORD** *of the Lord.*"
SBC > WH NU > NIV "*. . .* **the SPOKEN WORD** *of the Lord.*"

e) Dynamic equivalence changes in new versions

Psalm 138:2 (New versions do not teach that God's word is the most important revelation)
KJV "*. . . for thou hast magnified Thy word* **ABOVE** *all Thy name.*"
NASV *. . . for Thou hast magnified Thy word* **ACCORDING TO** *all Thy name.*"
NIV *. . . for you have exalted* **above all things** *your name AND your word.*"
ESV *. . . for you have exalted* **above all things** *your name and your word.*

3) Occult Gnostic revelations form the basis for the Bible and are superior to the Bible which is Incomplete

a) Rejected truth

II Timothy 3:16-17–"*All Scripture is given by inspiration of God and is profitable for doctrine, for reproof, for correction, for instruction in righteousness: that the man of God* **MAY BE PERFECT**, **THROUGHLY FURNISHED** *unto all good works.*"

b) Gnostic doctrine

MASONIC "*The world-Bibles, then, are fragments. . . of Revelation . . . The next deeper sense of the word describes the* **MASS OF TEACHING HELD BY THE GREAT BROTHERHOOD OF SPIRITUAL TEACHERS** *in trust for men; this teaching is embodied in books, written in symbols. . .* **THIS IS THE REVELATION**. *This is the priceless treasure which the Guardians of humanity hold in charge, and* **FROM WHICH THEY SELECT, from time to time, FRAGMENTS TO FORM THE BIBLES OF THE WORLD**." (Book #1, p. 277)

"*. . . it was held by a vast number, even during the preaching of Paul, that the* **WRITINGS OF THE APOSTLES WERE INCOMPLETE** *that they contained only the* **GERMS OF**

ANOTHER DOCTRINE, which must receive from the hands of *PHILOSOPHY*, not only the systematic arrangement. which was wanting, but all the development which lay concealed therein." (Book #6, p. 248)

". . . all the Gnostic sects had Mysteries and an initiation. They all claimed to possess a secret doctrine, coming to them directly from Jesus Christ, different from that of the Gospels and Epistles *AND SUPERIOR TO THOSE COMMUNICATIONS*, which in their eyes, were merely exoteric." (Book #6, p. 542)

SCHAFF "*Finally, human comprehension, finite as it is, will be able to grasp only selected aspects of the infinite divine truth. Therefore, creeds are **ALSO ONLY PARTIAL MANIFESTATIONS OF THE CHRISTIAN TRUTH**, even though for this very reason they are complementary and not contradictory in nature, so that **ONLY TOGETHER WILL THEY FULLY MANIFEST THE DIVINE TRUTH**.*" (Book #191 p. 275)

c) Gnostic scriptures

d) Greek changes

4) Jesus revealed gnostic Scriptures secretly to the apostles after he died

a) Rejected truth

John 18:20–"*Jesus answered him, **I SPAKE OPENLY TO THE WORLD**; I ever taught in the synagogue, and in the temple, whither the Jews always resort; **AND IN SECRET HAVE I SAID NOTHING**.*"

II Timothy 1:13–"*Hold fast the form of sound words, which thou hast heard of me. . .*"

II Timothy 2:2–"*And the things that thou hast heard of me **AMONG MANY WITNESSES**, the same commit thou to faithful men, who shall be able to teach others also.*"

b) Gnostic doctrine

OPHITES "*Christos and Wisdom . . . restored Jesus to life and gave Him an ethereal body, in which He remained 18 months on earth, and receiving from Wisdom the perfect knowledge (. . . Gnosis), communicated it to a small number of His apostles, and then arose. . .*" (Book #6, p. 563-564)

c) Gnostic scripture

APOCRYPHON OF JOHN-- (Book #12, p. 30)
"*James writes to . . . thus: . . . Since you asked that I send you **A SECRET BOOK** which was revealed to me and Peter by the Lord, I could not turn you away. . . or gainsay you; but I have written it in the Hebrew alphabet and sent it to you, and you **ALONE**.*"

d) Greek changes

5) The purpose of revelation is to reveal man's deepest self (transcendental self is the god within)

a) Rejected truth

John 20:31–"*But these are written, that ye might believe that Jesus is the Christ, the Son of God; and that believing ye might have life through His name.*"

b) Gnostic doctrine

"*. . . spiritual man . . . becomes conscious of his deepest self when he hears the word of revelation.*" (Book #2, p. 567)

c) Gnostic scriptures

d) Greek changes

6) Present new revelations are given by "spirit guides," and are superior to revelation as found in the written Word of God

a) Rejected truth

Revelation 22:18–"*For I testify unto every man that heareth the words of the prophecy of this book, If any man shall **ADD UNTO THESE THINGS**, God shall add unto him the plagues that are written in this book.*"

b) Gnostic doctrine

"*Gnosis meant pre-eminently knowledge of God. . . On the one hand it is closely bound up with **REVOLUTIONARY EXPERIENCE** . . . either through sacred and secret lore or through **INNER ILLUMINATION**.*" (Book #20, p. 34-35)

"*Non-conformism was almost a principle of the gnostic mind and was closely connected with the doctrine of the **SOVEREIGN 'SPIRIT' AS A SOURCE OF DIRECT KNOWLEDGE AND ILLUMINATION**.*" (Book #20, p. 42)

"*. . . every one of them generates **SOMETHING NEW**, day by day, according to his ability; for no one is deemed 'perfect' who does not develop among them some mighty fictions.*" (Book #24, Vol.1, p. 343, IRENAEUS quote)

c) Gnostic scriptures

d) Greek changes

Acts 4:25
BY2 > KJV-- "*Who by the mouth of thy servant David hast said*"
SBA > WH NU > NASV NIV ESV by (A) **HOLY SPIRIT** by mouth of **OUR FATHER** David your servant did say

b. Inspiration

1) God did not superintend every word of Scripture

a) Rejected truth

II Timothy 3:16–"***ALL*** *Scripture is given by inspiration of God and is profitable. . .*"

Proverbs30:5–"***EVERY WORD*** *of God is pure. . .*"

b) Gnostic doctrine

HORT – ". . . *Westcott is just coming out with his 'The Elements of the Gospel Harmony.' I have seen the first sheet on* ***INSPIRATION****, which is a wonderful step in advance of* ***COMMON ORTHODOX HERESY****.*" (Book #10, Vol.1, p. 181)

"*If you make a decided conviction of the* ***ABSOLUTE INFALLIBILITY OF THE NEW TESTAMENT*** *. . . I fear I could not join you. . . .I recognize 'Providence' in Biblical writings. Most strongly I recognize it; but I am not prepared to say that it necessarily involves* ***ABSOLUTE INFALLIBILITY****.*" (Book #10, Vol.1, p. 420-421)

"*If I am ultimately driven to admit* ***OCCASIONAL ERRORS****, I shall be sorry; but it will not shake my conviction of the providential ordering of human elements in the Bible.*" (Book #10, Vol .1, p. 421-422)

"*I am convinced that any view of the Gospels, which distinctly and consistently recognizes for them* ***A NATURAL AND HISTORICAL ORIGIN*** *(whether under a special Divine superintendence or not) and assumes that they did not drop down ready-made from heaven must and will be startling to an immense proportion of educated English people. . . But so far, at least,* ***WESTCOTT AND I ARE PERFECTLY AGREED*** *. . .*" (Book #10, Vol.1, p. 420)

c) Gnostic scriptures

d) Greek textual changes

Matthew 15:6 (Critical text teaches that the traditional text is **NOT** God's word)
BYZ > KJV ". . . *Thus have ye made the* ***COMMANDMENT*** *of God of none effect by your tradition.*"
ORIGEN> SB) WH NU > NASV NIV ESV . . . **WORD** of God. . .

Luke 4:4
BYZ, >KJV–". . . ***BUT BY EVERY WORD OF GOD***"
BS > WH NU> NASV NIV ESV ESV **omit**

I Peter 1:23 (Critical text does not teach that God's preserved Word is eternally available to man
BYZ > KJV ". . . *word of God, which liveth and abideth* ***for ever****.*"
SBAC) WH NU> NASV NIV ESV **omits** "**for ever**"

2) Jesus did not say everything that is attributed to him in the Gospels

a) Rejected truth

Psalm 19:7–". . . the **_TESTIMONY OF THE LORD IS SURE_**, _making wise the simple_"

Psalm 119:152–"_Concerning thy testimonies, I have known of old that thou hast founded them **FOR EVER**._"

b) Gnostic doctrine

THE JESUS SEMINAR
"_82% of the words ascribed to Jesus in the gospels were **NOT ACTUALLY SPOKEN BY HIM**, according to the Jesus Seminar._" (Book #18, p. 5) (See following verses that change '**Jesus said**' to "**he said**" giving the impression that this is what the apostles remember He said, rather than His actual Words.)

". . . _of the Words attributed to Jesus in the Gospel of John the Fellows of the Seminar were **UNABLE TO FIND A SINGLE SAYING THEY COULD WITH CERTAINTY TRACE BACK TO THE HISTORICAL JESUS**_" (Book #18, p. 10)

c) Gnostic scriptures

d) Greek changes

Mark 6:11
BYZ A > KJV "**_VERILY I SAY UNTO YOU, IT SHALL BE MORE TOLERABLE FOR SODOM AND GOMORRAH IN THE DAY OF JUDGMENT, THAN FOR THAT CITY_**."
SBC > WH NU > NASV NIV ESV **omit**

Mark 15:34
BYZ AC > KJV   "_Jesus cried with a loud voice **SAYING**. . . My God, my God, Why hast thou forsaken me?_
SB > WH NU > NASV NIV ESV   **omit "saying"**

Luke 23:34
BYZ SA > KJV; (WH) (NU) > NASV NIV "**_THEN SAID JESUS, FATHER FORGIVE THEM FOR THEY KNOW NOT WHAT THEY DO._**"
SB **omit**

Luke 11:53 (Concerning the 6 Woes)
BYZ A > KJV-- "**_AND AS HE SAID THESE THINGS UNTO THEM_**,"
SBC > WH NU > NASV NIV ESV "**_AND AS HE WENT OUT THENCE_**"

These verses **omit "and the Lord said"** Luke 7:31, 22:31

This verse **omits "says to them Jesus"** Matthew 13:51

These verses **omit "saying"** when referring to Jesus
Mark 1:15. 1:25
Luke 4:4. 8:30, 18:40-41

These verses change "**Jesus said** (BYZ >KJV, NIV, ESV) to "**(he) said**" (variations of BSA> WH NU > NASV ESV) implying heresy or paraphrase rather than His actual Words.
Matthew 4:18-19, 9:12, 12:25, 15:16, 17:11, 17:20, 18:2-3, 22:37; 24:2; Mark 1:41, 7:27 8:1, 11:14, 11:15, 12:41, 14:22; 7:22, 8:38, 13:2, 23:43; John 4:16, 8:20, 8:21

3) The Word of God is full of errors

a) Rejected truth

Psalm 12:6-7"*The words of the Lord are **PURE** words: as silver tried in a furnace of earth, purified seven times.*"

Psalm 119:140–"*Thy word is **VERY PURE**: therefore thy servant loveth it.*"

Psalm 119:160–"*Thy word is **TRUE FROM THE BEGINNING**: . . .*"

II Timothy 2:19–"*Nevertheless the foundation of God **STANDETH SURE, HAVING THIS SEAL**,*"

b) Gnostic doctrine

SCHAFF--"*He also voted against the **INERRANCY STATEMENT ABOUT THE BIBLE**, committing himself to the authority of the Scriptures, but not to the **VERBAL THEORY OF INSPIRATION OF** the ultra-conservatives.*" (Book #11, p. 92)

c) Gnostic scriptures
TESTIMONY OF TRUTH--"*Rather, we have been born again by the word.*" (Book #12, p. 452)

d) Greek changes

c. Preservation

1) The Apostolic Bible is only a temporary substitute until the real Gnostic one is revealed to future generations

a) Rejected truth

Psalm 33:11–"*The counsel of the Lord **STANDETH FOR EVER**, the thoughts of his heart **TO ALL GENERATIONS**.*"

Psalm 100:5–". . . *His truth **ENDURETH TO ALL GENERATIONS**.*"

Psalm 119:160–". . . "*every one of thy righteous judgments **ENDURETH FOR EVER**.*"

Isaiah 40:8–*"The grass withereth, the flower fadeth; but the word of our God shall **STAND FOREVER**."*

Matthew 24:35–*"Heaven and earth shall pass away, but **MY WORDS SHALL NOT PASS AWAY**."*

II Timothy 2:19–*"... the foundation of God **STANDETH SURE, HAVING THIS SEAL** ..."*

I Peter 1:25– *"But the word of the Lord **ENDURETH FOR EVER**."*

b) Gnostic doctrine

MASONIC--Initiation for Master Mason's degree:

*"... and as **THE MASTER'S WORD IS NOW LOST, THE FIRST WORD SPOKEN AFTER THE BODY IS RAISED** (Christ) **SHALL BE A SUBSTITUTE FOR THE MASTER'S WORD UNTIL FUTURE GENERATIONS SHALL FIND OUT THE RIGHT ONE**."* (Book #17, p. 36)

Initiation for Royal Master's Degree:

"... this word should ... not be given until the temple was completed ..." (Book #17, p. 80)

Initiation for Prince of Rose-Croix Degree:

*"... **THE SACRED WORD IS LOST**; therefore it is impossible we can give it to you, nevertheless it is not our intention to remain inactive: we will endeavor to recover it. Are you disposed to follow us? ... The black apron with which I invest you ... will also serve to show you those who are in search of the true word ..."* (Book #17, p. 163) (Answer - The Rosicrucians)

c) Gnostic scriptures

THE NAG HAMMADI LIBRARY
"Opens the secrets of a religion which the Gnostics themselves had hoped would be kept sealed until the Last Day." (Book #12, Back Cover comment)

d) Greek changes

Matthew 15:6
BYZ > KJV *"Thus have ye made the **COMMANDMENT** of God of none effect ..."*
ORIGEN > SB > WH NU > NASV NIV ESV-- *"... the **WORD** of God"*

1 Peter 1:23
BYZ > KJV - *"word of God which liveth and abideth **for ever**"*
SBAC > WH NU > NASV NIV ESV - **omit "for ever"**

II John 9

BYZ > KJV–"*he that abideth in the doctrine **OF CHRIST**, he hath both the Father and the Son.*"
AB > WH NU > NASV NIV-- **omit "of the Christ"**

d. Authority

1) Only Gnostic scriptures are authoritative

a) Rejected truth

II Thessalonians 2:15–"*Therefore, brethren, stand fast, and **hold the TRADITIONS** which ye have been taught, whether by word, or our epistle.*"

b) Gnostic doctrine

"*In this life the 'pneumatics,' as the possessors of gnosis called themselves, are set apart from the great mass of mankind. The immediate illumination not only **MAKES THE INDIVIDUAL SOVEREIGN IN THE SPHERE OF KNOWLEDGE** . . . but also determines the sphere of action.*" (Book #20, p. 46)

"*The **traditional canon** of texts **NO LONGER HAS AUTHORITY**"* (Book #12 p. 548)

MASONIC–"*Modern Christianity no longer gives to the world a sufficiently definite, clear, simple, exact and unequivocal, or **AUTHORITATIVE expression** of the Great 'Word of Instruction'"* (Book #13 p. 149)

HORT–"*There are, I fear, still more **SERIOUS DIFFERENCES BETWEEN US ON THE SUBJECT OF AUTHORITY, AND ESPECIALLY THE AUTHORITY OF THE BIBLE** . . . The errors and prejudices, which we agree in wishing to remove, can surely be more wholesomely and. . . effectually reached by individual efforts of an indirect kind than by combined open assault. **AT PRESENT VERY MANY ORTHODOX BUT RATIONAL MEN ARE BEING UNAWARES ACTED ON BY INFLUENCES WHICH WILL ASSUREDLY BEAR GOOD FRUIT IN DUE TIME**, if the process is allowed to go on quietly; but I cannot help fearing that a premature crisis would frighten back many into the merest traditionalism.*" (Book #10, Vol.1:400)

c) Gnostic scriptures

d) Greek textual changes

Luke 4:4 (Critical text does not teach that **EVERY WORD** in Scripture is authoritative)
BYZ, A> KJV - "***BUT BY EVERY WORD OF GOD***"
BS> WH NU > NASV NIV ESV - **omitted**

Luke 6:48 (**Critical text does not teach that God's word is the church's authority and is an unchanging foundation**)
BYZ > KJV - "*it **WAS FOUNDED UPON A ROCK**"*
SB > WH NU > NASV NIV ESV --- "*it **WAS WELL BUILT**"*

(Note- the Critical text uses any Greek text to justify its denial of the authority of each book of the New Testament)

Matthew 28:20
BYZ > KJV -"*AMEN*"
ORIGEN > SBA > WH NU > NASV NIV ESV - <u>omit</u>

Mark 16:20
BYZ, AC > KJV- "*AMEN*"
A > WH NU > NASV NIV ESV- <u>omit</u>

Luke 24:53
BYZ, BA > KJV - "*AMEN*"
S > WH NU > NASV ESV - <u>omit</u>

John 21:25
BYZ > KJV- "*AMEN*"
SBAC> WH NU > NASV NIV ESV - <u>omit</u>

Romans 16:24
BYZ > KJV - "*AMEN*"
ORIGEN > BSAC > WH NU > NASV NIV ESV- <u>omit</u>

1 Corinthians 16:24
BYZ, SAC > KJV, NASV - "*AMEN*"
B > WH NU > NIV-- <u>omit</u>

II Corinthians 13:13, Ephesians 6:24, Philippians 4:23, Colossians 4:18, I Thessalonians 5:28, II Thessalonians 3:18, I Timothy 6:21. Titus 3:15, Philemon 25, Hebrews 13:25, I Peter 5:14, II Peter 3:18, I John 5:21, II John 13, Revelation 22:21
KJB- "*AMEN*"
NASV NIV-- <u>omit</u>

e. Propagation

1) The true word of God is kept secret through an oral tradition

a) Rejected truth (The written word is the same as the oral tradition)

II Thessalonians 2:15 " . . . *hold fast the traditions which ye have been taught,* ***WHETHER BY WORD, OR OUR EPISTLE*.*"

Exodus 24:4 "*And Moses* ***WROTE ALL THE WORDS OF THE LORD*** *. . .*"

Deuteronomy 27:8 "*And thou shalt* ***WRITE UPON THE STONES ALL THE WORDS OF THIS LAW*** *very plainly.*"

II Kings 23:2 ". . . *and he read in their ears* ___ALL THE WORDS OF THE BOOK OF THE COVENANT___ *which was found in the house of the Lord.*"

Jeremiah 16:10 ". . . *Thou shalt shew this people* ___ALL THESE WORDS___, . . ."

Jeremiah 30:2 ". . . *write thee* ___ALL THE WORDS THAT I HAVE SPOKEN UNTO THEE IN A BOOK___."

Jeremiah 36:2 "*Take thee a roll of a book, and write therein* ___ALL THE WORDS___ *that I have spoken unto thee. . .*"

      b) Gnostic doctrine

"*These little Gnostic sects and groups all lived in the conviction that they possessed a secret and mysterious knowledge* ___IN NO WAY ACCESSIBLE___ *to those outside, which was not to be proved or* ___PROPAGATED___, *but believed in by the initiated, and anxiously guarded as a secret.*" (Book #3, p. 153)

MASONIC "___THE WRITINGS OF THE APOSTLES___, *they (the Gnostics) said, in addressing themselves to mankind in general,* ___ENUNCIATED ONLY THE ARTICLES OF THE VULGAR FAITH___; *but transmitted the mysteries of knowledge to* ___SUPERIOR MINDS___, *to the Elect,* ___MYSTERIES HANDED DOWN FROM GENERATION TO GENERATION IN ESOTERIC TRADITIONS___; *and to this science, of the mysteries they gave the name of (Gnosis).*" (Book #6 p. 248)

      c) Gnostic "scriptures"

THE SENTENCES OF SEXTUS (Book #12, p. 506)
"*Do not give the word of God to everyone.*"

      d) Greek changes

Luke 22:61
BYZ A KJV> NASV?- "*Peter remembered* ___THE WORD___ *of the Lord.*"
SBC > WH NU >NIV-- "*Peter remembered* ___THE SPOKEN WORD___ *of the Lord.*"

Acts 12:24
BYZ > KJV; NU > NIV ESV- "*the word of* ___GOD___ *grew and multiplied*"
? > WH > NASV-- "*the word of* ___THE LORD___ . . ."
1.f.1)

f. Interpretation

1) The Bible can only be understood in the light of other documents.

      a) Rejected truth

Psalm 119:130 "*The entrance of thy words giveth light; it giveth understanding unto the simple.*"

1 Corinthians 2:13-14 *"Which things also we speak, **NOT IN WORDS WHICH MAN'S WISDOM TEACHETH, BUT WHICH THE HOLY GHOST TEACHETH; COMPARING SPIRITUAL THINGS WITH SPIRITUAL**. But the natural man receiveth not the things of the Spirit of God: for they are foolishness unto him; **NEITHER CAN HE KNOW THEM**, because they are spiritually discerned."*

b) Gnostic doctrine

LIGHTFOOT *"was convinced of **THE NECESSITY OF DEALING WITH THE NEW TESTAMENT, NOT IN ISOLATION** as was the usual practice, but **IN RELATION TO THE ENTIRE CORPUS OF EARLY CHRISTIAN WRITINGS** . . . . In the 20th century Walter Bauer . . . argued that in many places the earliest discernible form of Christianity was often a form that later came to be labeled as heresy. . . . H. Koester . . . **PLACES THE NEW TESTAMENT WRITINGS IN THE LARGER CONTEXT OF THE APOSTOLIC FATHERS AS WELL AS GNOSTIC AND APOCRYPHAL DOCUMENTS**"* (Book #7, p. 14-15)

SCHAFF *". . . human comprehension, finite as it is, will be able to grasp only selected aspects of the infinite divine truth. Therefore, creeds are **ALSO ONLY PARTIAL MANIFESTATIONS** of the Christian truth, even though for this very reason they are complementary and not contradictory in nature, **SO THAT ONLY TOGETHER WILL THEY FULLY MANIFEST THE DIVINE TRUTH**."* (Book #19, p. 275)

c. Gnostic scriptures

d. Greek changes

2) The Bible is to be interpreted allegorically

a) Rejected truth

Deuteronomy 27:8-- *"And thou shalt write upon the stones all the words of this law **VERY PLAINLY**."*

Habakkuk 2:2--*"And the Lord answered me and said, Write the vision and **MAKE IT PLAIN UPON TABLES**, that he may run that readeth it."*

II Corinthians 11:3-- *"But I fear, lest by any means, as the serpent beguiled Eve through his subtilty, so your minds should be corrupted from the **SIMPLICITY THAT IS IN CHRIST**."*

b) Gnostic doctrine

*"Irenaeus provided two guidelines for drawing the boundary that would exclude **GNOSTIC** teachers from the Christian community . . . The second guideline is Irenaeus's rejection of **GNOSTIC ALLEGORIZATION OF SCRIPTURE**. He insists that biblical passages must mean what they appear to mean and that they must be interpreted within their contexts."* (Book #2, p. 579)

PLATO– "*. . . justly says, that spiritual things can be made intelligible only through FIGURES; and the forms of ALLEGORICAL EXPRESSION which, in a rude age, had been adopted unconsciously, were designedly chosen by the philosopher as the most appropriate vehicles for theological ideas.*" (Book #6, p. 678)

PHILO-- "*The JEWISH-GREEK SCHOOL OF ALEXANDRIA is known only by two of its Chiefs, Aristobulus and Philo, both Jews of Alexandrian in Egypt . . . Philo . . . endeavored to show that the Hebrews writings, by their system of ALLEGORIES, were the true source of all religious and philosophical doctrines. According to him the literal meaning is for the vulgar alone.*" (Book #6, p. 250)

ORIGEN-- "*. . . held that the Gospels were not to be taken in their literal sense. . .* " (Book #6, p. 266)

HORT-- "*The authors of the Article doubtless ASSUMED THE STRICTLY HISTORICAL CHARACTER OF THE ACCOUNT OF THE FALL IN GENESIS. THIS ASSUMPTION IS NOW, IN MY BELIEF, NO LONGER REASONABLE. But the early chapters of Genesis remain a DIVINELY APPOINTED PARABLE . . .* " (Book #10, V.2, p. 329)

c) Gnostic scriptures

d) Greek changes

3) Only the spiritually mature can understand the Bible's hidden allegorical meaning

a) Rejected truth

1 Corinthians 2:16– "*For who hath known the mind of the Lord, that he may instruct him? But **WE HAVE THE MIND OF CHRIST**.*"

b) Gnostic doctrine

ORIGEN-- "*It was Origen who systematically developed this method of interpretation . . . Origen needs this **ALLEGORICAL** method in order to establish the system of his peculiar doctrines and material . . . First, the Scriptures have a **SOMATIC OR LITERAL SENSE** upon which the simpler souls of the multitude depend. Exegesis is to find out that sense, but must remember withal that it is intended only to **CONCEAL THE TRUE SENSE**. Second, the Scriptures have a **PSYCHICAL OR MORAL SENSE** which refers to the individual soul in this life and to its ethical relations, including its relations to God. And third, the Scriptures have a **PNEUMATIC OR SPECULATIVE SENSE** . . . the profounder meaning which is sealed to all save the mature believer. There are cases where the literal sense must be rejected altogether (as for instance, Genesis 19; 20 ff; 25:1 ff; 29:27 f; 30:3,9). The literal sense is intended to conceal the spiritual sense in order that pearls may not be cast before swine. But **THE MATURE BELIEVER WILL PRESS BEYOND THE LITERAL SENSE AND DISCOVER THE ESOTERIC TENETS OF THE DIVINE WORD**.*" (Book #7 p. 36)

*"**THE DOCTRINE OF DIFFERING DEGREES OF KNOWLEDGE** may be best illustrated by Origen's treatment of the primitive eschatology. The hope of the second coming of Christ is taken in a literal and material sense by simple believers. Origen does not attack their belief; it is better that they should believe the right thing in the wrong way*

Stop Being Conceited!

Here is another Greek present prohibition. It means to stop an action already in progress. Paul was telling these believers to "*stop being wise in your own conceits.*" They were apparently all puffed up and filled with self, and selfish things, rather than what they could do for someone else. Paul says "*Stop doing that and being wise in your own conceit. Think of others.*"

*Zvzthan not believe it at all, and it is the best of which they are capable. But the Christian preacher has a responsibility to educated minds who, so Origen observes, are often distressed by this article of the creed. **THE SPIRITUAL, SYMBOLIC MEANING OF THE DOCTRINE** of the second coming may be either the universal expansion of the Church throughout the world, bringing all men to obedience of Christ, or the inward coming of Christ to the soul, when he comes not in humiliation but in glory, uniting the believer to himself in a union so intense that the believer leaves behind the limitations of this mortal state, and is raised to be one spirit with the Lord.*" (Book #8 p. 77-78)

MASONIC-- "*We have seen that **ORIGEN**, one of the sanest of men and versed in occult knowledge, teaches that the Scriptures are threefold, consisting of Body, Soul, and Spirit. He says that the Body of the Scriptures is made up of the outer words of the histories and the stories, and does not hesitate to say that these are **NOT LITERALLY TRUE**, but are only stories for the **INSTRUCTION OF THE IGNORANT**. He even goes so far as to remark that statements are made in those stories that are obviously untrue, in order that the glaring contradictions that lie on the surface may stir people up to inquire as to the real meaning of these impossible relations. He says that so long as men are ignorant the Body is enough for them . . . As the mind grows, as the intellect develops . . . when he is stirred up to seek for a deeper meaning, and he begins to find the Soul of the Scriptures. That Soul is the reward of the intelligent seeker, and he escapes from the bonds of the letter that killeth. The Spirit of the Scriptures may only be seen by the spiritually enlightened man; only those in whom the Spirit is evolved can understand the spiritual meaning . . . The reason for this method of Revelation is not far to seek; it is the only way in which one teaching can be made available for minds at different stages of **EVOLUTION**. . . .*" (Book #1 p. 275-276)

c) Gnostic scriptures

d) Greek textual changes

Ephesians 3:9 (**Critical texts do not teach that all believers understand God's mystery**)
BYZ > KJV; (NU) > NIV ESV-- "*And to make **ALL** see what is the fellowship of the mystery, which from the beginning of the world hath been hid in God. . . .*"
ORIGEN > SA > WH > NASV-- **omits "all**"

Colossians 2:7 (B,A,C) (**Critical texts do not teach that all believers are able to abound IN the teachings of the faith**)
BYZ > KJV (WH)-- "*abounding **THEREIN** with thanksgiving.*"
SAC > NU > NASV NIV ESV-- **omits "therein**"

I Thessalonians 2:7 (<u>**Critical text teaches that the Thessalonians were "*spiritually ignorant*"**</u>)
BYZ > KJV; NASV NIV ESV - "we were **<u>GENTLE</u>** in your midst"
SBC > WH NU-- "we were **<u>SIMPLE</u>** in your midst"

I John 2:20 (S,B) (<u>**Critical text does not teach that all believers can know EVERY TRUTH in Scripture**</u>)
BYZ, AC > KJV-- "But ye have an unction from the Holy One, and <u>*ye know ALL THINGS*</u>."
SB > WH NU > NASV NIV ESV-- ". . . and <u>**YOU ALL know**</u>"

2. THEOLOGY (God)

Jude 4– "For there are certain men crept in unawares, who were before of old ordained to this condemnation, ungodly men . . . **<u>DENYING THE ONLY LORD GOD, AND OUR LORD JESUS CHRIST</u>**."

a. Person of God

1) There Is an Unknown God who Is not the Creator

a) Rejected truth

Acts 17:23-24-- "For as I passed by, and beheld your devotions, 1 found an altar with this inscription, **<u>TO THE UNKNOWN GOD</u>**. Whom therefore ye ignorantly worship, him declare I unto you. **<u>GOD THAT MADE THE WORLD AND ALL THINGS THEREIN</u>**, seeing that He is Lord of heaven and earth, dwelleth not in temples made with hands."

Romans 1:19-21-- "that which may be known of God is manifest in them; for God hath. shewed it unto them. For the **<u>INVISIBLE THINGS OF HIM</u>** from the creation of the world **<u>ARE CLEARLY SEEN</u>**, being understood by the things that are made, even His eternal power and Godhead; so that they are without excuse. Because that when they knew God, they glorified him not as God, . . ."

b) Gnostic. doctrine

"The transcendent God Himself is hidden from all creatures and is **<u>UNKNOWABLE BY NATURAL CONCEPTS</u>**. Knowledge of Him requires supranatural revelation and illumination and even then can hardly be expressed otherwise than in negative terms." (Book #20, p. 42-43)

PHILO OF ALEXANDRIA-- ". . . calls the Logos, who is instrumental in creation, both 'a second god' and 'archangel' on the one hand, and 'Lord' (YHVH) and 'Name' (i.e. YHVH) on the other. Jewish Gnostics such as Simon and Cerinthus affirm that the *demiurge (identified with YHVH) was in fact this angel of the Lord, who had not yet rebelled against God. In the Apocryphon of John the angel is called Saklas (Aramaic for 'fool') because he does not know that there is a God greater than he."* (Book #2, p. 569)

VALENTINUS, MARCION, APELLES-- *". . . were familiar with the myth contained in the Apocryphon of John, all held that the demiurge was an angel. This is a typically Jewish concept."* (Book #2 p. 569) (Demiurge being the evil creator)

MARCION-- *". . . one overpowering idea: God, the Father of Jesus was not the Hebrew YHVH. Like the gnostics, he distinguished between **UNKNOWN GOD** (whom he felt to be the only genuine God) and a lower divinity, the demiurge, who is responsible for creation and interacts with man."* (Book #2, p. 571)

c) Gnostic scriptures

APOCRYPHON OF JOHN-- *". . . can be summarized as follows: from the Unknown God (who exists beyond thought and name) and his spouse (who is his counterpart and mirror) issued the spiritual world. The last of the spiritual entities, Sophia, became wanton and brought forth a monster, the Demiurge. He organized the zodiac and the seven planets. He proclaimed: 'I am a Jealous god, apart from me there is no other.' Then a voice was heard, teaching him that above him existed the Unknown God and his spouse."* (Book #2, p. 570)

d) Greek changes

2) God is a monad existing in three forms--Father, Mother, Son

a) Rejected truth

Genesis 1:26-- *"And God said, Let **US** make man in **OUR** image. . ."*
Matthew 28:19-- *". . . baptizing them in the name of the **FATHER**, and of the **SON**, and of the **HOLY GHOST**."*
II Corinthians 13:14-- *"The grace of the **LORD JESUS CHRIST**, and the love of **GOD**, and the communion of the **HOLY GHOST**, be with you all."*

b) Gnostic doctrine

MASONIC-- *"This Trinity is the divine Self, the divine Spirit, the was and is and is to come. . ."* (Book #1, p. 195-6)

c) Gnostic scriptures

THE APOCRYPHON OF JOHN (Book #12, p. 105-106)
*"Straightway the heavens opened and the whole creation which is below heaven shone, and the world was shaken . . . I was afraid, and. behold I saw in the light .a youth who stood by me. While I looked at him he became like an old man. And he changed his likeness again becoming like a servant. **THERE WAS NOT A PLURALITY BEFORE ME, BUT THERE WAS A LIKENESS WITH MULTIPLE FORMS** in the light, and the likenesses appeared through each other, and the likeness had three forms. He said to me, John . . . I am the one who is with you always. **I AM THE FATHER, I AM THE MOTHER, I AM THE SON** . . . The **MONAD** is a monarchy with nothing above it. It is he who exists as God and Father of everything, the invisible One who is above everything, who exists as incorruption, which is in the pure light into which no eye can look."*

GOSPEL OF EGYPTIANS (Book #12, p. 209)
*"Three powers came forth from him; they are **THE FATHER, THE MOTHER**, (and) **THE SON** . . . From that place the three powers (came) forth, the three ogdoads that (the Father brings) forth, in silence with his providence, from his bosom, i.e. the **FATHER, THE MOTHER, (AND) THE SON**. The first ogdoad . . . the **ANDROGYNOUS FATHER**. The second ogdoad-power, **THE MOTHER**, the virginal Barbelon . . . The third ogdoad-power, the **SON OF THE SILENT SILENCE**."*

d) Greek changes

I John 5:7-8 BYZ > KJV-- *"for there are three that bear record **IN HEAVEN, THE FATHER, THE WORD, AND THE HOLY GHOST: AND THESE THREE ARE ONE. AND THERE ARE THREE THAT BEAR WITNESS IN EARTH**, the Spirit, and the water, and the blood: and these three agree in one."*
CLEMENT > BYZ SBAC > WH NU > NASV* NIV ESV*
"Three there are who bear witness, the Spirit and the water and the blood."

3) God has a fallen nature

a) Rejected truth

Deuteronomy 32:4-- *"He is the Rock, his work is perfect: for all His ways are judgment: a God of truth and **WITHOUT INIQUITY**, just and right is He."*

Matthew 5:48-- *"Be ye therefore perfect, even as your Father which is in heaven is **PERFECT**."*

b) Gnostic doctrine

". . . *Gnostic systems make great use of the idea of a **FALL OF THE DEITY HIMSELF; BY THE FALL OF THE GODHEAD** into the world of matter, this matter, previously insensible, is animated into life and activity, and then arise the powers . . . who hold sway over this world.*" (Book #3, p. 154)

c) Gnostic scriptures

PARAPHRASE OF SHEM-- (Book #12, p. 353-354)
"*When he will have appeared, O Shem, upon the earth, (in) the place which will be called Sodom, (then) safeguard the insight which I shall give you. For those whose heart was pure will congregate to you, because of the word which you will reveal. For when you appear in the world, **DARK NATURE WILL SHAKE AGAINST YOU**, together with the winds and a demon, that they may destroy the insight. But you, proclaim quickly to the Sodomites your universal teaching, for they are, your members. For the demon of human form (Lot) will part from that place by my will, since he is ignorant. He will guard this utterance. But the Sodomites according to the will of the Majesty, will bear witness to the universal testimony. They will rest with a pure conscience in the place of their repose, which is the unbegotten Spirit. And as these things will happen, **SODOM WILL BE BURNED UNJUSTLY BY A BASE NATURE**. For the evil will not cease, in order that your majesty may reveal that place.*

THE TESTIMONY OF TRUTH-- (Book #12, p. 455)
"*But what sort is this God? First (He) **MALICIOUSLY** refused Adam from eating of the tree of knowledge. And secondly he said, Adam, where are you? **GOD DOES NOT HAVE FOREKNOWLEDGE**; otherwise, would he not know from the beginning? And afterwards he said, Let us cast him out of this place, lest he eat of the tree of life and live forever. **SURELY HE HAS SHOWN HIMSELF TO BE A MALICIOUS GRUDGER**. And what kind of God is this*"?

d) Greek changes reflected in Versions

Matthew 19:17
BYZ) KJV-- "Why **CALLEST THOU ME** good? there is **NONE** good **BUT ONE, THAT IS, GOD**:"
ORIGEN) SB) WH NU) NASV NIV ESV-- "*Why **ASK ME CONCERNING THE** good? **ONE** is good.*"

4) God is androgynous

a) Rejected truth

John 1:18-- *"No man hath seen **GOD** at any time; the only begotten Son, who is in the bosom of **THE FATHER**, he hath declared him*
*(*God is always referred to as He, Him, His)

b) Gnostic doctrine

*"PRE-CHRISTIAN GNOSIS: . . . The ancient Egyptians spoke freely about . . . the **HOMOSEXUAL BEHAVIOR OF THEIR GODS**."* (Book #2, p. 566)

*"The first God, Nous or Intellect, is **ANDROGYNOUS** . . . male function and female substance, coexist in him. His goodness itself makes him generate a **SECOND GOD**, a most beautiful Anthropos, **WITH WHOM HE FALLS IN LOVE** and to whom he entrusts his creatures."'* (Book #28, p. 107)

MASONIC-- (Book #6, p. 849-850)
*"Reversing the letters of the Ineffable Name, and dividing it, it becomes BI-SEXUAL, as the word . . . JAH is. . . (Jehovah) . . . The Word is the First and Only-begotten of the Father; and the awe with which the Highest Mysteries were regarded has imposed silence in respect to the Nature of the Holy Spirit . . . You see at the beginning of this reading, an old Hermetic Symbol copied from the 'Materia Prima' of **VALENTINUS** . . . Upon it you see a Triangle upon a Square, both of these contained in a circle; and above this, standing upon a **DRAGON**, a human body, with two arms only, but two heads, **ONE MALE AND THE OTHER FEMALE**. By the side of the male head is the Sun, and by that of the female head, the Moon . . . And the hand on the male side holds a Compass, and that on the female side, a Square."*

ORIGEN-- *"He (Christ) is the pre-existent eternal Logos through whom we pray to the Father, one whom we may even . . . describe as a '**SECOND GOD**' beside the Father."* (Book #8, p. 91-92)

c) Gnostic scriptures

GOSPEL OF THE EGYPTIANS (Book #12, p. 209)
*"The first ogdoad . . . is the . . . . **ANDROGYNOUS FATHER**."*

TRIMORPHIC PROTENNOIA (Book #12, p. 519)
*"I am **ANDROGYNOUS**. I am Mother and I am Father since I copulate with myself. I*

copulated with myself and with those who through me alone that the All stands firm."

d) Greek changes

e) Bible versions

THE NEW TESTAMENT AND PSALMS: AN INCLUSIVE VERSION
". . . removes or changes Bible verses that could prove offensive. God isn't referred to as 'Our Father' anymore. He, or it, is 'Father-Mother.'"

5) The term 'Lord' refers to 'the Father', not Jesus

a) Rejected truth

Romans 10:9-- *"That if thou shalt confess with thy mouth **THE LORD JESUS** and shalt believe in thine heart that God hath raised him from the dead, thou shalt be saved."*

b) Gnostic doctrine

HORT--commentary on Revelation
Revelation I:8-- *"I am the Alpha and Omega, the beginning and the ending, saith the Lord (God), which is, and which was, and which is to come, the Almighty."*
*"This verse must stand alone. **THE SPEAKER CANNOT BE OUR LORD**, when we consider 1:4, . . . and **ALL SCRIPTURAL ANALOGY IS AGAINST THE ATTRIBUTION OF 'THE LORD GOD' WITH OR WITHOUT 'ALMIGHTY' TO CHRIST** (Book #16, p. 26)–See Revelation 1:8 below."*

c) Gnostic scriptures

THE GOSPEL OF THOMAS (Book #12, p. 127)
"Jesus said, I All NOT YOUR MASTER (LORD)."

ASCLEPIUS (Book #12, p. 332)
*"And now listen! **GOD AND THE FATHER, EVEN THE LORD**, created man subsequent to the gods . . ."*

d) Greek changes

James 3:9
BYZ > KJV-- *"therewith bless we **GOD**, even the Father;"*
SBA > WH NV > NASV NIV ESV-- *"we bless **THE LORD** and Father"*

Revelation 1:8
BYZ pt) > KJV-- "*saith the Lord, which is, and which was, and which is **to come, the Almighty**.*"
BYZ (pt) SAC > WH NU > NASV NIV-- "*says the Lord **GOD** who is **. . .***"

6) The Son is not equal to the Father

a) Rejected truth

Philippians 2:5-6-- ". . . *Christ Jesus, who, being in the form of God, thought it not robbery **TO BE EQUAL WITH GOD**.*"

b) Gnostic doctrine

ORIGEN-- "*The Logos is the image of the Father's power - not an image of the Father so identical with the archetype that he can be said to be as much Father as the Father himself . . . The Logos is therefore God in relation to the lower order; he is God immanent (indwelling).*" (Book #8, p. 84)

". . . *the eternal Logos . . . describe(d) as a 'second God' beside the Father.*" (Book #8, p. 92)

HORT-- "*Thousands of persons who do not dream of rejecting St. John's gospel, would be horrified at its distinct enunciation, concluding (correctly enough according to logic) that **IT IS INCOMPATIBLE WITH THE BELIEF   OF THE EQUALITY OF THE THREE PERSONS OF THE TRINITY**. And I am now persuaded that this same scepticism of the carnal understanding is what makes us confound obedience on earth with slavery, authority with tyranny; and set down freedom as inconsistent with obedience. And I am likewise persuaded that practically men gain this seemingly impossible reconciliation in and through that same Spirit in whom **THE SON AND THE FATHER ARE–(I DO NOT NOW SAY ONE--THAT IS ANOTHER QUESTION) EQUAL**.*" (Book #10, Vol.1, p. 136)

c) Gnostic scriptures

d) Greek changes

Mark 12:32
BYZ > KJV NIV ESV– "***GOD** is one.*"
BYZ (Part) SBA) WH NU) NASV ESV-- "***HE** is one.*"

7) The Son is wiser than the Father

a) Rejected truth

Romans 16:27— *"To God only wise, be glory through Jesus Christ for ever."*

b) Gnostic doctrine

c) Gnostic scriptures

d) Greek changes reflected in Versions

I Timothy 1:17
BYZ > KJV-- *"only **WISE God**"*
BSAC > NASV, NIV ESV - <u>omits 'wise'</u>

Jude 25
BYZ) KJV-- *"only **WISE God** our Saviour,"*
BSAC> NASV, ESV - <u>omits 'wise'</u>

8) The Third Person of Gnostic Trinity is the Great Mother who is the personification of Wisdom (Sophia) and the Holy Spirit

a) Rejected truth

b) Gnostic doctrine

*"In almost all systems an important part is played by the **GREAT MOTHER** who appears under the most varied forms. At an early period and notably in the older systems of the Ophites . . . the (Mother) is the most prominent figure in the light-world, elevated above the (seven) and the great mother of the faithful. The sect of the Barbelo-gnostics takes its name from the 'female figure of the Barbelo (perhaps a corruption of . . . **'VIRGIN'** in Epiphanius. . .). But Gnostic speculation gives various accounts of the descent or fall of this **GODDESS OF HEAVEN** . . . The kindred idea of the light-maiden . . . has also a central place in the Manichaean scheme of salvation . . . In the Pistis-Sophia . . . with this figure of the mother-goddess who descends into the lower world seems to be closely connected the idea of the fallen **SOPHIA**, which is so widespread among the Gnostic systems. This Sophia . . . is a lower aeon at the extreme limit of the world of light, who sinks down into matter . . . or turns in presumptuous love towards the **SUPREME GOD**, and thus brings the Fall into the world of the aeons. This Sophia then appears as the mother of the 'seven' gods . . . There can hardly be any doubt that the figure of the great*

mother-goddess or goddess of heaven, who was worshipped throughout Asia under various forms and names (Astarte, Beltis, Atargatis, Cybel, the Syrian Aphrodite), was the prototype of the (mother) of the Gnostics. The character of the great goddess of heaven is still in many places fairly exactly preserved in the Gnostic speculations." (Book #3, p. 155-156)

*"In Mandaean lore Sophia appears in degraded form as a mean and lewd creature called the **HOLY SPIRIT**."* (Book #2, p. 570)

c) Gnostic scriptures

THE GOSPEL OF PHILIP (Book #12, p. 143)
*"Some said Mary conceived by the **HOLY SPIRIT**. They are in error. They do not know what they are saying. When did a woman ever conceive **BY A WOMAN**? Mary is the virgin whom no power **DEFILED**."*

d) Greek changes

9) God is the Universal Father of all mankind (All mankind are His sons)

a) Rejected truth

John 1:12-- *"But as many as received Him, to them gave he power **TO BECOME THE SONS OF GOD**, even to them that believe on His name."*

Romans 8:15-16-- *". . . ye have received the Spirit of **ADOPTION**, whereby we cry, Abba, Father. The Spirit itself beareth witness with our spirit that **WE ARE THE CHILDREN OF GOD**."*

Romans 9:26-- *"And it shall come to pass, that in the place where it was said unto them, **YE ARE NOT MY PEOPLE**; there shall they be called the **CHILDREN OF THE LIVING GOD**."*

Galatians 3:26-- *"For ye are all the **CHILDREN OF GOD BY FAITH IN CHRIST JESUS**."*

Ephesians 1:5-- *"Having predestinated us unto the **ADOPTION OF CHILDREN BY JESUS CHRIST TO HIMSELF**. . ."*

I John 3:10-- *"In this the **CHILDREN OF GOD** are manifest, and the **CHILDREN OF THE DEVIL** . ."*

John 8:41-44-- *". . . Then said they to him, We be not born of fornication; **WE HAVE ONE FATHER, EVEN GOD**. Jesus said unto them, **IF GOD WERE YOUR FATHER, YE WOULD LOVE ME . . . YE ARE OF YOUR FATHER THE DEVIL**."*

b) Gnostic doctrine

WESTCOTT-- *(concerning John 10:29) "The thought, which is concrete in v.28, is here traced back to its most absolute form as resting on the essential power of God in His relation of **UNIVERSAL FATHERHOOD**."* (Book #14, p. 159)

c) Greek changes

John 1:18
BYZ A > KJV-- *"only begotten **SON**"*
CLEMENT ORIGEN) SBC > WH NU > NASV NIV ESV-- *"only begotten **GOD**"*

The following verses **could refer to anyone's only begotten son**
John 3: 16
BYZ A > KJV NASV NIV ESV-- *"For God so loved the world that he gave **HIS** only begotten son . . ."*
SBC) WH NU) NASV-- *"**THE Son** the only begotten"*

John 3:17
BYZ A) KJV -- *"for God sent not **HIS Son** into the world . . ."*
SBC > WH NU > NASV-- *"for sent not God **THE son** . . ."*

(Please note that **the Critical text uses any Greek text to justify its position on the Universal Fatherhood of God**)

Matthew 24:36
BYZ > KJV-- *"**MY Father**"*
SS > WH NU > NASV NIV ESV-- *"**THE Father**"*

John 6:65
BYZ) KJV-- *"**MY Father**"*
SBC > WH NU > NASV NIV ESV-- *"**THE Father**"*

John 8:28
BYZ, B) KJV-- *"**MY Father**"*
S) WH NU > NASV NIV ESV-- *"**THE Father**"*

John 8:38
BYZ, SC > KJV-- *"**MY Father**"*
ORIGEN > B > WH NU) NASV NIV-- *"**THE Father**"*

John 14:28, 16:10, 20:17 KJV-- *"**MY Father**"*

NASV NIV ESV-- "*THE Father*"

II Thessalonians 1:2
BYZ, SA > KJV; (NU) - "*God OUR Father*"
B > WH > NASV NIV-- "*God THE Father*"

I Timothy 1:2
BYZ > KJV-- "*God OUR Father*"
SA) WH NU > NASV NIV-- "*God THE Father*"

Ephesians 3:14
BYZ > KJV-- "*I bow my knees unto the Father OF OUR LORD JESUS CHRIST.*"
ORIGEN > SBA > WH NU > NASV NIV-- "*I bow my knees to the Father*"

b. Works of God

1) An evil God (Demiurge) or 7 powers created the world which is also evil--see also section 5.a.1)

a) Rejected truth

Deuteronomy 32:4-- "*He is the Rock, HIS WORK IS PERFECT: for all His ways are judgment: a God of truth and WITHOUT INIQUITY, just and right is he.*"

b) Gnostic doctrine

"*Another characteristic feature of the Gnostic conception of the universe is the role played in almost all Gnostic systems by THE SEVEN WORLD-CREATING POWERS. There are indeed certain exceptions; for instance, in the systems of the Valentinian schools there is the figure of the one DEMIURGE WHO TAKES THE PLACE OF THE SEVEN.*" (Book #3, p. 154)

"*The Archons are also the creators of the world, except where this role is reserved for their leader, who then has the name of 'demiurge' . . . and is often painted with the distorted features of the Old Testament God.*" (Book #20, p. 43-44)

c) Gnostic scriptures

d) Greek changes reflected in Versions

Matthew19:17

BYZ C > KJV-- *"Why CALLEST THOU good? THERE IS NONE good BUT ONE, THAT IS, GOD."*
ORIGEN >SB) WH NU > NASV NIV ESV-- *"Why ASK ME CONCERNING THE good? ONE is good."*

Mark 10:6
BYZ, A> KJV NIV ESV-- **"GOD made them** male and female."
SB) WH NU) NASV-- ("**'God' omitted**, thus "**'he' made them**.")
Acts 4:24
BYZ > KJV-- *"Lord, thou ART GOD, WHICH hast made heaven, and earth,"*
SSA > WH NU > NASV NIV ESV-- *"Lord, you made the heaven and earth."*

Ephesians 3:9
BYZ > KJV-- *"created all things BY JESUS CHRIST."*
BSA > WH NU > NASV NIV ESV- **"omits 'by Jesus Christ'"**

c. Worship of God

1) Serpents are worshipped as God

a) Rejected truth

b) Gnostic doctrines

*". . . in others (sects) again appears the **WORSHIP OF SERPENTS**, which here appears to be connected in various and often very loose ways with the other ideas of these Gnostics, hence the names of the 'Ophites' and Naasseni."*   (Book #3, p. 158)

c) Gnostic scriptures

d) Greek changes

d. Abiding place of God

1) Androgynous God and his Spirit is within every man

a) Rejected truth

John14:23-- *"Jesus answered and said unto him, If a man love me, he will keep my words: and my Father will love him, and WE WILL COME UNTO HIM, AND MAKE OUR ABODE WITH HIM."*

b) Gnostic doctrine

c) Gnostic scriptures

TRIMORPHIC PROTENNOIA (Book #12, p. 519)
"*I am androgynous. I am Mother and I am Father . . . And* ***I HID MYSELF IN EVERYONE*** *and revealed myself within them, and every mind seeking me longed for me, for it is I who gave shape to the All when it had no form . . . And I cast into them the eternally holy Spirit and I ascended and entered my Light.*"

d) Greek changes

Luke 11:2
BYZ, AC > KJV-- "***OUR Father WHICH ART IN HEAVEN***,"
ORIGEN > SB > WH NU > NASV NIV ESV-- "***Father***"

II Thessalonians 2:10
BYZ> KJV-- "*and with all deceivableness of unrighteousness **IN** them that perish.*"
SBA > WH NU NASV NIV-- "*. . . unrighteousness **TO** them that perish.*"

3. CHRISTOLOGY (Christ)

I1 Corinthians 11:4– "*For if he that cometh **preacheth ANOTHER JESUS** whom we have not preached . . . ye might well bear with him.*"

Jude 4-- "*For there are certain men crept in unawares . . . **denying . . . our Lord Jesus Christ**.*"

a. The preexistence of Christ

1) The Christ was a created being and therefore had a beginning in time.

a) Rejected truth

Hebrews 13:8-9-- "*Jesus Christ the same yesterday, and today, and for ever. Be not carried about with divers and strange **DOCTRINES**.*

b) Gnostic doctrine

ORIGEN-- "*He called Him a creature, but only in so far as He is generated of God and does not have a life independent of God.*" (Book #7. p. 87)

HORT--from his commentary on Revelation 1-3
Revelation 3:15 -- "*The words **MIGHT NO DOUBT BEAR THE ARIAN MEANING 'THE FIRST THING CREATED'** . . . .*" (Book #16, p. 26)

WESTCOTT--from his commentaries on John and Hebrews

John 1:15--("*He that cometh after me is preferred before me.*") "*The SUPPOSED REFERENCE TO THE PRE-EXISTENCE OF THE WORD SEEMS TO BE INCONSISTENT with the argument which points to a present-consequence . . .* " (Book #16, p. 21)

John 17:24-- ("*Before the foundation . . .*") "*The words distinctly IMPLY THE PERSONAL PRE-EXISTENCE OF CHRIST.*" (Book #16, p. 21)

Hebrews 7:1– "*Two other STRANGE OPINIONS may be noticed. Some orthodox Christians SUPPOSED THAT Melchisedec WAS AN INCARNATION OF THE SON OF GOD or perhaps simply a CHRISTOPHANY.*" (Book #16, p. 22)

c) Gnostic scriptures

TRIMORPHIC PROTENNIOA (Book #12 p. 515)
"*They blessed the Perfect Son, the Christ, the ONLY-BEGOTTEN GOD . . . Then moreover, the GOD WHO WAS BEGOTTEN gave them (the Aeons) a power of life on which they might rely and he established them. . . Now these Aeons were begotten by THE GOD WHO WAS BEGOTTEN--THE CHRIST--and these Aeons received as well as gave glory. They were the first to appear, exalted in their thought, and each Aeon gave myriads of glories within great untraceable lights and they all together blessed the Perfect Son, THE GOD WHO WAS BEGOTTEN.*"

PISTIS SOPHIA   (Book #15, p. 467)
"*MELCHISEDEC, the Great Receiver or Collector of Light.*"

d) Greek changes

John 1:18
BYZ, A) KJV– "*only begotten SON*"
VALENTINIANS CLEMENT ORIGEN > BSC > WH NU > NASV NIV ESV– "*only begotten GOD*"

Hebrews 7:21 (**The Critical Text does not extend His priesthood to eternity past, but only eternity future, seeing that Melchisedec was without beginning or ending**)
BYZ > KJV-- "*Thou art a priest for ever AFTER THE ORDER OF MELCHISEDEC.*"
BSC > WH NU > NASV ESV-- "*You are a priest forever*" only

e) O.T. changes

Micah 5:2
KJV-- "*. . . whose GOINGS FORTH have been from of old, from everlasting.*"
NASV– "*. . . His goings forth are from long ago, from the days of eternity*"
NIV– "*. . . whose ORIGINS are from of old, from ancient times*"
ESV– "*. . . whose coming forth is from of old, from ancient days.*"

2) The Logos is the angel of the Lord (a.k.a Demiurge) before his rebellion against God.

   a) Rejected truth

John 14:31– "... *as the Father gave me commandment, even so I do....*"

John 15:10-- "*... I have kept my Father's commandments....*"

Hebrews 10:9– "*Then he said, Lo, I come to do thy will, 0 God.*"

   b) Gnostic doctrine

PHILO OF ALEXANDRIA-- "*... calls the Logos, who is instrumental in creation, both 'a second god' and 'archangel' on the one hand and 'Lord' (YHVH) and 'Name' (i.e. YHVH) on the other. Jewish gnostics such as Simon and Cerinthus affirm that the **DEMIURGE** (identified with YHVH) was in fact this angel of the Lord, **WHO HAD NOT YET REBELLED AGAINST GOD**.*" (Book #2, p. 569)

WESTCOTT--commentary on Gospel of John

John 1:18-- "***HE DOES NOT EXPRESSLY AFFIRM BUT ASSUMES*** the identification of the ***WORD WITH JESUS CHRIST***." (Book #16, p. 28)

   c) Gnostic scriptures

   d) Greek changes

3) The Logos was defective (sinful) before he was illuminated

   a) Rejected truth

Hebrews 13:8-- "*Jesus Christ **the SAME** yesterday, and today, and forever.*"

   b) Gnostic doctrine

   c) Gnostic scripture

TRIPARTITE TRACTATE-- "*When the **LOGOS WHICH WAS DEFECTIVE** was illumined, his Pleroma began ... He stripped off that **ARROGANT THOUGHT**.*" (Book #12, p. 79)

   d) Greek changes.

1 John 3:5– (Critical change could refer to **His sins**.)
BYZ SC) KJV NIV ESV-- "*he was manifested to take away **OUR sins**;*"
BA) WH NU > NASV ESV- **omits 'our'**

Revelation 16:5

BYZ (pt)) KJV-- *"Thou art righteous, **LORD**, which art, and wast, and shalt be, . . ."*

BYZ (pt) S > WH NU > NASV NIV ESV-- "righteous are You, who are and who was **THE HOLY ONE**. . . ."

4) The living Word is the son of the Christ

a) Rejected truth

b) Gnostic doctrine

c) Gnostic scripture

THE GOSPEL OF THE EGYPTIANS

*"There the great self-begotten living Word came forth, the true god, the unborn physis, he whose name I shall tell . . . who is the **SON OF THE GREAT CHRIST** . . ."* (Book #12, p. 211)

". . . the great Logos, the divine Autogenes, and the incorruptible man Adam as mingled with each other. A Logos of man came into being. However, the man came into being through a word." (Book #12, p. 212)

d) Greek changes

5) The Primal Man revealed himself in Christ

a) Rejected doctrine

b) Gnostic doctrine

"Another characteristic figure of Gnosticism is that of the Primal Man . . . Thus in the system of the Niaasseni . . . the Primal Man has a central and predominant position . . . Among the Barbelo-gnostics, the Primal Man (Adamas, homo perfectus et verus) and Gnosis appear as a pair of aeons, occupying a prominent place in the whole series . . . The figure in the Mandaean system most closely corresponding to the Primal Man . . . is that of Manda d'hayye (cf. the pair of aeons, Adamas and Gnosis . . .). Finally in the Manichaean system . . . the Primal Man again assumes the predominant place." (Book #3, p. 356)

c) Gnostic scriptures

*". . . in the text on which are based the pseudo-Clementine writings (**RECOGNITIONS** . . . and **HOMILIES** . . .) as in the closely related system of the Ebionites in Epiphanus . . . we meet with **THE MAN WHO EXISTED BEFORE THE WORLD**, the prophet who goes through the world in various forms, and finally reveals himself in Christ."* (Book #3, p. 156)

PISTIS SOPHIA– "*. . . even in the Pistis-Sophia the Primal Man 'Ieu' is frequently alluded to as the King of the Luminaries.*" (Book #3, p. 156)

d) Greek changes

6) The Primal Man (Christ) is androgynous (bisexual)

a) Rejected truth

b) Gnostic doctrine

"*. . . before Philo there must have been Jewish thinkers who claimed that the heavenly Man was **ANDROGYNOUS**. Such circles originated the Anthropos model of gnosis, which is found in the doctrine of Saturninus.*" (Book #2, p. 568)

MANI-- "*. . . relates that in the beginning the Primal Man is sent out to combat the powers of darkness. This Archanthropos is overpowered and forced to leave 'the Maiden who is his soul' embedded in matter. The entire world process is necessary to shape the Perfect Man so that the original state of **ANDROGENY** (male and maiden at the same time) will be restored. All these speculations presuppose the god Man of Ezekiel 1:26. Moreover it is possible that Paul was familiar with the same concept when he said that Christ was both the power(dunamis) and the wisdom (sophia) of God.*" (1 Corinthians1:24) (Book #2, p. 568)

VALENTINUS-- "*Christ and Sophia (Wisdom) are a couple (separated for awhile on. account of the trespass and fall of Sophia but in the end happily reunited).*" (Book #2, p. 571)

c) Gnostic scripture

"*Variations of the myth of Saturninus are Found in quite a few of the **WRITINGS FROM NAG HAMADI**.*" (Book #2, p. 568)

POIMANDRES-- "*The same figure is to be found in the Hermetic Poimandres, clearly influenced by Alexandrian Jews. This writing relates how God generated a son to whom he delivered all creatures. **THE SON IS ANDROGYNOUS**, equally Phos (Man, Adam, Light) and Zoe (Eve, Life).*" (Book #2, p. 568)

THE SOPHIA OF JESUS CHRIST
"*I want you to know that First Man is called Begetter, Self-Perfected Mind. He reflected with Great Sophia, his consort, and revealed his **FIRST-BEGOTTEN ANDROGYNOUS SON** . . . Now **FIRST-BEGOTTEN IS CALLED 'CHRIST'**" (Book #12, p. 231)

"*The perfect Savior said: Son of Man consented with Sophia, his consort, and revealed a great **ANDROGYNOUS** light. His male name is designated 'Savior, Begetter of All Things.' His female name is designated 'All-Begettress Sophia.' Some call her 'Pistis.'*"

EUGNOSTOS THE BLESSED (Book #12 p. 231)
"*When he received the consent of his consort, Great Sophia, he revealed that **FIRST-BEGOTTEN ANDROGYNE, WHO IS CALLED FIRST-BEGOTTEN SON OF GOD**.*"

d) Greek changes

7) The serpent in the garden was the luminous Jesus

a) Rejected truth

John 14:30-- "*Hereafter I will not talk much with **YOU: FOR THE PRINCE OF THIS WORLD COMETH, AND HATH NOTHING IN ME**.*"

b) Gnostic doctrine

MANI-- "*Augustine, the former Manichaean, describes Gnostic beliefs with clarity and indignation: 'They assert . . . that **CHRIST WAS THE ONE CALLED BY OUR SCRIPTURES THE SERPENT**, and they assure us that they have been given insight into this in order to open the eyes of knowledge and to distinguish between Good and Evil.*" (Book #22, p. 41)

c) Gnostic scriptures

"*In a Manichaean version of Genesis it is Eve who gives life to Adam, while **THE SERPENT, THE LUMINOUS JESUS**, is a liberating figure urging the first couple to take the first step toward salvation by eating from the Tree of Gnosis.*" (Book #22, p. xviii)

d) Greek changes

I Peter 4:14
BYZ KJV-- "***ON THEIR PART HE IS EVIL SPOKEN OF, BUT ON YOUR PART HE IS GLORIFIED***."
BSAC WH NU) NASV NIV ESV <u>omit</u>

b. The Incarnation and birth of Jesus Christ

1) Jesus was not God incarnate and did not have all of God's attributes

a) Rejected truth

Colossians 2:9-- "*For in Him dwelleth all the fulness of the Godhead bodily.*"

b) Gnostic doctrine

ORIGEN
"*He is the pre-existent eternal Logos . . . described as a 'second god' beside the Father.*"

(Book #8, p. 91-92)

"*God . . . reveals himself to those who are pure in heart . . . through the* **INCARNATE LOGOS**." (Book #8, p. 83)

"*When . . . we consider these great and marvellous truths about the nature of the Son of God, we are lost in the deepest amazement that such a being . . . should have '*__EMPTIED HIMSELF__*' of his majestic condition and become man and dwelt among men . . .*" (Book #8, p. 109)

". . . *when he dwelt on earth among men in a body like ours . . . it was then possible to think of him as* **BEING ENCLOSED IN SOME ONE PLACE**." (Book #8, p. 153)

c) Gnostic scriptures

THE GOSPEL OF THOMAS (Book #12, p. 133)
"Jesus said to her, I am he who exists from the undivided. I was given **SOME OF THE THINGS OF MY FATHER**."

d) Greek changes

I Timothy 3:16
BYZ) KJV-- "*. . . great is the mystery of godliness:* **GOD** *was manifest in the flesh.*"
SAC > WH NU) NASV NIV ESV-- ". . . *(HE) WHO was manifest in the flesh.*"

I John 4:3
BYZ > KJV-- "*And every spirit that confesseth not that Jesus* **CHRIST IS COME IN THE FLESH** *is not of God: and this is that spirit of antichrist, . . .*"
BA > WH NU > NASV NIV ESV-- **omit 'Christ is come in the flesh'**

The following verses deny some of the attributes of Christ

John 8:59   (**omnipotence**)
BYZ > KJV-- "**GOING THROUGH THE MIDST OF THEM, AND SO PASSED BY**"
ORIGEN > SBC > WH NU > NASV NIV ESV-- **omit**

John 3:13   (**omnipresence**)
BYZ A > KJV-- "*no man hath ascended up to heaven, but he that came down from heaven, even the Son of man* **WHICH IS IN HEAVEN.**"
ORIGEN > SB > WH NU > NASV NIV ESV-- **omit 'which is in heaven'**

Matthew 12:25
BYZ C) KJV -- "*and* **JESUS** *knew their thoughts, and said unto them,*"
SB > WH NU > NASV ESV-- **omit 'Jesus'**

Matthew 24:36 (**implies universal fatherhood**)

"But of that day and hour knoweth no man, no, not the angels of heaven, but __my__ Father only."
ORIGEN > SB > WH NU > NASV NIV ESV– *"but __the__ father only"*

John 13:3   **(Question omniscience)**
BYZ A > KJV -- "__*JESUS*__ *knowing that the father had given all things into his hands,"*
SB > WH NU > NASV-- __omits 'Jesus'__

John 7:53--8:11   **(Question Omniscience)**
BYZ > KJV--INCLUDE these 12 verses
    BSAC > WH (NU) (NASV) (NIV) ESV– either __OMIT__ or set them apart in brackets, footnotes, or
                   other ways)

Matthew 24:36   **(Question Omniscience)**
BYZ > KJV– *"But of that day and hour knoweth no man, no, not the angels of heaven, but my Father
only."*
ORIGEN > SB > WH NU > NASV NIV ESV– *". . . not even the angels of the heaven,* __*NOR THE SON*__*,
but my Father only."*

2) The Savior became manifest in an INVOLUNTARY suffering

a) Rejected truth

Hebrews 10:5-7-- *". . . but a body hast thou prepared me . . . Then said I, Lo, I come (in the volume of the
book it is written of me,)* __*TO DO THY WILL, O GOD*__*."*

Matthew 26:39-- *"O my Father, if it be possible, let this cup pass from me: nevertheless not as I will,* __*BUT
AS THOU*__ *(wilt)."*

Matthew 26:42-- "O My Father, if this cup may not pass away from me, except I drink it, __*THY WILL BE
DONE*__*."*

b) Gnostic doctrine

c) Gnostic scriptures

THE TRIPARTATE TRACTATE   (Book #12, p. 92)
"He it was who was our Savior in willing compassion, who is that which they were. For
it was for their sake that he **BECAME MANIFEST IN AN INVOLUNTARY
SUFFERING**."

d) Greek changes

Luke 24:46
BYZ A > KJV-- "Thus it is written, __AND THUS IT BEHOOVED__ Christ to suffer,"
BSC > WH NU > NASV NIV ESV-- __omit "and thus it behooved"__

3) Joseph, not God, was the father of Jesus

a) Rejected truth

b) Gnostic doctrine

c) Gnostic scriptures

d) Greek changes

Matthew 8:29
BYZ) KJV-- *"What have we to do with thee, **JESUS**, thou Son of God?"*
SBC > WH NU > NASV NIV ESV--**omit 'Jesus'**

Mark 1:1
BYZ BAS) KJV; (NU) > NASV* NIV* ESV–"Jesus Christ, the **SON OF GOD**."
ORIGEN) S* > WH--**omit 'Son of God"**

Luke 2:33
BYZ > KJV-- "**JOSEPH** and HIS mother"
ORIGEN > SB > WH NU > NASV ESV-- "**HIS FATHER** and mother"

John 3:16
BYZ A > KJV NASV –*"For God so loved the world, that he gave **HIS** only begotten Son,"*
SBC > WH **NU–omit "*his*"**

John 3:17
BYZ A > KJV N1V–*"for God sent not **HIS** Son into the world to condemn the world;"*
SBC > WH NU > NASV-- **omit '*His*'**

John 5:17
BYZ A > KJV; (NU) > NIV ESV-- "But ***JESUS*** answered them, My Father worketh hitherto, and I work."
SB > WH > NASV-- "***HE*** answered. . ."

Acts 3:26
BYZ A > KJV-- *"God, having raised up His Son **JESUS**,"*
SBC > WH NU > NASV NIV ESV--**omit '*Jesus*'**

Acts 8:37
BYZ > KJV (NASV)–". . . ***I BELIEVE THAT JESUS CHRIST IS THE SON OF GOD***."
BYZ SBAC > WH NU > NIV ESV--**omit**

Ephesians 3:14
BYZ) KJV-- *"I bow my knees unto the Father **OF OUR LORD JESUS CHRIST**,"*

ORIGEN > SBA > WH NU > NASV NIV ESV--<u>omit 'of our Lord Jesus Christ'</u>

(Note that Westcott and Hort were so determined to undermine this doctrine that they used any Greek text that supported their view)

Matthew 24:36, John 6:65, 10:32, 16:10, 20:17
(Origen) BYZ > KJV-- "***MY*** *Father*"
SB > WH NU > NASV NIV ESV-- "***THE*** *Father*"

John 8:28, 8:38
BYZ > KJV-- "***MY*** *Father*"
S > WH NU > NASV NIV ESV (8:28) - **THE** Father

John 14:28
BYZ.> KJV–"***MY*** *Father*"
BA > WH NU) NASV NIV ESV–"***THE*** *Father*"

4) The Incarnation of Christ is a continuing process, not an historical event

a) Rejected truth

Hebrews 9:26-- "*. . . but now* ***ONCE*** *in the end of the world* ***HATH HE APPEARED*** *to put away sin by the sacrifice of himself.*"

b) Gnostic doctrine

"'*Christ' stands for man's OWN inner divine nature, which must be* ***BROUGHT TO BIRTH . . . IN EACH INDIVIDUAL*** *. . . . Christ is the divine spark in each one of us. . .*" (Book #25, p. 42)

MANI– "Christ . . . is the suffering form of Primal Man. This original and profound interpretation of the figure of Christ was an important article of the Manichaean creed and is known as the doctrine of **JESUS PATIBILIS**, and 'passible Jesus' who 'hangs from every tree' . . . '**EVERY DAY IS BORN, suffers and dies**'" (Book #20, p. 229)

ORIGEN-- "*Origen made a larger contribution to the dogma of the Trinity, by speaking of an* ***ETERNAL GENERATION****.* ***The Father IS ALWAYS BEGETTING THE SON****.*" (Book #7, p. 86)

SCHAFF-- "*With reference to an article by Schaff, the critic said: 'The affirmation he makes that '****THE LORD IS PERPETUALLY BORN ANEW IN THE . . . HEARTS OF BELIEVERS****' sounds strangely to our ears . . . Again: 'the commencement . . . of Church history, is strictly the incarnation of the Son of God, or the entrance of the new principle of light and life into humanity.*" (Book #14, p. 151)

c) Gnostic scriptures

d) Greek changes

5) Jesus was begotten by the Logos (he is not the Logos)

a) Rejected truth

b) Gnostic doctrine

c) Gnostic scripture

THE GOSPEL OF THE EGYPTIANS
"... *Logos-begotten one, even Jesus the living one, even he whom the great Seth has put on.*"

d) Greek changes

c. The life and person of Jesus

1) Jesus is not the 'Lord God Almighty'

a) Rejected truth

Romans 10:9,13-- *"That if thou shalt confess with thy mouth the **LORD JESUS**, and shalt believe in thine heart that God hath raised him from the dead, thou shalt be saved. . . . For whosoever shall call upon the name of the **LORD** shall be saved.*

b) Gnostic doctrine

HORT-- "Statements from his commentary on Revelation 1-3, and I Peter 1-3."
I Peter 1:3-- "*(Blessed be the God and Father of our **LORD** Jesus Christ) In **ALL** this early usage **'Kurios'** probably represents **NOT ADON**, but the nearly equivalent Aramaic 'Mar', sometimes **APPLIED TO TEACHERS BY DISCIPLES** . . ."* (Book #16. p. 25)

Revelation 1:1-- "*The conception of the book is **NOT THAT THE PRIMARY REVEALER IS CHRIST... BUT THAT THE PRIMARY REVEALER IS GOD**.*" (Book #16, p. 7)

Revelation 1:2-- "*John's conveyance of the revelation to the churches just as he had received it from the angel and the angel from Christ, **AND CHRIST FROM GOD**.*" (Book #16, p. 26)

Revelation 1:8-- "*(I am the Alpha and Omega, the beginning and the ending, saith the Lord (God), which is, and which was, and which is to come, the Almighty)" "This verse must stand alone. **THE SPEAKER CANNOT BE OUR LORD**, when we consider 1:4 . . . and **ALL SCRIPTURAL ANALOGY IS AGAINST THE ATTRIBUTION OF 'THE LORD GOD' WITH OR WITHOUT 'ALMIGHTY' TO CHRIST**.*" (Book #16, p. 26) See

Revelation 1:8 below.

WESTCOTT-- From his commentary on the Gospel of John
John 20:28-- "*(And Thomas answered and said unto him **MY GOD**) . . . and the words which follow shew that the Lord accepted the declaration of **HIS DIVINITY AS THE TRUE EXPRESSION OF FAITH. HE NEVER SPEAKS OF HIMSELF DIRECTLY AS GOD** (comp. v. 18) **BUT THE AIM OF HIS REVELATION WAS TO LEAD MEN TO SEE GOD IN HIM**.*" (Book #16, p. 26)

c) Gnostic scriptures

THE GOSPEL OF THOMAS (Book #12, p. 127)
"*Jesus said, **I AM NOT YOUR MASTER**. (Lord)*"

GOSPEL OF PHILIP
"*Those who say 'There is a **HEAVENLY MAN** and there is one above him,' are wrong. For it is the first of these two heavenly men, the one who is revealed, that they called 'the one who is below'; and he to whom the hidden belongs is (supposed to be) that one who is above him.*" (Book #12, p. 150) - note. 1 Corinthians15:47 below

ASCLEPIUS (Book #12, p. 332)
"*And now listen! God and the Father, **EVEN THE LORD**, created man subsequent to the gods . . .*"

d) Greek changes

Revelation 1:8
BYZ (pt) > KJV–"*saith the Lord which is **and which was, and which is to come, the Almighty**.*"
BYZ SAC) WH NU > NASV NIV-- "*says the Lord GOD **who is** . . .*"

I Corinthians 11:29
BYZ S > KJV. -- "*not discerning the **Lord's body**.*"
S*BA WH NU) NASV ESV-- **omits "Lord's body"**

I Corinthians15:47
BYZ A) KJV-- "*. . . the second man is **THE LORD** from heaven.*"
ORIGEN > S*BC > WH NU > NASV ESV--**omit "the Lord"**

This verse uses "**Lord**" when referring to the **Father** (v.33) implying "**Lord**" **Jesus as being equal with the Father**.

Matthew 18:26
BYZ S > KJV-- "***LORD** have patience.*"
ORIGEN > B > WH NU > NASV ESV-- **omit "Lord"**
The following verses **delete "Lord"** when referring to Jesus, or **delete "Jesus"** when. referring to "Lord"

Matthew 8:5
BYZ) KJV NIV–"*and when **JESUS** was entered into Capernaum there came unto Him a centurion, beseeching him, and saying, Lord, . . .*"
SBC.) WH NU > NASV ESV–<u>**omit "Jesus"**</u>

Matthew 13:51
BYZ C.> KJV–"*Yea. **LORD**.*"
BS) WH NU > NASV NIV ESV–<u>**omit "Lord"**</u>

Matthew 28:6
BYZ AC > KJV–"*the place where **THE LORD** lay.*"
ORIGEN) SB > WH NU) NASV NIV ESV–"*the place where **HE** lay.*"

Mark 9:24
BYZ > KJV–"***LORD**, I believe; help thou mine unbelief.*"
BSAC > WH NU > NASV NIV ESV– <u>**omit "Lord"**</u>

Luke 9:57
BYZ AC > KJV–– "***LORD**, I will follow thee whithersoever thou goest.*"
SB > WH NU NASV NIV ESV–– <u>**omit "Lord"**</u>

Luke 9:59
BYZ SAC) KJV; (NU) > NIV–"***LORD**, suffer me*"
B) WH) NASV–– <u>**omit "Lord"**</u>

Luke 9:60 (see v.59)
BYZ AC > KJV NIV–– "***JESUS** said unto him,*"
SB > WH NU > NASV–– "*but **HE** said to him.*"

Luke 23:42
BYZ A > KJV– "*And he said UNTO JESUS, **LORD**, remember me.*"
SBC > WH NU > NASV NIV ESV–– "*He said, Jesus, Remember me.*"– <u>**omit "LORD"**</u>

Luke 24:36 (v.34– "*the **LORD** is risen, . . .*")
BYZ A > KJV NIV–– "and as they thus spake, **JESUS** himself stood in the midst of them."
SBC > WH NU. > NASV– "*. . . **HE** stood in their midst.*"

Acts 9:6
BYZ > KJV–– "<u>**AND HE TREMBLING AND ASTONISHED SAID, LORD, WHAT WILT THOU HAVE ME TO DO? AND THE LORD SAID UNTO HIM,**</u>"
BYZ SBAC > WH NU > NASV NIV ESV–– <u>**omit all these words**</u>

Acts 10:48
BYZ) KJV–"*baptized in the name **OF THE LORD**.*"
BYZ SBA > WH NU > NASV ESV– "*. . . name of* **JESUS CHRIST**

Acts 17:27
BYZ > KJV-- *"that they should seek THE LORD,"*
SBA > WH NU > NASV NIV ESV-- "to seek **GOD**"

Acts 18:25
BYZ > KJV-- *"he spake and taught diligently the things of THE LORD,"*
BYZ SBA > WH NU > NASV NIV ESV– ". . . **concerning JESUS**"

James 1:12
BYZ > KJ (NASV)-- *"the crown of life which THE LORD hath promised . . ."*
SBA) WH NU) NIV (God)-- ". . . **HE** *promised*"

Verses that change '**Lord' to 'God**'-- Luke 2:38, Acts 21:20

Verses that **add to Lord 'and our God'** (See Hart's commentary on Revelation 1:8)

Verses that **omit 'And the Lord said'**--Luke 7:31, 22:31

Verses that **omit 'Says the Lord'**--Hebrews 10:30

Verses that **change "word of THE LORD"** to '**word of GOD**'--Acts 13:48, 16:32

Verses that **omit "Lord" from 'LORD Jesus'**--I1 Corinthians 4:14, Galatians 6:17
90 3.c.1)

Verses that **omit "Lord" from 'LORD Jesus Christ'**--Romans 6:11 , I Timothy 1:1, 5:21, II Timothy 4:1, II John 3

Verses that **omit "Jesus" from "Lord JESUS"**--Acts 9:29, 19:10, 1 Corinthians 5 :5

Verses that **omit "Jesus" from "Lord JESUS Christ"**--Romans 16:18

2) The Son of Man is separate from Jesus Christ

a) Rejected truth

John 20:26-27– *"For as the Father hath life in himself: so hath he given the **SON** to have life in himself. And hath given him authority to execute judgment also, **BECAUSE HE IS THE SON OF MAN**."*

b) Gnostic doctrine

MARCUS–*". . . the Holy Spirit . . . spoke through the mouth of Jesus in the Gospel narratives, and proclaimed **ITSELF** as Son of Man, and revealed the Father, **DESCENDING ON JESUS AND BECOMING ONE WITH HIM**. It was this Saviour who put an end to death, by the removal of ignorance, and Jesus made Him known as His Father, the Christ."* (Book #15, p. 378)

WESTCOTT from his Commentary on the Gospel of John--
John 12:34 (Who is this Son of man) *"The question--**CLEARLY SHOWS THAT THE TITLE THE SON OF MAN WAS NOT NECESSARILY IDENTIFIED WITH 'THE CHRIST'**"* (Book #12, p. 30)

c) Gnostic scriptures

d) Greek changes

Matthew 16:13
BYZ) KJV-- *"Whom do men say that **I** the son of man am?"*
ORIGEN > B > WH-NU > NASV NIV ESV– **Omits 'I'**

Matthew 18:11
BY2) KJV (NASV)– *"**FOR THE SON OF MAN IS COME TO SAVE THAT WHICH WAS LOST**."*
ORIGEN > WH NU > ESV-- **omit verse**

Matthew 25:13
BYZ > KJV– *"For ye know neither the day nor the hour **WHEREIN THE SON OF MAN COMETH**."*
SBAC > WH NU > NASV NIV ESV--**omit 'wherein the Son of Man cometh.'**

Luke 9:56
BYZ > KJV (NASV)–*"**FOR THE SON OF MAN IS NOT COME TO DESTROY MEN'S LIVES, BUT TO SAVE THEM**."*
BYZ SBA > WH NU > ESV-- **omit these words**

John 3:13 (**The Critical texts omit the presence of the Son of Man in heaven and on earth at the same time--omnipresence**)
BYZ A > KJV–*"and no man hath ascended up to heaven, but he that came down from heaven, even the Son of man **WHICH IS IN HEAVEN**."*
ORIGEN >SS) WH NU > NASV NIV ESV--**omit "which is in heaven"**

3) Jesus had a sin nature like every other man

a) Rejected truth

Hebrews 4:15–*"For we have not an high priest which cannot be touched with the feeling of our infirmities; but was in all points tempted like as we are, yet **WITHOUT SIN**."*

Hebrews 7:26–*"For such an high priest became us, who is holy, harmless, **UNDEFILED, SEPARATE FROM SINNERS**, and made higher than the heavens;"*

b) Gnostic doctrine

WESTCOTT--from his commentaries on Gospel of John and Hebrews John 1:51–*"**ALL** that *TRULY BELONGS TO HUMANITY, ALL* therefore *THAT TRULY BELONGS TO EVERY INDIVIDUAL IN THE WHOLE RACE, BELONGS ALSO TO HIM*." (Book #16, p. 27)

Hebrews 2:10—"*The conception of teleiosai (to make perfect) is that of bringing Christ to the FULL MORAL PERFECTION OF HIS HUMANITY (Cf. Luke xiii.32) which carries with it the completeness of power and dignity . . . THIS 'PERFECTION' WAS NOT REACHED. TILL AFTER DEATH . . .*" (Book #16, p. 27)

Hebrews 5:7-- "*The question has been asked for what did Christ pray? . . . Perhaps it is BEST TO ANSWER, generally, FOR THE VICTORY OVER DEATH THE FRUIT OF SIN.*" (Book #16, p. 30)

c) Gnostic scriptures

d) Greek changes (**All involving the Attributes of God in Jesus) These verses deny/omit that Jesus was good/sinless**

Matthew 19:16
BYZ) KJV-- "**GOOD** Master"
ORIGEN) SB > WH NU > NASV ESV-- **omit "good"**

Matthew 19:17
BYZ > KJV-- "Why **CALLEST THOU ME** good?"
ORIGEN > Se > WH NU > NASV NIV ESV-- "*Why* **CALLEST THOU ME** *the good*?"

Luke 20:23 (**Critical texts omit implication that He cannot be tempted, i.e. his eternal goodness** - see
BYZ, AC) KJV-- "*WHY TEMPT YE ME*?"
SB > WH NU) NASV NIV ESV-- **omit these words**

Philemon 6
BYZ > KJV-- "*every good thing which is in you in Christ JESUS*"
SAC) WH NU) NASV NIV ESV-- **omit 'Jesus'**

Matthew 27:24
BYZ) KJV-- "*JUST person*"
Origen > B) WH NV > NASV NIV ESV-- **omit 'JUST'**

Revelation 16:5
BYZ (pt) > KJV-- "*thou art righteous, O LORD, which art and wast, . . .*"
SAC) WH NV) NASV NIV ESV-- **omit *O LORD***

These verses can deny/omit that Jesus was truthful

Mark 12:41

BYZ A) KJV NIV ESV-- "*and **JESUS** sat over against the treasury . . .*"
SS) WH NV) NASV-- **omit 'Jesus'**

Luke 23:43
BYZ AC > KJV -- "*and JESUS said unto him, Verily I say unto thee*"
SB) WH NU NASV ESV **(HE)** *said to him . . .*"

John 7:8 (Jesus did go to the feast, so the Critical text makes him a liar)
BYZ > KJV; (WH) NIV-- "*I go not up **YET** unto this feast.*"
S > NV > NASV ESV-- "*I not am going up to this feast.*"

These verses can be used to deny Jesus was pure (He could have been purified of his own sin. Gnostic view of re-incarnation is that it is necessary due to imperfection in past life)

Hebrews 1:3
BYZ) KJV-- "*when he had **BY HIMSELF** purged **OUR** sins,*"
BSAC> WH NV > NASV NIV ESV-- **omit OUR** and **BY HIMSELF**

I John 3:5
BYZ SC > KJV NIV-- "*He was manifested to take away **OUR** sins;*"
BA) WH NV > NASV ESV-- **omit 'our'**

4) The Christ is separate from Jesus

    a) Rejected truth

    b) Gnostic doctrine

    WESTCOTT - commentary on Hebrews
    Hebrews 5:5-- *(So Christ (the Christ) also . . .)* "*it is **NOT SAID THAT 'JESUS' GLORIFIED NOT HIMSELF, BUT THE CHRIST** the appointed Redeemer, glorified not Himself.*" (Book #16, p. 30)

    c) Gnostic scriptures

    d) Greek changes

Luke 4:41
BYZ A) KJV-- "*Thou art **CHRIST** the Son of God.*"
SBC > WH NU) NASV NIV ESV **omit 'Christ'**

John 4:42
BYZ A > KJV-- "*For we have heard him ourselves, and know that this is indeed **THE CHRIST**, the Saviour of the world.*"
SBC) WH NU) NASV NIV ESV-- **omit 'the Christ'**

John 6:69
BYZ) KJV-- *"Thou art **THE CHRIST, THE SON OF THE LIVING** God."*
SBC > WH NU > NASV NIV ESV-- *"You are **THE HOLY ONE OF** God."*

Acts 9:20
BYZ > KJV-- *"and straightway he preached **CHRIST** in the synagogues, that he is the Son of God."*
BYZ (pt) SBAC > WH NU) NASV NIV ESV-- *"he was proclaiming **JESUS** that he is the Son of God."*

Verses where **'Christt' is omitted from 'Jesus Christ'** I1 Corinthians4:6, I John 1:7, 4:3, Revelation 1:9

Verses where **'Christ' is omitted from 'Christ Jesus'** Acts 19:4, Hebrews 3:1

Verses where **'Christ' is omitted from "(our) Lord Jesus Christ"**
Acts 15:11, 16:31, 20:21, 28:31, Romans 16:20, 1 Corinthians 5:4, 9:1, 16:23, I1 Corinthians11:31, I Thessalonians2:19, 3:11, 3:13, II Thessalonians1:8, 1:12, Revelation 22:21

Verses where **'Jesus' is omitted from 'Jesus Christ'** Romans 15:8, 11 Corinthians 5:18

Verses where **'Jesus' is omitted from 'Christ Jesus'** Acts 24:24, Colossians 1:28, I Peter 5:10, 5:14

Verses where **'Jesus' is omitted from 'Lord Jesus Christ'** Romans 16:18

Verses where **'Jesus Christ' is omitted** Titus 2:13, Philemon 9

Verses where **'Jesus Christ' is omitted from 'Lord Jesus Christ'** 1 Corinthians16:22, II Timothy 4:22

5) The Christ came upon Jesus at his baptism in order to enlighten and perfect him, and left him before he died

   a) Rejected truth

Hebrews 13:8-- *"Jesus Christ **the same yesterday, and today, and for ever.**"*

Colossians 2:3-4-- *"**in whom (Christ) are hid all the treasures of wisdom and knowledge**. And this I say lest any man should beguile you with enticing words."*

   b) Gnostic doctrine

*"When the time was right, Jesus was **ENLIGHTENED AT HIS BAPTISM** in the river Jordan . . . He is considered to be the prototype of all spiritual men, who through his revealing word **BECAME CONSCIOUS OF THEIR INNERMOST BEING, THE SPIRIT**, and rise up to the spiritual realm."* (Book #2, p. 571)

OPHITES AND SETHIANS

"... *Christ, united to Sophia, descended into him (Jesus), and thus Jesus Christ was produced* ... *They affirm that many of his disciples were not aware of the descent of Christ into him; but that **WHEN CHRIST DID DESCEND ON JESUS**, he then began to work miracles, and heal, and announce the unknown Father, and openly to confess himself as the son of the first man* ... *They say: that **CHRIST HIMSELF, along with Sophia, DEPARTED FROM HIM** into the state of an incorruptible Aeon, **WHILE JESUS WAS CRUCIFIED** ... They strove to establish the descent and ascent of Christ, by the fact that neither before his baptism, nor after his resurrection from the dead, do his disciples state that he did any mighty works.*" (Book #33, p. 357 Irenaeus Against Heresies, 1.30.12-14)

WESTCOTT--from his commentary on Gospel of John
John 1:33-34-- "*At the same time we cannot but believe (so far as we realize the perfect humanity of Christ) that **CHRIST AT THIS CRISIS FIRST BECAME CONSCIOUS AS MAN OF A POWER OF THE SPIRIT WITHIN HIM**.*" (Book #16, p. 14-15)

John 1:42--(Thou art) "***THIS IS NOT NECESSARILY A PROPHETIC DECLARATION BY DIVINE KNOWLEDGE**.*" (Book #16 p. 22)

John 2:24-25--(he knew what was in man) "*Only on rare occasions does He ask anything, **AS IF ALL WERE NOT ABSOLUTELY CLEAR BEFORE HIS EYES** ... But St John exhibits this attribute of **COMPLETE HUMAN KNOWLEDGE** most fully, ... At other times it appears to be the **RESULT OF AN INSIGHT** which came from a perfect spiritual sympathy, found in some degree among men. ... A careful study of these passages seems to shew beyond doubt that the **KNOWLEDGE OF CHRIST**, ... **HAS ITS ANALOGUES IN HUMAN POWERS. HIS KNOWLEDGE** appears to be truly the **KNOWLEDGE OF THE SON OF MAN, AND NOT MERELY THE KNOWLEDGE OF THE DIVINE WORD**, though at each moment and in each connection it was, in virtue of His perfect humanity, **RELATIVELY COMPLETE**.*" (Book #16, p. 22)

John 1:48–"(*when thou wast under the fig tree, I saw thee*) ... *the Lord shewed His **DIVINE INSIGHT** into the heart of man.*" (Book #16, p. 22)

John 4:1--("*When therefore the Lord knew ...*") "***NOTHING IMPLIES THAT THE KNOWLEDGE OF THE LORD WAS SUPERNATURAL**.*" (Book #16, p. 23)

d) Gnostic scriptures

d) Greek changes.

Matthew 24:36 (**Critical text teaches that Jesus Christ the Son of God was not eternally omniscient**)
BYZ > KJV-- "*But of that day and hour knoweth no man, no not the angels in heaven, but my father only.*"
ORIGEN > SB > WH NU > NASV NIV ESV-- **these add** "***NOR THE SON***"

Mark 14:68
BYZ > KJV-- "***AND THE COCK CREW***"
SB > WH NU > NASV NIV **omit these words**

Mark 14:72 (The Critical text is still determining whether to agree with Westcott and Hort. See note in NA text)
BYZ > KJV NU-NASV NIV ESV-- "*and **THE SECOND TIME** the cock crew*."
WH - **omits "the second time"**

John 7:53--8:11 (**These verses teach that Jesus was able to convict these men because He knew their individual sins of adultery--verses 8:6-9**)
BYZ > KJV--**INCLUDE**
SBAC> WH omit NU favors omission (A rating- see note) **NASV NIV--(bracketed) ESV Omitted**

I Timothy 1:16
BYZ > KJV NASV–"***JESUS CHRIST** might show forth **ALL** longsuffering*."
A > (WH) NU > NIV ESV-- "***CHRIST JESUS** might show forth **PERFECT** longsuffering*."

6) Jesus Christ was deified in stages by the Logos and did not have a spirit until later in life (probably at His baptism or death)

a) Rejected truth

b) Gnostic doctrines

ORIGEN-- "*The Logos . . . has a controlling influence over the Man Jesus. The influence of the Logos **DEIFIES THE HUMANITY OF CHRIST MORE AND MORE**. Origen went so far as to say that, because of its virgin-birth, the body of Christ was from the act of incarnation **EVEN MORE DIVINE THAN OUR BODIES** . . . The Logos gradually absorbed the body of Jesus until **finally He WAS TRANSFORMED INTO Spirit and ADMITTED INTO UNION WITH THE GODHEAD** . . .* " (Book #7 p. 90)

c) Gnostic scriptures

d) Greek changes

Luke 2:40
BYZ A > KJV-- "and the child *grew, and waxed strong **IN SPIRIT**,*"
BS > WH NU) NASV NIV ESV-- **omit 'in spirit'**

Luke 10:21
BYZ AC) KJV NIV-- "*in that hour **JESUS** rejoiced in spirit,*"
SB > WH NU) NASV ESV-- "***(HE)** rejoiced in the Holy Spirit*"

I Peter 3:18
BYZ > KJV NIV-- "*Christ . . . being put to death in the flesh but quickened **BY THE Spirit**:*"
BYZ SBAC > WH NU > NASV ESV-- "*Christ . . . put to death in flesh but made alive **IN spirit**.*"

d. The Words of Jesus Christ

1) The Words of Jesus don't cause man to have eternal life

a) Rejected truth

John 6:63– "*. . . the **WORDS** that I speak unto YOU, they are spirit, and they are **LIFE**.*"

John 6:68-- "*Then Simon Peter answered him, Lord, to whom shall we go? **THOU HAST THE WORDS OF ETERNAL LIFE**.*"

b) Gnostic doctrine

c) Gnostic scripture

THE APOCRYPHON OF JAMES (Book #20, p. 31)
"*Henceforth, waking or sleeping, remember that you have seen the Son of Man and spoken with him in person, and listened to him in person. Woe to those who have seen the Son of Man: **BLESSED WILL THEY BE** who have not seen the man, and they who have not consorted with him, and they who have not spoken with him, and they **WHO HAVE NOT LISTENED TO ANYTHING FROM HIM**: **YOURS IS LIFE**.*"

d) Greek changes

Acts 13:48
BYZ SAC > KJV NU**NASV* NIV*-- "*glorified the word of **THE LORD**.*"
B > WH– "*word of **GOD***"

Acts 16:32
BYZ SAC > KJV; NU* > NASV NIV-- "*And they spake unto him the word of **THE LORD**.*"
SB > WH–" *. . . word of **GOD***"

Acts 19:10
BYZ) KJV-- "*so that all they which dwelt in Asia heard the word of the Lord **JESUS**,*"
SBA > WH NU > NASV NIV ESV-- **omit 'Jesus'**
All the verses found in - 1.b.2)

e. The work of Jesus Christ

1) The saviour came to destroy bad people and save good people

a) Rejected truth

Romans 3:12– "*. . . there is none that doeth good, no, not one.*"

b) Gnostic doctrine

SATORNINOS (according to Irenaeus) (Book #26, p. 162)
*"Indeed there are - he says - two human races which were modeled by the angels, one wicked and one good. And . . . the **SAVIOR CAME FOR THE DESTRUCTION OF BAD HUMANS BEINGS** and demons **AND FOR THE SALVATION OF GOOD ONES**."*

c) Gnostic scriptures

d) Greek changes.

Matthew 18:11
BYZ > KJV (SV) -- "***FOR THE SON OF MAN IS COME TO SAVE THAT WHICH WAS LOST***."
ORIGEN) 86 > WH NU) ESV-- **omit**

Matthew 25:13
BYZ > KJV– "ye know neither the day nor the hour **WHEREIN THE SON OF MAN COMETH**."
SBAC > WH NU > NASV NIV ESV--**omit 'wherein the Son of Man cometh'**

Luke 9:56
BY2 > KJV (NASV)– "***FOR THE SON OF MAN IS NOT COME TO DESTROY MEN'S LIVES, BUT TO SAVE THEM***."
BYZ SBA) WH NU) NIV ESV-- **omit**

2) Jesus does not call people to enter the heavenly kingdom

a) Rejected truth

John 10:16-- *"And other sheep I have, which are not of this fold: them also I must bring, and **THEY SHALL HEAR MY VOICE;** . . ."*

I Thessalonians 4:16-- *"For **THE LORD HIMSELF SHALL** descend from heaven with a **SHOUT**, with the voice of the archangel, and with the trump of God: and the dead in Christ shall rise first: . . ."*

b) Gnostic doctrine

c) Gnostic scripture

THE APOCRYPHON OF JAMES. (Book #12, p. 31)
*"He (Jesus) said, Verily I say unto you **NO ONE WILL EVER ENTER THE KINGDOM OF HEAVEN AT MY BIDDING**, but only because you yourselves are full."*

d) Greek changes

Matthew 9:13
BYZ C > KJV– *"for I am not come to call the righteous, but sinners **TO REPENTANCE**."*
BYZ BS. > WH NU > NASV N1V ESV-- **omit 'to repentance'**

Acts 16:10
BYZ > KJV-- *"assuredly gathering that **THE LORD** had called us for to preach the gospel unto them."*
SBA > WH NU) NASV NIV ESV-- *"concluding that had called us **GOD**. . ."*

1 Corinthians 7:17
BYZ > KJV-- *"but as **GOD** hath distributed to every man, as **THE LORD** hath called every one."*
SBAC > WH NU) NASV NIV ESV-- *"only to each as divided **THE LORD**, each as has called **GOD**."*

1 Peter 5:10
BYZ A) KJV (NU)-- *"But the God of all grace who hath called us unto his eternal glory by Christ **JESUS**."*
SB > WH > NASV NIV ESV-- <u>omit 'Jesus'</u>

f. The miracles of Christ

1) Walking on the water was symbolic (The main purpose of this segment is to show how Gnostic scriptures influenced the Greek change)

a) Rejected truth

b) Gnostic doctrine

c) Gnostic scriptures

THE TESTIMONY OF TRUTH
*"They boarded the ship, and at about **THIRTY STADES**, they saw Jesus walking on the sea. These are empty martyrs, since they bear witness only to themselves."*

d) Greek changes

Matthew 14:24
BY2 SC > KJV-- *"But the ship **WAS NOW IN THE MIDST OF THE SEA**, tossed with waves:"*
B > WH NU > NASV NIV ESV-- *"But the ship now **MANY STADIA FROM THE LAND WAS DISTANT**, tossed by the waves."*

g. The suffering and death of Christ

1) The Primal Man is slain for man's redemption at the beginning of creation and continues to die daily (This is the basis for the daily sacrifice of the Mass in the Catholic church)

a) Rejected truth

Hebrews 9:25-28-- *"Nor yet that He should offer himself often . . . for then must He often have suffered since the foundation of the world: but now **ONCE IN THE END OF THE WORLD** hath He appeared to put away sin by the sacrifice of himself. And as it is appointed unto men **ONCE TO DIE**, . . . **SO CHRIST WAS ONCE OFFERED** to bear the sins of many; . . ."*

b) Gnostic doctrine

*"The question of the derivation of the myth of the Primal Man is still one of the unsolved problems of religious history . . . According to the old Persian myth also,the development of the world begins with the **SLAYING OF THE PRIMAL MAN** . . . .further, that the Primal Man ('son of man' = man) also plays a part in Jewish apocalyptic literature (. . . Enoch). . . .**THE DOGMA OF CHRIST'S DESCENT INTO HELL IS DIRECTLY CONNECTED WITH THIS MYTH** . . . It is certainly true that in some way an essential part in the formation of the myth has been played by the **SUN-GOD**, who **DAILY** descends into darkness, to rise from it again victoriously."* (Book #3, p. 156)

MANI– *" . . . Christ. . . is the suffering form of Primal Man. This original and profound interpretation of the figure of Christ was an important article of the Manichaean creed and is known as the doctrine of the **JESUS PATIBILIS**, the 'passible Jesus' who . . . 'EVERY DAY IS BORN, SUFFERS AND DIES.' He is dispersed into all creation, but his most genuine realm and embodiment seems to be the vegetable world . . . "* (Book #20, p. 229)

c) Gnostic scriptures

THE GOSPEL OF PHILIP (Book #12, p. 142)
*" . . . he voluntarily laid down his life from the **VERY DAY THE WORLD CAME INTO BEING**."*

d) Greek changes

Mark 15:44
BYZ > KJV-- "whether he had been **ANY WHILE** dead."
ORIGEN > B > WH NU > NASV NIV-- *"if **ALREADY** He died"*

Ephesians 4:9
BYZ > KJV-- *"he descended **FIRST**"*
ORIGEN > SA > WH NU > NASV NIV ESV-- *"he descended"*

2) Jesus Christ did not fulfill the Messianic sufferings because He is not the only Christ

a) Rejected truth

Acts 3:18-- *"But those things, which God before had shewed by the mouth of all **HIS PROPHETS, THAT CHRIST SHOULD SUFFER, HE HATH SO FULFILLED**."*

b) Gnostic doctrine

HORT-- his commentary on I Peter
I Peter1:11-- "(the sufferings destined for Messiah) **THIS CANNOT POSSIBLY MEAN THE *SUFFERINGS OF CHRIST*** in our sense of the words, i.e. the sufferings which as a matter of history **BEFELL THE HISTORICAL CHRIST**." (Book #16, p. 28)

I Peter 1:11-- *"Touch not mine anointed ones . . . and do my prophets no harm, where the Divine anointing of **CHRISTHOOD** and prophethood are set in parallelism as kindred attributes of the children of Israel . . . The prophet, the people to whom he belongs and to whom he speaks, and the dimly seen Head and King of the people ALL pass insensibly one into the other in the language of prophecy; **THEY ALL ARE PARTAKERS OF THE DIVINE ANOINTING, AND THE MESSIAHSHIP WHICH IS CONFERRED BY IT.**"* (Book #16, p. 28)

c) Gnostic scriptures

d) Greek changes

Matthew 27:35
BYZ) KJV-- *"**THAT IT MIGHT BE FULFILLED WHICH WAS SPOKEN BY THE PROPHET, THEY PARTED MY GARMENTS AMONG THEM, AND UPON MY VESTURE DID THEY CAST LOTS.**"*
BYZ SBA) WH NU > NASV NIV ESV-- **omit**

Mark 1:2
BYZ A) KJV-- *"as it is written in **THE PROPHETS.**"*
ORIGEN > SB > WH NU) NASV NIV ESV-- *"as it has been written in **ISAIAH THE PROPHET.**"*

Luke 7:19
BYZ SA) KJV-- *"And John calling unto him two of his disciples sent them to **JESUS,** saying, Art though he that should come?"*
B > WH NU > NASV ESV-- *"John sent them to **THE LORD** saying . . ."*

\

3) The Savior did not die on the cross, but rather another Jesus who was demon possessed

a) Rejected truth

I Corinthians 15:3-4-- *"For I delivered unto you first of all that which I also received, how that **CHRIST DIED** for our sins according to the scriptures; and that **HE WAS BURIED**, and that he rose again the third day according to the scriptures."*

II Corinthians 11:4-- *"For if he that cometh preacheth **ANOTHER JESUS**, whom we have not preached, . . . ye might well bear with him."*

b) Gnostic doctrine

c) Gnostic scriptures

APOCALYPSE OF PETER (Book #12, p. 377)

*"The Savior said to me, He whom you saw on the tree, glad and laughing, this is the living Jesus. But this one into whose hands and feet they drive the nails is his fleshly part, which **IS THE SUBSTITUTE** being put to shame, **THE ONE WHO CAME INTO BEING IN HIS LIKENESS**. But look at him and me . . . And I saw someone--about-to approach us resembling him, even him who was laughing on the tree. And he was filled with a Holy Spirit, and he is the Savior . . . And he said to me, Be strong, for you are the one to whom these mysteries have been given, to know them through revelation, that **HE WHOM THEY CRUCIFIED IS THE FIRST-BORN, AND THE HOME OF DEMONS**, and the stony vessel in which they dwell, Elohim, of the cross which is under the Law. But he who stands near him is the living Savior. . ."*

d) Greek changes

Acts 2:30
BYZ> KJV-- *"**ACCORDING TO THE FLESH, HE WOULD RAISE UP CHRIST** . . ."*
SEA > WH NU > NASV NIV ESV-- <u>omit</u>

Romans 8:34
BYZ B > KJV-- *"It is **Christ** who died"*
ORIGEN) SA) WH NU) NASV NIV ESV-- *"it is **Christ JESUS** who died"*

h. The resurrection of Christ

1) The resurrection of Christ was spiritual and figurative, not bodily .

a) Rejected truth

John 20:27-- *"Then saith he to Thomas, Reach hither thy finger, and behold MY hands; and reach hither thy hand, and thrust it into my side: and be not faithless, but believing."*

b) Gnostic doctrine

*"**Christ is the divine spark in each one of us: buried, obscured, 'crucified' because of our lower, sinful nature. He must 'rise again from the dead' in each one of us**. . ."* (Book #25, p. 42)

WESTCOTT--*commentary on the Gospel of John*
*John 2:19-- (Destroy this temple, and in three days I will raise it up) "On the other hand **the RESURRECTION OF CHRIST was the raising again of the Temple**, the complete **RESTORATION OF THE TABERNACLE OF GOD'S PRESENCE TO MEN**, perpetuated **IN THE CHURCH, WHICH IS CHRIST'S BODY**." (Book #16, p. 33)*

*John 6:62--(What and if ye shall see the Son of Man **ASCEND UP** where he was before?) "This incomplete question . . . has been interpreted in **TWO** very different ways . . . According to the **FIRST INTERPRETATION the 'ASCENDING UP'** is the **ASCENSION AS THE FINAL SPIRITUALIZING OF THE LORD'S PERSON**,*

WHEREBY THE OFFENCE OF THE LANGUAGE AS TO HIS FLESH WOULD BE REMOVED by the apprehension of the truth as to His SPIRITUAL HUMANITY. In the SECOND the *'ASCENDING UP' is referred to the 'ELEVATION' ON THE CROSS . . . EACH OF THESE TWO INTERPRETATIONS APPEAR TO CONTAIN ELEMENTS OF THE FULL MEANING*." (Book #16, p. 29)

Comment by Dr. Waite– "*. . . To say that Christ's 'ASCENDING UP' refers to the cross is ridiculous . . . The Lord said 'ascend up where he was before' and He most certainly was never on the cross before! Here is an obvious desire to escape the literal, physical, bodily ASCENSION of the Lord into heaven.*")

c) Gnostic scriptures

d) Greek changes

Luke 24:51
BYZ SBAC > KJV (WH) NU) NIV-- "*AND CARRIED UP INTO HEAVEN*"
S*) NASV-- <u>omit</u>

John 16:16
BYZ A > KJV-- "**BECAUSE I GO TO THE FATHER.**"
SB > WH NU) NASV NIV ESV-- <u>omit</u>

Acts 2:30
BYZ > KJV-- "*ACCORDING TO THE FLESH, HE WOULD RAISE UP CHRIST*."
SBAC) WH NU) NASV NIV ESV-- <u>omit</u>

Ephesians 5:30
BYZ > KJV-- "*OF HIS FLESH, AND OF HIS BONES*."
BSAC > WH NU > NASV NIV ESV-- <u>omitted</u>

Colossians 2:12
BY2 B > KJV NASV NIV-- "*God, who hath raised Him from THE DEAD.*"
SAC > WH NU– ". . . *from DEATH*

I Thessalonians 1:10
BYZ SB > KJV; (WH) (NU) > NASV NIV ESV-- "H*is Son from heaven, whom He raised from THE DEAD.*"
AC– ". . . *from DEATH*"

I Peter 3:18
BYZ) KJV NIV-- "*Christ . . . put to death in the flesh, but quickened BY THE Spirit.*"
BYZ SBAC > WH NU > NASV ESV– ". . . *but made alive IN spirit*"

2) The resurrection of Jesus happened before he died

a) Rejected truth

1 Corinthians15:3-4– "... *Christ died for our sins according to the scriptures: and that he was **BURIED**, and that he **ROSE AGAIN** the third day according to the scriptures.*"

b) Gnostic doctrine

c) Gnostic scriptures

THE GOSPEL OF PHILIP (Book #12, p. 144)
"*Those who say that the lord died first and then rose up are in error, for **HE ROSE UP FIRST AND THEN DIED**. If one does not first attain the resurrection he will not die.*"

d) Greek changes

I1 Corinthians 4:14
BYZ SC > KJV;
(WH) NU* > NASV NIV ESV-- *He which raised up **THE LORD** Jesus*"
B– **omit "Lord"**

Ephesians 4:9
BYZ BS > KJV-- "*he also descended **FIRST** into the lower parts of the earth?*"
CLEMENT ORIGEN >AS) WH NU) NASV ESV-- **omit "first"**

Colossians 2:12
BYZ B) KJV NASV -- "*God, who hath raised Him from **THE DEAD**.*"
SAC > WH NU– "*. . . from **DEATH**"

3) The resurrected Christ meets with his disciples through divination in order to reveal to them his secret plan.

a) Rejected truth

Deuteronomy 18:10-12-- "*There shall not be found among you any one that maketh his son or his daughter to pass through the fire, or that useth **DIVINATION**, or an observer of times, or an enchanter, or a witch, or a charmer, or a consulter with familiar spirits, or a wizard, or a necromancer. For all that do these things are an abomination unto the Lord: . . .*"

I1 Corinthians11:14-- "*And no marvel; for **SATAN HIMSELF IS TRANSFORMED INTO AN ANGEL OF LIGHT**.*"

b) Gnostic doctrine

c) Gnostic scriptures

SOPHIA OF JESUS CHRIST (Book #12, p. 222)
"After he arose from the dead, his twelve disciples and seven women continued to be his followers and went to Galilee onto the mountain called '__DIVINATION__ and Joy.' When they gathered together and were perplexed about the underlying reality of the universe and the plan and the holy providence and the power of the authorities and about everything that the Savior is doing with them in the secret of the holy plan, __THE SAVIOR APPEARED__, not in his previous form, but in the invisible spirit. And __HIS LIKENESS RESEMBLES A GREAT ANGEL OF LIGHT__."

d) Greek changes

I. The return of Jesus Christ

II Peter 3:3-4-- *"Knowing this first, that there shall come in the last days scoffers, walking after their own lusts, and saying, __WHERE IS THE PROMISE OF HIS COMING__?. . ."*

1) The second coming of Christ is not literal but figurative and refers to the spiritual coming of Christ into the life of the believer

a) Rejected truth

Titus 2:13-- *"Looking for that blessed hope, and the glorious __APPEARING__ of the great God and our Saviour Jesus Christ.*

Revelation 22:20- Surely I come __QUICKLY__. . ."

b) Gnostic doctrine

ORIGEN-- *"The __spiritual, symbolic meaning__ of the doctrine of the __SECOND COMING__ maybe either the universal, expansion of the Church throughout the world, bringing all men to the obedience of Christ, or __the inward coming of Christ to the soul__. . . ."* (Book #8, p. 77)

HORT-- His Commentaries on I Peter 1:I-2:17 and Revelation
I Peter 1:7-- (at the revelation of Jesus Christ) *"There is nothing in either this passage __OR OTHERS ON THE SAME SUBJECT__, apart from the __FIGURATIVE LANGUAGE__ OF Thessalonians, to show that the revelation here spoken of is to be __LIMITED TO A SUDDEN PRETERNATURAL THEOPHANY. IT MAY BE A LONG AND VARYING PROCESS__., though ending in a climax."* (Book #16, p. 17)

Revelation 1:8-- (I am the Alpha and Omega, the beginning and the ending, saith the Lord (God), which is, and which was, and which is to come, the Almighty) "This verse must stand alone. **THE SPEAKER CANNOT BE OUR LORD**, when we consider 1:4, . . . and **ALL SCRIPTURAL ANALOGY IS AGAINST THE ATTRIBUTION OF 'THE LORD GOD' WITH OR WITHOUT 'ALMIGHTY' TO CHRIST** (Book #16 p. 26)
See Revelation 1:8 below

c) Gnostic scriptures

d) Greek changes

Matthew 25:13
BYZ) KJV-- "***WHEN THE SON OF MAN COMETH***."
SBAC > WH Nil) NASV NIV ESV-- <u>omit</u>

I Thessalonians 2:19
BYZ) KJV-- "in the presence of our Lord Jesus **CHRIST** at His coming?"
BYZ SBA > WH Nil > NASV NIV ESV-- **omit 'Christ'**

I Thessalonians 3:13
BYZ > KJV-- "*the coming of our Lord Jesus **CHRIST** with all His saints.*"
BYZ SBA.) WH NU NASV NIV ESV-- **omit "Christ"**

Revelation 1:8
BYZ (pt) > KJV-- "*saith the **Lord**, which is, and which was, and which is to come, the Almighty.*"
BYZ SAC > WH NU > NASV NIV ESV - says the **Lord GOD** who is. . . .

Revelation 11:17
BYZ > KJV-- "**AND ART TO COME**"
A > WH NU > NASV NIV ESV-- <u>omit</u>

4. PNEUMATOLOGY (Holy Spirit)

I1 Corinthians 11:4– *"For if . . . ye receive **ANOTHER SPIRIT**, which Ye have not received . . . ye might well bear with him."*

a. Person of the Holy Spirit

1) Sophia Is a/the Holy Spirit

a) Rejected truth

b) Gnostic doctrine

HORT--commentary on I Peter
I Peter 1:12-- (*by A holy spirit sent from heaven . . .*) (Book #16, p. 15)

c) Gnostic scriptures

WISDOM OF SOLOMON
"*In the Wisdom of Solomon, part of the Greek and Roman Catholic Bible, **WRITTEN IN ALEXANDRIA** close to the beginning of the Christian era, personified wisdom, called Sophia, is said to be **A HOLY SPIRIT OR THE HOLY SPIRIT**, which penetrates the All.*

*She is also referred to as the effluence of God's glory; an emanation of **ETERNAL LIGHT**, and an **IMMACULATE MIRROR** of God's activity. She is described as the beloved both of the wise man and of God, even more as the spouse of the Lord." (8:30)"* (Book #2, p. 568)

d) Greek changes

Acts 6:3
BY2 AC*) KJV-- *"full of the **HOLY GHOST** and wisdom"*
SB WH. NU > NASV NIV ESV-- *"full of **spirit** and wisdom"*

Ephesians 5:9
BYZ > KJV-- *"fruit of the **SPIRIT**"*
ORIGEN) SBA) WH NU >NASV NIV ESV-- *"fruit of the **LIGHT**"*

2) The Sophia Spirit reveals herself as a saint and as a whore

a) Rejected truth

Mark 3:29-- *"But he that shall blaspheme against the Holy Ghost hath never forgiveness, but is in danger of eternal damnation:"*

b) Gnostic doctrine

SIMON-- *"According to Simon, Wisdom—finally came to dwell as a **WHORE** in a brothel of Tyre in Phoenicia where Simon, 'the great power' of God, found and redeemed her."* (Book #29 p. 569)

MANDAEANS-- *"In Mandaean lore Sophia appears in degraded form as **A MEAN AND LEWD CREATURE** called the Holy Spirit"* (Book #2, p. 569)

c) Gnostic scripture

THUNDER, WHOLE MIND
*"In the Thunder, Whole Mind . . . . Sophia manifests herself as the wisdom of the Greeks and the gnosis of the barbarians, the **SAINT AND THE WHORE** the bridegroom and the bride. Over and over, she introduces these startling and paradoxical revelations with the formula 'I AM.'"* (Book #2, p. 568)

d) Greek changes

John 7:39
BYZ) KJV-- *"for the **HOLY GHOST** was not yet given;"*
ORIGEN > S > WH NU') NASV NIV ESV-- **omit 'Holy'**

Acts 6:3

BYZ AC* > KJV-- *"full of the __HOLY__ Ghost"*
SB. > WH NU) NASV NIV ESV-- <u>omit 'Holy'</u>

Acts 8:18
BYZ AC). KJV-- *"through laying on of the of apostles' hands the __HOLY__ Ghost was given,"*
SB > WH NU > NASV NIV ESV-- <u>omit 'Holy'</u>

I Corinthians 2:13
BYZ) KJV-- *"but which the __HOLY__ Ghost teacheth;"*
SBAC > WH NU >NASV ESV-- <u>omit 'Holy'</u>

b. Works of the Spirit

1) The Sophia Spirit created the world

   a) Rejected truth

   b) Gnostic doctrine

   SAMARITANS - *"The Samaritans . . . transmit a certain tradition about __Wisdom__ as the personal __creator of the world__."* (Book #2, p. 568)

   c) Gnostic scriptures

   d) Greek changes

Acts 4:24
BYZ) KJV-- *"Lord, thou art __GOD__, which hast made heaven,"*
SBA) WH NU) NASV NIV ESV-- <u>omit 'God'</u>

Ephesians 3:9
BYZ > KJV-- *"created all things __BY JESUS CHRIST__:"*
BSA > WH NU) NASV NIV ESV-- <u>omit 'by Jesus Christ'</u>

2) The Spirit is the source of DIRECT revelation

   a) Rejected truth

Il Corinthians 11:14– ". . . Satan himself is transformed into an angel of __LIGHT__."

I Timothy 4:1-- *"Now the Spirit speaketh expressly, that in the latter times some shall depart from the faith, giving heed to __SEDUCING SPIRITS__, and doctrines of devils;"*

   b) Gnostic doctrines

   "Non-conformism was almost a principle of the gnostic mind and was closely connected with the doctrine of the sovereign '__SPIRIT' AS A SOURCE OF DIRECT KNOWLEDGE__

AND ILLUMINATION.'" (Book #20, p. 42)

c) Gnostic scriptures

d) Greek changes

Acts 4:25
BYZ > KJV-- *"who by the mouth of thy servant David hast said,"*
SBA > WH NU > NASV NIV ESV-- *"who by (A) **HOLY SPIRIT** by mouth of **OUR FATHER** David Your servant did say."*

c. Indwelling of the Spirit

1) The Sophia Spirit is incarnated and reincarnated in human bodies

a) Rejected truth

b) Gnostic doctrine

SIMON-- *"According to Simon, **Wisdom**, the spouse of the Lord, was also called Holy Spirit and God's first idea, the mother of all . . .   She was even **INCARNATED AND REINCARNATED** in human bodies, such as that of the Helen of Greek myth and poetry."* (Book #2, p. 569)

WESTCOTT-- commentary on 1-3 John
I John 4:4-- *"he that is in you, that is in the **CHRISTIAN SOCIETY** . . . The Divine Person is **UNDEFINED**. We think naturally of God in Christ."* (Book #16, p. 15)

c) Gnostic scriptures

d) Greek changes

5. ANTHROPOLOGY (Man)

Romans 1:25–*"Who changed the truth of God into a lie, and **WORSHIPPED AND SERVED THE CREATURE** more than the Creator. . ."*

a. The creation of man

1) The angels created man

a) Rejected truth

1 Corinthians 8:6-- "But to us there is but one God the Father, of whom are all things, and we in him: and one **LORD JESUS CHRIST BY WHOM ARE ALL THINGS, AND WE BY HIM**."

Colossians 1:16-- *"For by him were all things created, that are in heaven and that are in earth , . . ."*

b) Gnostic doctrine

"*A parallel myth to that of the Primal Man are the accounts to be found in most of the Gnostic systems of the creation of the first man. In all these accounts the idea is expressed that so far as his body is concerned, **MAN IS THE WORK OF THE ANGELS WHO CREATED THE WORLD**. So . . . Satornil related that a brilliant vision appeared from above to the world creating angels; they were unable to hold it fast but formed man after its image. And as the man thus formed was unable to move, but could only crawl like a worm, the supreme Power put into him a spark of life, and man came into existence.*" (Book #3, p. 156)

c) Gnostic scriptures

d) Greek changes

Acts 4:24
BYZ > KJV-- "*Lord, thou art GOD which hast made heaven, and earth, and the sea, and all that in them is:*"
SBA > WH NU > NASV NIV ESV-- **omits "God"**

Ephesians 3:9
BYZ > KJV-- "*created all things **BY JESUS CHRIST**:*"
BSA > WH NU > NASV NIV - omit 'by Jesus Christ'

b. The person of man

1) Before a person is born he was pre-existent and one with God

a) Rejected truth

b) Gnostic doctrine

WESTCOTT
John 3:12-- "*Such was the full revelation of the Son, involving the redemption of the world and the **REUNION OF MAN WITH GOD**.*" (Book #16, p. 1 B)

John 10:16-- (bring) "*This could only be by His death, which **REUNITES MAN WITH GOD**. . .*" (Book #16, p. 18)

c) Gnostic scriptures

d) Greek changes

2) Man sinned in his pre-existent state before he was born and became a soul

a) Rejected truth

John 9:2-3-- *"And his disciples asked him, saying, Master, who did sin, this man, or his parents, that he was born blind? Jesus answered, Neither hath this man sinned, nor his parents: but that the works of God should be made manifest in him."*

b) Gnostic doctrine

ORIGEN– *". . . **before the ages** minds were all pure, both daemons and **SOULS** and angels . . . But the devil . . . desired to resist God . . . With him revolted **ALL THE OTHER POWERS**. Some sinned deeply and became daemons, others less and became angels; others still less and became-archangels . . . But there remained some SOULS who had not sinned so greatly as to become daemons, nor . . . so very lightly as to become angels. God therefore made the present world and bound the soul to the body as a punishment . . . It is clear that God made one a daemon, one a soul and one an angel as a means of punishing each in proportion to its sin. For **if this were not so, and SOULS HAD NO PRE-EXISTENCE, WHY DO WE FIND SOME NEW-BORN BABES TO BE BLIND**, when they have committed no sin, while others are born with no defect at all?"* (Book #21, p. 67)

c) Gnostic scriptures

d) Greek changes

3) The divine spark (Christ) is in all of mankind, and all have potential to become Christs, divine, and God

a) Rejected truth

Ephesians 2:12-- *"That at that time ye were **WITHOUT CHRIST**, being aliens from the commonwealth of Israel, and strangers from the covenants of promise, having no hope, **AND WITHOUT GOD IN THE WORLD**."*

1 Corinthians 1:13-- *"is Christ divided? . . ."*

Galatians 2:6-- *"As ye have therefore **RECEIVED CHRIST JESUS THE LORD**, so walk ye in Him:"*

Matthew 24:4-5-- *"And Jesus answered and said unto them, Take heed that no man deceive you. For many shall come **IN MY NAME** saying, **I AM CHRIST**; and shall deceive many.*

b) Gnostic doctrine

*"Enclosed in the soul is the spirit, or 'pneuma' (called also the 'spark'), a portion of the **DIVINE SUBSTANCE** from beyond which has fallen into the world . . . In its unredeemed state the pneuma thus immersed in soul and flesh is unconscious of itself, benumbed, asleep, or intoxicated by the poison of the world: in brief, it is 'ignorant.' Its awakening and liberation is effected through knowledge (Gnosis)."*   (Book #20, p. 44)

*"**CHRIST IS THE DIVINE SPARK IN EACH ONE OF US**: buried, obscured, 'crucified' because of our lower, sinful nature. **He must 'rise again from the dead' in each one of us**.*

. .” (Book #25, p. 42)

ORIGEN-- *"Now some of our predecessors have observed that in the New Testament, whenever the Spirit is mentioned without its qualifying adjective, the expression should be understood to refer to the Holy Spirit . . . We . . . think that this particular use may be observed in the Old Testament also, as when it says, 'he that giveth spirit to the people who are upon the earth, and spirit to them that walk thereon. . . ' For undoubtedly EVERY ONE WHO WALKS UPON THE EARTH, THAT IS TO SAY, EVERY EARTHLY AND CORPOREAL BEING, IS A PARTAKER OF THE HOLY SPIRIT, WHICH HE RECEIVES FROM GOD."* (Book #21, p. 31-32)

"That the activity of the Father and the Son is to be found BOTH IN SAINTS AND IN SINNERS is clear from the fact that ALL RATIONAL BEINGS are partakers of the word of God, that is of reason, and so HAVE IMPLANTED WITHIN THEM SOME SEEDS . . . OF WISDOM AND RIGHTEOUSNESS, WHICH IS CHRIST . . . Certainly the apostle Paul shows that WE ALL HAVE A SHARE IN CHRIST. (Book #21, p. 34-35)

HORT
John 17:22-- *"Viewed from another point of sight it is the revelation of the DIVINE IN MAN realized in and through Christ."*   (Book #16, p. 10)

l John 2:18– *". . . the lie of Antichrist was to teach that MAN IS DIVINE APART FROM GOD IN CHRIST."* (Book #16, p. 10)

WESTCOTT
Hebrews 2:7-8-- *"In spite of his frailty MAN RECOGNIZES HIS DIVINE AFFINITY."* (Book #16, p. 11)

I John 3:23-- *"Thus in the three cases the Sonship of Jesus Christ is regarded in relation to God as the Father, to God as God, and to God as perfectly satisfying the DIVINE IDEAL WHICH MAN IS ABLE TO FORM."* (Book #16, p. 12)

I John 2:18-- *"The teaching of Antichrist leaves God and the world still un-united. THE PROCLAMATION OF THE UNION IS THE MESSAGE OF THE GOSPEL."* (Book #16, p. 19)

c) Gnostic scriptures

DEAD SEA SCROLLS
"The biblical Book of Genesis relates that God blew the breath of life into the nose of Adam, transforming him into a living being (Genesis 2:7) Already in certain passages of the Old Testament (Job 34:13-15, Psalm 104:29-30), this breath is identified with the spirit of God. THIS IS ESPECIALLY CLEAR IN THE DEAD SEA SCROLLS: 'I, the creature of dust, have known through the spirit, that Thou hast given me'. THE ALEXANDRIAN JEWS have integrated and amplified this concept. They were familiar with Greek philosophy and knew that the Orphics, Plato, and the Stoics considered the human soul to be a part of the deity. They were influenced by the Stoic Posidonius according to whom

'the daimon in us (the spirit) is akin to and of the same nature as **THE DAIMON** *(God)* **WHO PERVADES THE ALL**.*"* (Book #2, p. 569)

SEPTUAGINT

"The oldest translators - of the Septuagint Tendered 'breath' in Genesis 2:7 as 'spirit' (pneuma). This variant is evidenced by the Old Latin Version translated from the Septuagint. Philo polemicizes against this particular translation because **IT DEIFIES SINFUL MAN**.*"* (Book #2, p. 569)

WISDOM OF SOLOMON

"And yet the Alexandrian 'Wisdom of Solomon' still included in every Roman Catholic Bible, **DECLARES EXPLICITLY THAT GOD'S INCORRUPTIBLE PNEUMA IS IN ALL THINGS (12:1). MOST GNOSTICS PRESERVED THIS TENDENTIOUS TRANSLATION AND MADE IT THE BASIS FOR THEIR MYTHOLOGICAL SPECULATIONS**. *It enabled them to tell how it came to pass that* **the Spirit sleeps in man** *and how it can be made conscious. So it is with Valentinus and Mani. Few people nowadays are aware that these mythologems presuppose a consensus of virtually all Greek philosophers* **AND HAVE A BIBLICAL FOUNDATION**.*"* (Book #2, p. 569)

THE PRAYER OF THANKSGIVING (Book #12, p. 329)
"We rejoice, having been illuminated by Your knowledge. . . We rejoice because while we were in (the) body, **YOU HAVE MADE US DIVINE** *through Your knowledge (Gnosis)."*

ASCLEPIUS (Book #12 p. 333)
"Therefore **MAN HAS BECOME AKIN TO THE GODS**, *and they know the affairs of each other with certainty. The gods know the things of men, and men know the things of the gods.* **AND I AM SPEAKING ABOUT MEN**, *Asclepius,* **WHO HAVE ATTAINED LEARNING AND KNOWLEDGE** *(gnosis). But about those who are more vain than these, it is not fitting that we say anything base,* **SINCE WE ARE DIVINE** *and are introducing holy matters . . . For just as the Father, the Lord of the universe, creates gods in this very way* **MAN TOO**. . . . *also himself . . .* **CREATES GODS** . . . **NOT ONLY IS HE GOD, BUT HE ALSO CREATES GODS**. *Are you astonished Asclepius? Are you yourself another disbeliever like the many"?*

THE SENTENCES OF SEXTUS (Book #12, p. 507)
"A man who is worthy of God, **HE IS GOD AMONG MEN**, *and he is the son of God."*

THE GOSPEL OF MARY (Book #12 p. 525)
"Beware that no one lead you astray, saying, Lo here! or Lo there! **FOR THE SON OF MAN IS WITHIN YOU**. *Follow after him!"*

d) Greek changes

Colossians 1:28
BYZ > KJV– *". . . that we may present every man perfect in Christ* **JESUS**.*"*
BSAC.> WH NU > NASV NIV ESV-- **omit "Jesus."**

II Thessalonians 2:10
BYZ > KJV-- "*and with all deceivableness of unrighteousness __IN__ them that perish*"
SBA > WH NU NASV NIV? ESV– "*. . . unrighteousness __TO__ them that perish*"?

e) Gnostic twisting of Scripture

Colossians 3:11– "*. . . Christ is all and in all (Gnostics say __He is in all mankind rather than in all believers__).*"

4) Man has a spiritual 'twin' which is his transcendental Self

a) Rejected truth

Deuteronomy 18:10-12– "*There shall not be found among you any one that maketh his son or his daughter to pass through the fire, or that useth divination or an oberver of times, or an enchanter, or a witch or a charmer, or a consulter with __FAMILIAR SPIRITS__, or a wizard, or a necromancer. For all that do these things are an abomination unto the Lord:*"

b) Gnostic doctrine

VALENTINUS– "*Man and his guardian angel, __OR TRANSCENDENTAL COUNTERPART__, celebrate the mystical marriage of bride and bridegroom.*" (Book #2, p. 571)

MANI-- "*Very much in the spirit of Valentinus was Mani's primary religious experience. The basis of his entire myth, the __ENCOUNTER WITH HIS 'TWIN' OR TRANSCENDENTAL SELF, IS GNOSTIC__, very much in the spirit of Valentinus 'I recognized him and understood that he was my Self from whom I had been separated.' Mani encountered his spiritual Self at the age of 12 and encountered it a second time at the age of 25. He felt constantly accompanied by his twin, and when he died a martyr in prison he was gazing at this __FAMILIAR__. The encounter with one's twin is central to the life of every Manichaean.*" (Book #2, p. 573).

c) Gnostic scriptures

THE GOSPEL OF THOMAS (Book #12, p. 135)
"*Jesus said, When you see __YOUR LIKENESS__, you rejoice. But when You see your images which came into being before you, and which neither die nor become manifest, how much YOU will have to bear!*"

THE BOOK OF THOMAS THE CONTENDER: "*The savior said, Brother Thomas . . . Now since it has been said that you are __MY TWIN__ and true companion, examine yourself and learn who you are, in what way you exist, and how you will come to be. . . .it is not fitting that you be ignorant of yourself . . . .You have in fact already come to know, and __YOU__ will be called 'the one who knows himself.' For he who has not known himself has known nothing, but he who has known himself has at the same time already achieved*" *knowledge about the depth of the all.*" (Book #12, p. 201)

d) Greek changes

5) Man becomes perfected through a series of reincarnations or evolutionary processes

a) Rejected truth

Hebrews 9:27– :*. . . it is appointed unto men **ONCE TO DIE**, but after this the judgment.*"

I John 1:8-- *"If we say that we have no sin, we deceive ourselves, and the truth is not in us.*"

b) Gnostic doctrine

"*A heavenly savior has been sent to awaken gnostic humanity, to give them acquaintance (gnosis) with themselves and god, to free their souls from destiny and from bondage to the material body, and to teach them how to escape the influence of malevolent rulers. To counteract the evil spirit of these rulers, a good spirit has been bestowed upon the gnostics. According as each soul responds and gains acquaintance, it either escapes and returns to god, or **BECOMES REINCARNATE** in another body. . .*" (Book #26, p. 17)

ORIGEN– "*. . . through their endurance of greater and more severe punishments of long duration, extending, if I may say so, OVER MANY AGES, are by these very stern methods of correction renewed and restored, first by the instruction of angels and afterwards by that of powers yet higher in rank, so that **THEY ADVANCE THROUGH EACH GRADE TO A HIGHER ONE**, until at length they reach the things that are 'invisible' and 'eternal.'*" (book #21, p. 57)

"*There is another paraphrase of this passage of Origen in Jerome . . . "the daemons themselves and the rulers of the darkness in any world or worlds, if they desire to turn to better things **BECOME MEN** and so revert, to their original condition in order that being disciplined by the punishments and torments which they endure for a long or short period while in the bodies of men they may in time reach the exalted rank of the angels. It follows logically from this that **ANY RATIONAL CREATURE CAN DEVELOP OUT OF ANY OTHER, NOT ONCE OR SUDDENLY BUT OVER AND OVER AGAIN**; that we may become angels, or, if we live carelessly, daemons, and on the other hand daemons, if they desire to possess virtue, may attain the dignity of angels. No opinion of Origen's was more vehemently opposed than this one which gave daemons and lost men a chance of restoration.*" (Book #21, p. 56, footnote Book #4)

"*. . . at the end of this world each man that must pass into another world will receive the beginnings of a **FRESH BIRTH**.*" (Book #21, p. 145)

HORT--(To Ellerton) "*The book which has most engaged me is **DARWIN**. Whatever may be thought of it, it is a book that one is proud to be contemporary with. I must work out and examine the argument more in detail, but at present my feeling is strong that the theory is* *unanswerable. If so, it opens up a new period in--I know not what.*" (Book #10, V.1 p. 416)

WESTCOTT (Commentary on Hebrews)
John 15:8-- "*(and so shall ye be (become) my disciple)* ***A CHRISTIAN NEVER 'IS', BUT ALWAYS 'IS BECOMING' A CHRISTIAN.*" (Book #16, p. 20)

Hebrews 1:2-- "*The universe may be regarded either in its actual constitution as a whole. . ., or as an order which exists through time* ***DEVELOPED IN SUCCESSIVE STAGES***. *There are obvious reasons why the* ***LATTER MODE*** *of representation should be adopted here.*" (Book #16, p. 11)

Hebrews 5:7-- "*We can indeed form no clear conception of 'immortal,' 'incorruptible' flesh; but the phrase represents to us the continuance under new conditions of all that belongs to the* ***PERFECTION OF OUR NATURE***." (Book #16, p. 12)

Hebrews 7:10-- "*Each man is at once an individual of a race and a new power in the* ***EVOLUTION OF THE RACE***." (Book #16, p. 11)

I John 3:14-- '*To enter into life'* . . . *In this largest sense 'life'* . . . *is the fulfillment of the* ***HIGHEST IDEA OF BEING: PERFECT TRUTH IN PERFECT ACTION***." (Book #16, p. 20)

I John 4:2-3-- "*The INCARNATE Saviour is the* ***PLEDGE OF THE*** *complete redemption and* ***PERFECTION OF MAN***,. . ." (Book #16, p. 19)

SCHAFF-- "*There is, therefore, no room for a conflict between the Bible and Science, faith and reason . . . They run in parallel lines, independent, and yet friendly and mutually helpful, tending to the same end--salvation and* ***PERFECTION OF MAN IN THE KINGDOM OF GOD***." (Book #19, p. 334) ("*When Schaff refers to 'the kingdom of God', he is speaking of the earthly kingdom brought about by man's own efforts– p. lxvi -- he attempted throughout his long career . . . to achieve or maintain an evangelical consensus and to restore the unity of the church, viewing both as means toward the ultimate goal of establishing* ***GOD'S KINGDOM ON EARTH***.")

"*Shortly before his death . . .* ***Schaff publicly embraced Darwin's theory of EVOLUTION***, *affirming it as the counterpart in the natural sciences to his cherished notion of historical development.*" (Book #19, p. lxvii)

"*The theory of historical development, which corresponds to the theory of* ***PHYSICAL EVOLUTION***, *and preceded it, was first denounced by orthodox divines . . . as a dangerous error leading to infidelity, but is now adopted by every historian.* ***IT IS ENDORSED BY CHRIST HIMSELF*** *in the twin parables of the mustard seed and the leaven.*" (Book #19 p. 333)

c) Gnostic writings

THE ARCHONTICS ACCORDING TO ST. EPIPHANIUS

"*. . . Adam united with Eve his wife and begot Seth, his own physical son. And next . . . the higher power descended, accompanied by the ministering angels of the good god, and caught up Seth himself, . . . carried him somewhere above and cared for him for a while, lest he be slain; and after a long time* **BROUGHT HIM BACK DOWN INTO THIS WORLD AND RENDERED HIM SPIRITUAL AND BODILY** *. . .*" (Book #26 p. 197-198)

d) Greek changes

6) Some races of man are inferior to other races due to evolution

a) Rejected truth

Romans 3:9-12– "*. . . both Jews and Gentiles . . . are all under sin; as it is written, There is none righteous, no, not one: there is none that understandeth, there is none that seeketh after God. They are all gone out of the way, they are together become unprofitable; there is none that doeth good, no, not one.*"

Romans 3:19– "*. . . every mouth may be stopped, and* **ALL THE WORLD** *may become guilty before God.*"

b) Gnostic doctrine

SATORNINOS (according to Irenaeus (Book #26, p. 162)
"*Indeed there are--he says--***TWO HUMAN RACES*** which were modeled by the angels, one wicked and the other good.*"

ORIGEN
"*For Origen, there were no hard-and-fast boundaries between angels and men. One fragment quotes him as teaching that 'angels may become men or demons, and again from the latter they may rise to be men or angels.' . . . Origen is also quoted as believing that these spirits who fell were those in whom the divine love had grown cold and states that these could have been 'hidden in gross bodies such as ours, and have been* **CALLED MEN**.*' In that statement, Origen evinces the belief that certain men are actually the embodiments of* **WICKED ANGELS**.*" (Book #29, p. 318-320)

SCHAFF– "*The Anglo-Saxon and the German, he would always believe formed the basis of the American national character; together they were destined to execute the designs of divine providence for the* **FURTHER PROGRESS OF CHRIST'S CHURCH AND THE HUMAN RACE** *. . . .He did not want to speculate what was to be 'the ultimate fate of the red man, the Negro and the Chinese who are* **SEPARATED FROM US BY INSURMOUNTABLE DIFFERENCES OF RACE**.*' The evidence was already conclusive, however, that all the civilized nations of Europe,* **ESPECIALLY THOSE OF GERMANIC ORIGIN, HAVE CONTRIBUTED AND WILL CONTRIBUTE TO OUR STOCK**.*'*" (Book #19, p. 156)

c) Gnostic scriptures

d) Greek changes
Acts 17:26
BYZ > KJV-- "*hath made of one **BLOOD** all nations of men*"
CLEMENT > SBA > WH NU > NASV NIV ESV-- "*he made from one man every nation*"

7) Perfect man is bi-sexual (This is the basis for Sodomy)

a) Rejected truth

Leviticus18:22-- "*Thou shalt not lie with mankind, as with womankind: it is an abomination.*"

II Peter2:6-8-- "*And turning the cities of **Sodom and Gomorrah into ashes** condemned them with an overthrow, making them an ensample unto those that after should live ungodly; and delivered just Lot, vexed with the **filthy conversation of the wicked**: (for that righteous man dwelling among them, in seeing and hearing, vexed his righteous soul from day to day with their unlawful deeds;)*"

b) Gnostic doctrine

"*The entire world process is necessary to shape the Perfect Man so that the original state: **ANDROGYNY** (male and maiden at the same time)will be restored.*" (Book #2 p. 568)

c) Gnostic scriptures

THE PARAPHRASE. OF SHEM
"*When he will have appeared, O Shem, upon the earth, in the place which will be called **SODOM**, then safeguard the insight which I shall give you. **FOR THOSE WHOSE HEART IS PURE WILL CONGREGATE TO YOU**, because of the word which you will reveal. For when you appear, in the world, dark Nature will shake against you, together with the winds and a demon, that they may destroy the insight. But you, proclaim quickly to the **SODOMITES** your universal teaching for they are your members. For the demon of human form (Lot) will part from that place by my will, since he is ignorant. He will guard this utterance. **BUT THE SODOMITES, ACCORDING TO THE WILL OF THE MAJESTY WILL BEAR WITNESS TO THE UNIVERSAL TESTIMONY. THEY WILL REST WITH A PURE CONSCIENCE** in the place of their repose, which is. the unbegotten Spirit. And as these things will happen, **SODOM WILL BE BURNED UNJUSTLY BY A BASE NATURE**.*" (Book #12, p. 353-354)

GOSPEL OF THOMAS
"*Jesus said to them, When you make the two one—and **WHEN YOU MAKE THE MALE AND THE FEMALE ONE AND THE SAME, SO THAT THE MALE NOT BE MALE NOR THE FEMALE FEMALE** then will you enter the kingdom.*" (Book #12 p. 129)

"*Simon Peter said to them, 'Let Mary leave us, for women are not worthy of life.' Jesus said, I myself shall lead her in order **TO MAKE HER MALE**, so that she too may become a living spirit resembling you males. For **EVERY WOMAN WHO WILL MAKE HERSELF MALE** will enter the kingdom of heaven.*" (Book #12, p. 138)

*"His disciples said, When will you become revealed to us and when shall we see you? Jesus said, When you **DISROBE** without being ashamed and take up your garments and place them under your feet like little children and tread on them, then will you see the son of the living one, and you will not be afraid."* (Book #12, p. 130)

d) Greek changes

e) Translation changes (Dynamic equivalence)

Deuteronomy 23:17
KJV-- *"There shall be no whore of the daughters of Israel, nor a **SODOMITE** of the sons of Israel."*
NIV-- *"No Israelite man or woman-is to become a **SHRINE PROSTITUTE**:"*
ESV--*None of the daughters of Israel shall be a **cult prostitute**, and none of the sons of Israel shall be a cult prostitute.*

1 Kings 14:24
KJV-- *"And there were **SODOMITES** in the land: and they did according to all the abominations of the nations which the Lord: cast out. before the children of Israel."*
NIV-- "There were even **MALE SHRINE PROSTITUTES** in the land. . . ."
ESV– *"and there were also male **cult prostitutes** in the land. They did according to all the abominations of the nations that the LORD drove out before the people of Israel."*

I Kings 15:12
KJV-- *"And he took away the **SODOMITES** out of the land, . . ."*
NIV-- "He expelled all the **SHRINE PROSTITUTES** from the land . . ."
ESV– *"He put away the male **cult prostitutes** out of the land and removed all the idols that his fathers had made."*

1 Kings 22:46
KJV-- *"And the remnant of the **SODOMITES** . . . he took out of the land."*
NIV– "*rest of the **SHRINE PROSTITUTES**"*
ESV– *"And from the land he exterminated the remnant of the **male cult prostitutes** who remained in the days of his father Asa."*

2 Kings 23:7
KJV-- "And he brake down the houses of the **SODOMITES** . . ."
NIV-- "He also tore down the quarters of the **MALE SHRINE PROSTITUTES** . . ."
ESV– *"And he broke down the houses of the **male cult prostitutes** who were in the house of the LORD, where the women wove hangings for the Asherah."*

8) Perfected man stops being a soul and becomes spirit (rejects that the soul is eternal)

a) Rejected truth

I Thessalonians 5:23-- *"And the very God of peace sanctify you wholly; and I pray God your whole spirit and **SOUL** and body **BE PRESERVED** blameless unto the coming of our Lord Jesus Christ."*

b) Gnostic doctrine

VALENTINUS-- *"The ultimate 'object' of gnosis is God: its event in the soul transforms the knower himself by making him a partaker of the divine essence. Thus in the more radical systems like the Valentinian the ... subject is **transformed (from 'soul' to 'spirit')** ..."* (Book #20, p. 35)

ORIGEN--*"And so the rational being, growing at each successive stage, not as it grew when **IN THIS LIFE IN THE FLESH; OR BODY AND IN THE SOUL** but increasing in mind and intelligence, advances as a mind already perfect knowledge no longer hindered by its form carnal senses..."*
(*Note Book #4-- Jerome's paraphrase of this passage is ... "And at the end of the second book, in the course of his argument about our final perfection, he says: When we have progressed so far that we are no longer flesh and bodies, and possibly not even souls..."*)
(Book #21, p. 152)

HORT (Westcott must agree--see I Peter 1:9 note)
I Peter 2:11-- *"It is by this time sufficiently recognized that the modern religious sense of the term **'SOUL' AS THE HIGHEST ELEMENT IN MAN IS FOUNDED ON A MISUNDERSTANDING OF THE N.T.** and it is dangerous to build an absolute psychology on such passages as I Thessalonians 1:23."* (Book #16, p. 12)

I Peter 1:5-- *"'salvation of souls' ... In these and similar phrases we must beware of importing ... modern associations connected with the **RELIGIOUS USE OF THE WORD 'SOUL' The 'SOUL' in the Bible IS SIMPLY THE LIFE** and 'to save a soul' is the opposite of 'to kill.'"* (Book #16, p. 12)

I Peter 1:9-- *"(salvation of souls) "Here again ... we have to be on our guard against interpreting the language of Scripture by the sharp limitations of modern usage. Salvation is deliverance from dangers and enemies and above all **FROM DEATH** and destruction. **THE SOUL IS NOT A PARTICULAR ELEMENT OR FACULTY OF OUR NATURE, BUT ITS VERY LIFE** (Cf. WESTCOTT of John xii.25).* (Book #16, p. 13)

c) Gnostic scriptures

GOSPEL OF PHILIP
*"The soul of Adam came into being by means of a breath. The partner of his soul is the spirit. His mother is the thing that was given to him. **HIS SOUL WAS TAKEN FROM HIM AND REPLACED BY A (SPIRIT)**."* (Book #12, p. 152)

d) Greek changes

Mark 12:33
BYZ A) KJV-- "and to love Him with all the heart, and with all the understanding, **AND WITH ALL THE SOUL**, and with all the strength,"
SB) WH NU) NASV ESV-- **omit 'and with all the soul'**

Luke 9:55
BYZ) KJV (NASV)-- "*AND SAID YE KNOW NOT OF WHAT SPIRIT YE ARE OF.*"
BYZ SBA > WH NU) NIV ESV-- <u>omit</u>

Luke 9:56
BYZ > KJV (NASV)– "**FOR THE SON OF MAN IS NOT COME TO DESTROY MEN'S LIVES, BUT TO SAVE THEM**."
BYZ SBA) WH NU-) NIV ESV-- <u>omit</u>

Acts 2:31
BYZ > KJV-- "**Christ, that <u>HIS SOUL</u> was not left in hell,**"
SBC) WH NU > NASV NIV ESV-- <u>omit 'his soul'</u>

Acts 18:5
BYZ > KJV-- "**Paul was pressed <u>IN THE SPIRIT</u>,**"
SBA > WH NU > NASV N1V ESV-- "*was pressed <u>**WITH THE WORD**</u> Paul.*"

c. The person of Mary

1) Mary was the Logos, the World Mother

a) Rejected truth

b) Gnostic doctrine

HORT-- "*1 have been persuaded for many years that <u>**MARY-WORSHIP AND JESUS-WORSHIP HAVE VERY MUCH IN COMMON IN THEIR CAUSES AND IN THEIR RESULTS**</u>.*"   (Book #10, Vol.2, p. 50)

c) Gnostic writings

BARTHOLOMEW II.
"*Then he said to me: Hail, you who are high favored, the chosen vessel.*" (Book #22, p. 354)

d) Greek changes

Luke 1:28
BYZ AC > KJV– "*. . . Hail, thou art highly favoured, the Lord is with thee: <u>**BLESSED ART THOU AMONG WOMEN**</u>.*"
SB > WH NU > NASV NIV ESV-- <u>omit 'blessed art thou among women'</u>

d. The propagation of man

1) Marriage and sexual propagation is evil

a) Rejected truth

Hebrews 13:4-- *"Marriage is honourable in all, and the bed undefiled: but whoremongers and adulterers God will judge."*

b) Gnostic doctrine

*"**Marriage and sexual propagation** are considered either as **absolute Evil** or as altogether **worthless**, and carnal pleasure is frequently looked upon as forbidden."* (Book #3, p. 157)

c) Gnostic scriptures

THE TESTIMONY OF TRUTH (Book #12, p. 450)
*"But the Son of Man came forth from Imperishability, being alien to defilement . . . And John bore witness to the descent of Jesus. For it is he who saw the power which came down upon the Jordan river; for he knew that the **DOMINION OF CARNAL PROCREATION HAD COME TO AN END**."*

d) Greek changes

Mark 10:7
BYZ KJV (NU) NIV-- "For this cause shall a man leave his father and mother, *AND CLEAVE TO HIS WIFE*;"
  SB) WH > NASV ESV-- omit "and cleave to his wife"

6. ANGELOLOGY (Angels)

Colossians 2:18-- *"Let no man beguile you of your reward in . . . **WORSHIPPING OF ANGELS**, intruding into those things which he hath not seen, . . ."*

a. Lucifer, Satan, Serpent, Devil

1) The Devil Is an Instrument of God and will ultimately be pardoned

a) Rejected truth

Revelation 20:10-- *"And **the devil** that deceived them was cast into the lake of fire and brimstone, where the beast and the false prophet are, and shall be **TORMENTED DAY AND NIGHT FOR EVER AND EVER**."*

b) Gnostic doctrine

c) Gnostic scriptures

CLEMENTINE HOMILIES (Book #3, p. 154)
*"After a preliminary examination all possible different attempts at a solution of the problem of evil, the attempt is here made to represent **the DEVIL AS AN INSTRUMENT OF GOD**. **CHRIST AND THE DEVIL ARE THE TWO HANDS OF GOD**, Christ the right hand and the devil the left, the devil having power over this world epoch and Christ over the next. The devil here assumes very much the characteristics of the punishing and*

*just God of the Old Testament, and the prospect is even held out of **HIS ULTIMATE PARDON**."*

d) Greek changes

2) Lucifer Is Christ and the God of truth

a) Rejected truth

John 8:44-- *"Ye are of your father the devil, and the lusts of your father ye will do. He was a murderer from the beginning, and **ABODE NOT IN THE TRUTH, BECAUSE THERE IS NO TRUTH IN HIM**. When he speaketh a lie, he speaketh of his own; for **HE IS A LIAR**, and the father of it."*

b) Gnostic doctrine

MANI-- *"Augustine, the former Manichaean, describes Gnostic beliefs with clarity and indignation: 'They assert . . . that **CHRIST WAS** the one called by our Scriptures **THE SERPENT**, and they assure us that they have been given insight into this in order to open the eyes of knowledge and to distinguish between good and evil.'"* (Book #22 p. 41)

*"In a Manichaean version of Genesis it is Eve who gives life to Adam, while **THE SERPENT, THE LUMINOUS JESUS** is a liberating figure urging the first couple to take the first step toward salvation by eating from the Tree of Gnosis."* (Book #22, p. xviii)

HORT-- *"The authors of the Article doubtless assumed the strictly historical character of the account of the fall in Genesis. **THIS ASSUMPTION IS NOW, IN MY BELIEF, NO LONGER REASONABLE**. But the early chapters of Genesis remain a **DIVINELY APPOINTED PARABLE** . . ."* (Book #10, p. 329)

c) Gnostic scripture.

THE TESTIMONY OF TRUTH (Book #12, p. 454-455)
*"This therefore, is the true testimony; When man comes to know himself and **GOD WHO IS OVER THE TRUTH**, he will be saved—The God gave a command to Adam, From every tree you may eat, but from the tree which is in the midst of Paradise do not eat, for on the day that you eat from it you will surely die. **BUT THE SERPENT WAS WISER** than all the animals that were in Paradise, and he persuaded Eve, saying, On the day when you eat from the tree . . . the eyes of your mind will be opened. And Eve obeyed . . . But God came . . . and he cursed the serpent, and called him Devil . . . But of what sort is this God? First he maliciously refused Adam from eating of the tree of knowledge."*

Again it is written (Numbers 21:9), *"He made a serpent of bronze and hung it upon a pole . . . and the one who will believe in this **bronze serpent** will be saved.' FOR THIS IS CHRIST; those who believed in him have received life."* (Book #12, p. 455)

d) Greek changes

e) Translation changes (Dynamic equivalence)

Isaiah 14:12 (In the new versions this verse confuses Lucifer with Jesus as the "Morning Star" in Revelation 22:16)
KJV-- "*How art thou fallen from heaven, **O LUCIFER**, son of the morning!*"
NASV-- "*How you have fallen from heaven, **O STAR OF THE MORNING**, son of the dawn.*"
NIV-- "*How you have fallen from heaven, **O MORNING STAR**, son of the dawn.*"
ESV-- "*How you are fallen from heaven, **O Day Star, son of Dawn**! How you are cut down to the ground, you who laid the nations low!*"

3) Satan is not a person, but rather an evil force

a) Rejected truth

b) Gnostic doctrine

HORT-- "*The discussion which immediately precedes these four lines naturally leads to another enigma most intimately connected with that of everlasting penalties, namely, that of the **PERSONALITY OF THE DEVIL**. It was Coleridge who some 3 years ago **FIRST RAISED ANY DOUBTS IN MY MIND ON THE SUBJECT--DOUBTS WHICH HAVE NEVER YET BEEN AT ALL SET AT REST**, one way or the other. The question still remains--**IS THIS CENTRAL ROOT** (of evil) **PERSONAL OR NOT**? Can the power of origination be in strict truth ascribed to anything except a will? **NOW IF THERE BE A DEVIL**, he cannot merely bear a corrupted and marred image of God; he must be wholly evil, his name evil, his every energy and act evil. Would it not be a violation of the divine attributes for the Word to be actively the support of such a nature as that? And so in the present day many avoid the difficulty by the monstrous fiction of a regenerated devil. Thus the author of Festus. . . supposes him finally restored through the medium of a genuine human affection! But does not this suggest that **NO IMAGE BUT GOD'S IMAGE IS POSSIBLE FOR A PERSON**?*" (Book #10, Vol.1, p. 121-122)

Revelation 2:13 (the throne of Satan) "*. . . but the visible supremacy of the **POWER OF EVIL**, inspiring to evil.*" (Book #16, p. 13)

WESTCOTT
I John 3:8-- "*From the very beginning we see **A POWER** in action hostile to God. Between these two, as between light and darkness, there can be no middle term.*" (Book #16, p. 13)

SCHAFF-- "*The **DELUSION** of witchcraft, which extended even to Puritan New England . . . has **DISAPPEARED** from all Christian nations forever.*" (Book #19, p. 332)

c) Gnostic scriptures

d) Greek changes

b. Angels

1) The angel of the Lord was the demiurge who had not yet rebelled against God

a) Rejected truth

b) Gnostic doctrine

PHILO–"... *Philo of Alexandria ... calls the Logos, who is instrumental in creation, both 'a second god' and 'archangel' on the one hand and 'Lord' (YHVH) and 'Name' on the other.*" (Book #2, p. 569)

SIMON AND CERINTHUS-- "*Affirm that the demiurge (identified with YHVH) was in fact this angel of the Lord, **WHO HAD NOT YET REBELLED AGAINST GOD**.*" (Book #2, p. 569)

VALENTINUS, MARCION, APELLES-- "*who were familiar with the myth contained in the **APOCRYPHON OF JOHN**, all held that the demiurge was an angel.*" (Book #2, p. 569)

c) Gnostic scriptures

d) Greek changes

2) Man's guardian angel is his transcendental Self

a) Rejected truth

b) Gnostic doctrine

"*Man and his **GUARDIAN ANGEL**, or transcendental counterpart, celebrate the mystical marriage of bride and bridegroom.*" (Book #2, p. 571-2)

VALENTINUS– "... *all the souls of the Gnostics who still languish in matter will become the **BRIDES OF THE ANGELS**.*" (Book #3, p. 157)

c) Gnostic scriptures

THE GOSPEL OF PHILIP (Book #12, p. 145)
"... *You who have joined the perfect light with the holy spirit, **UNITE THE ANGELS WITH US ALSO, AS BEING THE IMAGES**.*"

d) Greek changes

3) Man can see his guardian angels

a) Rejected truth

Colossians 2:18-- *"Let no man beguile you of your reward in . . . **WORSHIPPING OF ANGELS**, intruding into those things which he hath not seen,"*

b) Gnostic doctrine

MANI-- *"Man encountered his spiritual Self at the age of 12 and encountered it a second time at the age of 25. He felt constantly accompanied by his twin, and when he died a martyr in prison **HE WAS GAZING AT THIS FAMILIAR**."* (Book #2, p. 573)

HORT-WESTCOTT *". . . and I have started a society for the investigation of ghosts and **ALL SUPERNATURAL APPEARANCES** and effects, being all disposed to believe that such things really exist, and ought to be discriminated from hoaxes and mere subjective delusions . . . Our own temporary name is the 'Ghostly Guild'"* (Book #10, Vol.1, p. 211)

*"I sent you 2 'ghostly' papers . . . Macaulay is horrified at the paper. . . and some other eminent Edinburgh Reviewer . . . thinks it highly unphilosophical in us to assume the existence of **ANGELS**--which, by the way we don't do . . . though I don't suppose any of us would shrink from the 'assumption'"* (Book #10, Vol.1, p. 219)

c) Gnostic scriptures

GOSPEL OF THOMAS
*"Jesus said, **WHEN YOU SEE** one who was not born of woman, **PROSTRATE YOURSELF ON YOUR FACES AND WORSHIP HIM**. That one is your father."* (Book #12, p. 128)

d) Greek changes

Colossians 2:18
BYZ C > KJV-- *"worshipping of angels, intruding into those things which he hath **NOT** seen,"*
MARCION ORIGEN > SBA > WH NU > NASV NIV ESV-- **omit 'not'**

4) The guardian angel is our spirit guide

a) Rejected truth

b) Gnostic doctrine

c) Gnostic scriptures

d) Greek changes

Acts 10:6 (Critical text omits that God used Simon to instruct Paul)
BYZ > KJV-- *"**HE SHALL TELL THEE WHAT THOU OUGHTEST TO DO**."*

BYZ SBAC > WH NU > NASV ESV-- <u>omit</u>

7. HAMARTIOLOGY (Sin)

a. The causes of sin, evil

1) EROS (sex) is the origin of death

a) Rejected truth

Ezekiel 18:4– *". . . the soul that sinneth, it shall die."*

Romans 6:23-- *"For the wages of sin is death; . . ."*

Romans 5:12-- *"Wherefore, as by one man sin entered into the world, and **DEATH BY SIN**; and so death passed upon all men, for that all have **SINNED**:"*

James 1:15– *"Then when lust hath conceived, it bringeth forth sin: and **SIN**, when it is finished, **BRINGETH FORTH DEATH**."*

b) Gnostic doctrine

c) Gnostic scriptures

POIMANDRES-- *"The author expresses. . . 'Let spiritual man know himself, then he will know that he is immortal and that **EROS IS THE ORIGIN OF DEATH**, and he will know the All'"* (Book #2, p. 566)

d) Greek changes

2) Unconsciousness (lack of gnosis) and not sin is the cause of evil

a) Rejected truth

Matthew 15:19–*"For out of the **HEART** proceed evil thoughts, murders, adulteries, fornications, thefts, false witness, blasphemies:"*

b) Gnostic doctrine

*"Today Gnosticism is defined as a religion in its own right . . . Not sin or guilt, but **UNCONSCIOUSNESS, IS THE CAUSE OF EVIL**."* (Book #2, p. 567)

c) Gnostic scriptures

d) Greek changes

Acts 9:5
TR) KJV-- "***IT IS HARD FOR THEE TO KICK AGAINST THE PRICKS.***"
BSAC > NASV ESW-- <u>omit</u>

b. Freedom from the law

1) The law is to be rejected

a) Rejected truth

Matthew 5:18-- *"For verily I say unto you, Till heaven and earth pass, one jot or one tittle shall in no wise pass from the law, till all be fulfilled."*

II Peter 2:19-- *"While they **PROMISE THEM LIBERTY**, they themselves are the servants of corruption: "*

Jude 4–*"For there are certain men crept in unawares, . . . turning the grace of God into **LASCIVIOUSNESS**, . . ."*

b) Gnostic doctrine

*"Generally speaking, the pneumatic morality is determined by hostility towards the world and contempt for all mundane ties. From this principle however, two contrary conclusions could be drawn, and both found their extreme representatives: the ascetic and the libertine . . . The law of 'Thou shalt' and 'Thou shalt not' promulgated by the Creator is just one more form of the 'cosmic' tyranny. The sanctions attaching to its transgression can affect only the body and the psyche. As the pneumatic is free from the heimarmene (Universal Fate), so he is **FREE FROM THE YOKE OF THE MORAL LAW**. To him all things are permitted, since the pneuma is 'saved in its nature' .and can be neither sullied by actions nor frightened by the threat of archontic retribution. The pneumatic freedom however is a matter of more than mere indifferent permission: through **INTENTIONAL VIOLATION** of the demiurgical norms the pneumatic thwarts the design of the Archons (demons) and paradoxically contributes to the work of salvation."* (Book #20, p. 46)

c) Gnostic scriptures

d) Greek changes

Matthew 15:6
BYZ > KJV-- *"Thus have you made the **COMMANDMENT** of God of none effect by your tradition."*
ORIGEN >SB) WH NU > NASV NIV ESV–*"you made void the **WORD** of God on account of your tradition."*

c. Sinful acts

1) Idolatry is not sinful

a) Rejected truth

Exodus 20:4-5-- *"Thou shalt not make unto thee any **GRAVEN IMAGE**, or any likeness of any thing that is in heaven above, or that is in the earth beneath, or that is in the water under the earth: Thou shalt not bow down thyself to them, nor serve them. . ."*

I John 5:21-- *"Little children, keep yourselves from **IDOLS**."*

Revelation 2:14-- *"But I have a few things against thee, because thou hast there them that hold the doctrine of Balaam, who taught Balac to cast a stumblingblock before the children of Israel, to **EAT THINGS SACRIFICED UNTO IDOLS**, and to commit fornication.*

b) Gnostic doctrine

WESTCOTT-- *"After leaving the monastery we shaped our course to a little oratory (private chapel). Fortunately we found the door open. It is very small, with one kneeling place; and behind a screen was a 'Pieta' the size of life (i.e. a Virgin and dead Christ). **HAD I BEEN ALONE I COULD HAVE KNELT THERE FOR HOURS**."* (Book #23, Vol 1, p. 81)

'The face of the virgin is unspeakable beautiful. **I LOOKED TILL THE LIP SEEMED TO TREMBLE WITH INTENSITY OF FEELING**.' (Book #23, Vol.1, p. 183)

SCHAFF-- *"But as one might expect, Schaff proposed **to excise** the Confession's references to the papacy as 'antichrist' and to Roman Catholics **as 'IDOLATERS**.'"* (Book #19, p. 278)

c) Gnostic scriptures

d) Greek changes

Revelation 2:15 (**Nicolaitans were IDOLATERS--Revelation 2:14**)
BYZ > KJV-- *"that hold the doctrine the Nicolaitans, **WHICH THING I HATE**."*
BYZ SAC > WH NU > NASV NIV ESV-- **omit 'which thing I hate'**
xxx

2) Marriage and sexual propagation is evil,

a) Rejected truth

Hebrews 13:4-- *"**Marriage is honourable in all**, and the bed undefiled: . . ."*

I Timothy 4:1-3-- *"Now the Spirit speaketh expressly, that in the latter times some shall depart from the faith, giving heed to seducing spirits, and doctrines of devils; . . . **FORBIDDING TO MARRY**, . . ."*

b) Gnostic doctrine

MANI-- *"influenced by encratitic asceticism of the Aramaic Christians, Mani **REJECTED MARRIAGE** and the consumption of alcohol and meat. . ."* (Book #2, p. 573)

SATORNINUS-- *"They declare also that **MARRIAGE AND GENERATION ARE FROM SATAN**."* (Book #33, Vol.1, p. 348 Irenaeus 'Against Heresies' 1.24.2)

c) Gnostic scriptures

d) Greek changes

Mark 10:7
BYZ > KJV-- *"**AND CLEAVE TO HIS WIFE**."*
SB > NASV-- <u>omitted</u>

3) Prostitution, fornication, adultery is not evil

a) Rejected truth

Hebrews 13:4-- *"Marriage is honourable in all, and the bed undefiled: but **whoremongers and adulterers God will judge**."*

Romans 6:1-2– *". . . Shall we continue in sin, that **GRACE MAY ABOUND**? God forbid. How shall we that are dead to sin, live any longer therein?"*

b) Gnostic doctrine

*"In the systems of which the figure of the (mother-Sophia) plays a special part, **UNBRIDLED PROSTITUTION APPEARS AS A DISTINCT AND ESSENTIAL PART OF THE CULT** (cf. the accounts of particular branches of the GNOSTICS, NICOLAITINS.) The meaning of this cult is, of course, reinterpreted in the Gnostic sense: by this **unbridled prostitution** the Gnostic sects desired to **PREVENT THE SEXUAL PROPAGATION OF MANKIND**."* (Book #3, p. 156)

VALENTINIANS-- *". . . they themselves have GRACE as their own special possession, which has descended from above **BY MEANS OF AN UNSPEAKABLE AND INDESCRIBABLE CONJUNCTION; AND ON THIS ACCOUNT MORE WILL BE GIVEN UNTO THEM**. They maintain, therefore, that in every way **IT IS ALWAYS NECESSARY FOR THEM TO PRACTICE THE MYSTERY OF CONJUNCTION**. And that they may persuade the thoughtless to believe this, they are in the habit of using these very words, 'Whosoever being in this world **DOES NOT SO LOVE A WOMAN AS TO OBTAIN POSSESSION OF HER**, is not of the truth, nor shall attain to the truth."* (Book #33, Vol.1, p. 325-326 Irenaeus 'Against Heresies,' I. VI. 4)

c) Gnostic scriptures

d) Greek changes

Romans 1:29
BYZ KJV-- "*__FORNICATION__*,"
ORIGEN > SBA > NASV, NIV ESV-- <u>omitted</u>

Galatians 5:19
BYZ > KJV–"Now the *works of the flesh, are manifest, which are these;* *__ADULTERY__, fornication, uncleanness, lasciviousness,*"
SBAC) WH NU > NASV NIV ESV-- <u>omit 'adultery'</u>

4) Homosexuality is not sinful

a) Rejected truth

Genesis 13:13-- "*But __the men of Sodom were wicked and sinners before the Lord exceedingly__.*"

b) Gnostic doctrine

c) Gnostic scriptures

THE PARAPHRASE OF SHEM
"When he will have appeared, O Shem, upon the earth, in the place which will be called **SODOM**, then safeguard the insight which I shall give you. **FOR THOSE WHOSE HEART IS PURE WILL CONGREGATE TO YOU**, because of the word which you will reveal.... But **the SODOMITES** ... will bear witness to the universal testimony. They **will rest WITH A PURE CONSCIENCE** in the place of their repose."

d.) Greek changes

Mark 6:11
BYZ) KJV-- "*__VERILY I SAY UNTO YOU, IT SHALL BE MORE TOLERABLE FOR SODOM AND GOMORRAH IN THE DAY OF JUDGMENT, THAN FOR THAT CITY__.*"
SBC) NASV, NIV-- <u>omit</u>

Romans 1:29 (note **context as being the sins of homosexuals**- v.24-28)
BYZ > KJV– "*__FORNICATION__*,"
SBA, Origen > NASV, NIV ESV-- <u>omit</u>

5) Eating animal food is sinful

a) Rejected truth

I Timothy 4:3-- "*__COMMANDING TO ABSTAIN FROM MEATS__ which God hath created to be received with thanksgiving of them which believe and know the truth.*"

b) Gnostic doctrine

MANI-- "*Influenced by encratitic asceticism of the Aramaic Christians of Asia, Mani* **REJECTED marriage and THE CONSUMPTION OF alcohol and MEAT** . . ." (Book #2, p. 573)

c) Gnostic scriptures

THE PRAYER OF THANKSGIVING (Book #12, p. 329)
"*When they had said these things in the prayer . . . they went to eat their holy* **food, WHICH HAS NO BLOOD IN IT**."

THE DAMASCUS RULE. (Book #30, p. 96)
"**No man shall defile himself by eating any live creature** *or creeping thing, from the larvae of bees to all creatures which creep in water.*" (CD xii, p. 12-13)

d) Greek changes

I Corinthians 11:29 (Teaches that those who don't practice asceticism will be judged)
BYZ > KJV-- "*For he that eateth and drinketh* **UNWORTHILY**, *eateth and drinketh damnation to himself, not discerning the* **LORD'S** *body.*"
SBA > NASV, ESV-- "For he that eats and drinks, eats and drinks judgment to himself not discerning. the body."

6) Drinking alcohol is sinful (This explains why New Age Gnostics use AA for recruitment purposes)

a) Rejected truth [**I personally believe in total abstinence from alcohol. DAW**]

b) Gnostic doctrine

MANI-- "*Influenced by encratitic asceticism of the Aramaic Christians of Asia, Mani* **REJECTED marriage and the CONSUMPTION OF ALCOHOL and meat** . . ." (Book #2, p. 573)

c) Gnostic scripture
THE GOSPEL OF THOMAS (Book #26 p. 385).
"*Jesus said, 1 stood at rest in the midst of the world. And unto them I was shown forth incarnate; I found them all intoxicated And I found none of them thirsty. And my soul was pained for the children of humankind, for they are blind in their hearts and cannot see . . . now they are intoxicated. When they shake off their* **WINE** *then they will have a change of heart.*"

d) Greek changes

I Corinthians11:29 (Teaches that those who don't practice asceticism will be judged)

BYZ > KJV-- "*For he that eateth and drinketh UNWORTHILY, eateth and drinketh damnation to himself, not discerning the LORD'S body.*"
SBA > NASV, NIV, ESV-- "*For he that eats and drinks, eats and drinks judgment to himself not discerning the body.*"

Matthew 26:28
BYZ AC > KJV-- "*For this is my blood of the NEW testament,*"
SB > WH NU > NASV NIV ESV-- **omit "new"**

Mark 14:24
BYZ A > KJV-- "*This is my blood, of the NEW testament,*"
SBC > WH NU) NASV NIV ESV-- **omit "new"**

7) Killing people is sometimes necessary

a) Rejected truth

b) Gnostic doctrine

HORT-- "*Between the years 1846 and 1852 he appears to have made 24 speeches at Union debates; HE DEFENDED THE CRUSADES . . .*" (Book #10, Vol.1, p. 177)

c) Gnostic scripture

d) Greek changes

Luke 9:54
BYZ AC) KJV– ". . . wilt thou that we command fire to come down from heaven, and consume them, even **AS ELIAS DID**?"
SB > WH NU > NASV ESV-- **omit "as Elias did"**

Luke 9:55
BYZ > KJV (NASV)-- "*But he turned, and rebuked them, AND SAID, YE KNOW NOT WHAT MANNER OF SPIRIT YE ARE OF.*"
BYZ SBA > WH NU > NIV ESV-- omit "*and said, ye know not what manner of spirit ye are of.*"

Luke 9:56
BYZ > KJV (NASV)– "*FOR THE SON OF MAN IS NOT COME TO DESTROY MEN'S LIVES, BUT TO SAVE THEM.*"
BYZ SBA > WH NU > NIV ESV-- **omit**

Romans 12:14
BYZ SA) KJV, (NU*) NASV* NIV-- "*Bless them that persecute YOU: bless, and curse not.*"
CLEMENT > B > WH-- **omit you**

Galatians 5:21

BYZ AC > KJV-- "*envyings, **MURDERS**, drunkenness, . . .*"
MARCION CLEMENT ORIGEN >SB) WH NU > NASV NIV ESV-- **omit "murders"**

I Thessalonians 2:15
BYZ > KJV-- "*Who both killed the Lord Jesus, and **THEIR OWN** prophets,*"
ORIGEN) SBA) WH NU > NASV NIV ESV-- "*killed **THE** prophets*"

8) Pride is not a sin, but is the means of salvation

a) Rejected truth

Proverbs 11:2-- "*When pride cometh, then cometh shame: but with the lowly is wisdom.*"

Proverbs 16:18-- "*Pride goeth before destruction, and a haughty spirit before a fall.*"

Ezekiel 16:49-50-- "*Behold this was the iniquity of thy sister Sodom, **PRIDE**, fulness of bread, and abundance of idleness . . . neither did she strengthen the hand of the poor and needy. **AND THEY WERE HAUGHTY**, and committed abomination before me: therefore I took them away as I saw good.*"

Mark 7:21-23-- "*For from within, out of the heart of men proceed evil thoughts . . . **PRIDE**, foolishness: all these **EVIL THINGS** come from within, and defile the man.*"

b) Gnostic doctrine

c) Gnostic scripture

THE GOSPEL OF PHILIP
"*Those who think that sinning does not apply to them are called 'free' by the world. 'Knowledge' of the truth merely 'makes such people **ARROGANT**,' which is what the words 'it makes them free' mean. **IT EVEN GIVES THEM A SENSE OF SUPERIORITY OVER THE WHOLE WORLD**.*" (Book #12, p. 155)

d) Greek changes

I Timothy 6:5
BYZ > KJV-- "***PERVERSE DISPUTINGS** of men of corrupt minds, . . .*"
BYZ SA > WH NV > NASV NIV ESV-- "*useless **CONSTANT QUARRELINGS**. . .*"

8. SOTERIOLOGY (Salvation)

I1 Corinthians11:4-- "*For if he that cometh preacheth . . . **ANOTHER GOSPEL**, which ye have not accepted, ye might well bear with him.*"

a. Saviour of salvation

1) Lucifer is the Saviour

a) Rejected truth

Galatians 1:6-8-- *"I marvel that ye are so soon removed from him that called you into the grace of Christ unto __ANOTHER GOSPEL__: which is not another; but there be some that trouble you, and would __PERVERT THE GOSPEL OF CHRIST__, But though we, or an __ANGEL FROM HEAVEN__, preach any other gospel unto YOU than that ye have received, let him be accursed."*

Isaiah 14:12,20-- *"How art thou fallen from heaven, __O LUCIFER__, son of the morning! how art thou cut down to the ground, which didst weaken the nations! Thou shalt not be joined with them in burial, because __THOU HAST DESTROYED THY LAND; AND SLAIN THY PEOPLE__: the seed of evildoers shall never be renowned."*

John 14:30-- "Hereafter I will not talk much with you: **FOR THE PRINCE OF THIS WORLD COMETH, AND HATH NOTHING IN ME.**"

Il Corinthians 11:14– *". . . Satan himself is transformed into an angel of light."*

Il Corinthians 4:3-4-- *"But if our gospel be hid, it is hid to them that are lost: in whom the god of this world hath blinded the minds of them which believe not, lest the light of the glorious gospel of Christ, who is the image of God, should shine unto them."*

b) Gnostic doctrine

> *". . . revelation is needed . . . Its bearer is a messenger from the world of LIGHT (__Lucifer__) who penetrates the barriers of the spheres, outwits the Archons(demonic creators) awakens the spirit from its earthly slumber, and __IMPARTS TO IT THE SAVING KNOWLEDGE__ . . . " The mission of the transcendent savior begins even before the creation of the world . . . .The knowledge thus revealed, even though called simply 'the knowledge. of God' comprises the whole content of Gnostic myth. . ."* (Book #20, p. 45)

> MANI-- *"Augustine, the former Manichaean, describes Gnostic beliefs with clarity and indignation: 'They assert . . . that __CHRIST WAS__ the one called by our Scriptures __THE SERPENT__, and they assure us that they have been given insight into this in order to open the eyes of knowledge and to distinguish between Good and Evil."* (Book #22, p. 41)

> *"In a Manichaean version of Genesis it is Eve who gives life to Adam, while __THE SERPENT, THE LUMINOUS JESUS__, is a __LIBERATING FIGURE__ urging the first couple to take the __FIRST STEP TOWARD SALVATION__ by eating from the Tree of Gnosis."* (Book #22, p. xviii)

> HORT-- *"The authors of the Article doubtless assumed the strictly historical character of the account of __the fall in Genesis. THIS ASSUMPTION IS NOW, IN MY BELIEF, NO LONGER REASONABLE__. But the early chapters of Genesis remain a __DIVINELY APPOINTED PARABLE__ . . ."* (Book #10, Vol.2, p. 329)

NEW AGE
"Christ is the same force as Lucifer . . . Lucifer prepares man for the experience of Christhood . . . Lucifer works within each of us to bring us to wholeness as we move into the New Age." (Book #31, p. 73, quoting David Spangler)

c) Gnostic scriptures

THE TESTIMONY OF TRUTH (Exalts the Serpent)
*"This therefore, is the true testimony: When man comes to know himself and . . . **GOD WHO . . . IS OVER THE TRUTH, HE WILL BE SAVED**, and he will crown himself with the crown unfading. . . . It is written in the Law concerning this, when God gave a command to Adam, 'From every tree you may eat, but from the tree which is in the midst of Paradise do not eat, for on the day that you eat from it you will surely die.' **BUT THE SERPENT WAS WISER** than all the animals that were in Paradise, and he persuaded Eve. . . And Eve obeyed. . . . But God came at the time of evening walking in the midst of Paradise. When Adam saw him he hid himself. And he said, Adam where are you? . . . Who is it who has instructed you? . . . But of what sort is this God? First he maliciously refused Adam from eating of the tree of knowledge. And secondly he said, Adam, where are you? God does not have foreknowledge; otherwise, would he not know from the beginning?. . ."* (Book #12, p. 454)

*"Again it is written (Numbers 21:9), He made a serpent of bronze and hung it upon a pole—for the one who will gaze upon this bronze serpent, none will destroy him, and **the one who will believe in this bronze serpent will be saved**. For this is Christ; those who believed in him have received life."* (Book #12, p. 455)

d) Greek changes

e) Translation changes (Dynamic equivalence)

Isaiah14:12– "(**Purpose is to confuse this passage with Revelation 22:16, where Jesus Christ is mentioned as the 'Morning Star'**)
KJV-- *"How thou art fallen from heaven, **O LUCIFER**, son of the morning!"*
NASV-- *"How you have fallen from heaven, **O STAR OF THE MORNING**, son of the dawn!"*
NIV-- *"How you have fallen from heaven, **O MORNING STAR**, son of the dawn."*
ESV– *"How you are fallen from heaven, **O Day Star**, son of Dawn!"*

2) The apostles will save the world

a) Rejected truth

John 1:12-13-- *"**But as many as received him**, to them gave he power to become the sons of God, even to them that believe on his name; who were born, not of blood, **NOR OF THE WILL OF THE FLESH, NOR OF THE WILL OF MAN**, but of God."*

b) Gnostic doctrine

"The Revealer (Jesus) had in fact from the beginning chosen the Apostles as __HIS ASSISTANTS__ in his mission of salvation. Thus, when he had come down into the world, he had brought with him 12 forces (which come from the 12 pleromatic saviors) and introduced them into the bodies of the earthly mothers of the Apostles." (Book #28, p. 106)

c) Gnostic scriptures

THE APOCRYPHON OF JAMES (Book #12, p. 35)
"You are the beloved; __YOU__ are they who __WILL BE THE CAUSE OF LIFE IN MANY__. Invoke the Father, implore God often, and he will give to you."

PISTIS SOPHIA (Book #28, p. 106)
"These forces were given to you before all the world, because __IT IS YOU WHO WILL SAVE THE WORLD__ . . ."

d) Greek changes

John 9:4
BYZ AC) KJV-- *"I must work the works of him that sent __ME__,"*
ORIGEN) SB > WH NU > NASV NIV ESV-- *"__US__ it behooves to work . . ."*

3) Sophia is the redeemer

a) Rejected truth

b) Gnostic doctrine

"Sophia caused the demiurge to breathe the pneuma he had inherited from her into the face of his creature. So begins a long struggle between __THE REDEEMING SOPHIA__ and the malicious demiurge, the struggle for and against the awakening of human spiritual consciousness." (Book #2, p. 570)

c) Gnostic scriptures

d) Greek changes

4) The Soter (heavenly saviour) saves the Gnostics, while the earthly Saviour Jesus saves the Psychics

a) Rejected truth

Acts 4:12-- *"Neither is there salvation is any other: for there is none other name under heaven given among men, whereby we must be saved."* (*Name of Jesus Christ- v.10*)

b) Gnostic doctrine

VALENTINUS-- "*In the Valentinian system, the myth of the fallen Sophia and the Soter, or their ultimate union, their marriage and their 70 sons . . . has absolutely nothing to do with the Christian conceptions of salvation. The subject is here that of a high goddess of heaven (she has 70 sons) whose friend and lover finds her in the misery of deepest degradation, frees her, and bears her home as his bride. To this myth the idea of salvation through the earthly Christ can only be attached with difficulty. And it was openly maintained that **THE SOTER ONLY EXISTED FOR THE GNOSTIC**, (and) the **SAVIOUR JESUS WHO APPEARED ON EARTH ONLY FOR THE PSYCHICUS**.*"   (Book #3, p. I57)

c) Gnostic scriptures

d) Greek changes

John 11:50
BYZ A) KJV-- "*It is expedient for **US**, that one man should die for the people,*"
ORIGEN > B) WH NU > NASV NIV ESV-- "*it is profitable for **YOU**. . .*"

Ephesians 5:2
BYZ S > KJV; NU* > NIV ESV-- "*As Christ also hath loved **US**, and hath given himself for **US**.*"
CLEMENT) SAB) WH-- "*Christ loved **YOU** and gave himself up for **YOU**.*"
NASV– "*. . . loved **YOU**. . . for **US***"

I Peter 2:21
BYZ > KJV-- "*Christ also suffered for **US**, leaving **US** an example,*"
SBA > WH NU > NASV NIV ESV-- "*Christ suffered for **YOU**, **YOU** leaving a model.*"

I Peter 3:18
•BYZ A > KJV NASV-- "*Christ also hath once suffered for sins, . . .that he might bring **US** to God,*"
BY2 BC > WH NU > NIV ESV-- "*. . . that **YOU** He might bring to God.*"

b. Means of salvation

1) Man is saved through Gnosis (knowledge that he already is a son of God)

a) Rejected truth

1 Peter 1:23-- "*Being born again, **NOT OF CORRUPTIBLE SEED**, but of incorruptible, **BY THE WORD OF GOD**, which liveth and abideth for ever.*"

I Peter 1:25-- "*But the **WORD OF THE LORD** endureth for ever. And this is the word which by the gospel is preached unto you.*"

Genesis 3:4-5-- "And the **SERPENT SAID** unto the woman, Ye shall not surely die: for God doth know that in the day ye eat thereof **YOUR EYES SHALL BE OPENED**, and ye shall be as gods, **KNOWING** (ginosko> gnosis) **GOOD AND EVIL**."

b) Gnostic doctrine

". . . *spiritual man is alien to the natural world and related to the deity and becomes conscious of his deepest Self WHEN HE HEARS THE WORD OF REVELATION.*" (Book #2, p. 567)

"*The goal of gnostic striving is the release of the 'inner man' from the bonds of the world and his return to his native realm of light. The necessary condition for this is that he **KNOWS** about the transmundane (hidden) God and about himself, that is, **ABOUT HIS DIVINE ORIGIN** as well as his present situation . . .*" (Book #20, p. 44)

VALENTINUS-- "*The ultimate 'object' of gnosis is God :. . . in the more radical systems like the Valentinian the **'knowledge' is not only an INSTRUMENT OF SALVATION** but itself the very form in which the goal of salvation, i.e., ultimate perfection, is possessed.*" (Book #20, p. 35)

MANI
"*In a Manichaean version of Genesis . . . the Serpent, the Luminous Jesus, is a liberating figure urging the first couple to take **THE FIRST STEP TOWARD SALVATION BY EATING FROM THE TREE OF GNOSIS.**" (Book #22, p. xviii)

"*They assert . . . that **CHRIST** was the one called by our Scriptures **the Serpent**, and they assure us that they have been given INSIGHT into this in order to **OPEN THE EYES OF KNOWLEDGE** and to distinguish between Good and Evil.*" (Book #22, p. 41)

ORIGEN– ". . . the object of Christianity is that we should **become wise** . . ." (Book #1, p. 73)

WESTCOTT
I John 5:20-- "***ETERNAL LIFE IS*** *the never-ending effort after this **KNOWLEDGE OF GOD**.*" (Book #16, p. 20)

c) Gnostic scriptures

THE APOCRYPHON OF JAMES (Book #12, p. 33)
"*So also can you yourselves **receive the kingdom of heaven**; unless you receive this **THROUGH KNOWLEDGE**, you will not be able to find it.*"

THE GOSPEL OF THOMAS (Book #12, p. 126)
". . . *the kingdom is inside of you, and it is outside of you. **WHEN YOU COME TO KNOW YOURSELVES** . . . **YOU WILL REALIZE THAT IT IS YOU WHO ARE THE SONS OF THE LIVING FATHER.**"

THE BOOK OF THOMAS THE CONTENDER (Book #12, p. 201)
"*The savior said, Brother Thomas . . . Now since it has been said that you are my **TWIN** and true companion, examine yourself and **LEARN WHO YOU ARE**, in what way **YOU** exist,*

and how you will come to be. Since you will be called my brother, it is not fitting that you be **IGNORANT OF YOURSELF**. *And I know that you have understood, because you had already understood that I am the knowledge of the truth. So while you accompany me, although you are uncomprehending, you have (in fact) already come to know, and you will be called '**THE ONE WHO KNOWS HIMSELF**.' For he who has not known himself has known nothing, but he who has **KNOWN HIMSELF**, has at the same time already achieved knowledge of the depth of the all."*

THE TESTIMONY OF TRUTH
*"And they came to **KNOW THEMSELVES**, as to who they are, or rather, where they are now, and what is the place in which they will rest from their senselessness, arriving at knowledge. These Christ will transfer to the heights since they have renounced foolishness, and have advanced to knowledge."* (Book #12, p. 451)

*"**When man comes to KNOW HIMSELF** and God who is over the truth, **HE WILL BE SAVED**, and he will crown himself with the crown unfading."* (Book #12, p. 454)

PRAYER OF THANKSGIVING (Book #12, p. 329)
*"You have made us divine through Your **KNOWLEDGE**."*

d) Greek changes

Romans 10:17
BYZ A) KJV– *"So then faith cometh by hearing, and hearing by the word of **GOD**."*
ORIGEN) SBC) WH NV) NASV NIV ESV— *". . . word of **CHRIST**"*

Colossians 1:10
BYZ > KJV NASV-- *"increasing **IN** the knowledge of God;"*
SBAC > WH NU-- *"growing **BY** (through) knowledge"*

I John 2:20
BYZ AC) KJV-- *"But ye have an unction from the Holy One, and ye know **ALL THINGS**."*
SB > WH NV > NASV NIV ESV– *". . . and you **ALL** know."*

d) Greek changes

2) Man is saved by the symbolic death of Christ within man, not by the blood of Christ

a) Rejected truth

Hebrews 9:22– *". . . without the shedding of blood there is no remission."*

b) Gnostic doctrine

*"Christ is the divine spark in each one of us: buried, obscured, '**CRUCIFIED**' because of our lower, sinful nature. He must 'rise again from the dead' in each on of us; and it is only*

*as this resurrection is accomplished, only as **we realize the 'CHRIST IN US'** as the active principle of our lives, that we can **FREE OURSELVES** from the 'bondage of the flesh'* . . ." (Book #25, p. 42)

HORT-- "*I confess I have no repugnance to the primitive doctrine of a ransom paid to Satan, though neither am I prepared to give full assent to it. But I can see no other possible form in which the doctrine of a ransom is at all tenable; **ANYTHING IS BETTER THAN THE NOTION OF A RANSOM PAID TO THE FATHER**.*" (Book #10, Vol. 1, p. 428)

WESTCOTT
John 1:29-- (which taketh away the sin of the world) "*The parallel passage in the Epistle . . . shews that the **REDEMPTIVE EFFICACY OF CHRIST'S WORK IS TO BE FOUND IN HIS WHOLE LIFE CROWNED BY HIS DEATH**.*" (Book #16, p. 18)

John 10:16-- (bring) "*This could only be by **HIS DEATH, WHICH REUNITES MAN WITH GOD**. . .*" (Book #16, p. 18)

Hebrews 9:12-- "*I have endeavoured to shew elsewhere. . . that the Scriptural idea. . . of **BLOOD IS ESSENTIALLY AN IDEA OF LIFE AND NOT OF DEATH**.*" (Book #16, p. 36)

THE SEAL OF THE VALIDITY OF A COVENANT IS . . . through which the covenant blood . . . (Book #16, p. 56)

I Peter 1:2-- "*In the N.T. the **BLOOD OF CHRIST** is associated with various images which need to be clearly distinguished. There is **HERE NO DIRECT REFERENCE TO THE IDEA OF PURCHASE OR RANSOM**, as in vv.18,19 . . . **OR TO THE IDEAL OF SACRIFICIAL ATONEMENT**, as in several other books of the N.T.*" (Book #16, p. 37)

I Peter 1:19-- (But with the precious blood of Christ, as of a lamb without blemish and without spot) "*In this **ALLUSION TO THE BLOOD** of an unspotted lamb, what had St Peter in mind? Chiefly, I think, and perhaps **SOLELY THE PASCHAL LAMB** . . . .The true lesson is that the language which speaks of a **RANSOM IS BUT FIGURATIVE LANGUAGE** . . .*" (Book #16, p. 37)

c) Gnostic scriptures

THE APOCRYPHON OF JAMES (Book #12, p. 32)
"*Remember my cross and my **DEATH** and you will live . . . Verily I say unto you, none will be saved unless they believe in my cross. But those who have believed in my cross, theirs is the kingdom of God.*"

THE TREATISE ON THE RESURRECTION (Book #12, p. 55)
"*We are elected to salvation and redemption since we are predestined from the beginning not to fall into the foolishness of those who are without knowledge, but we shall enter into the wisdom of those who have known the Truth . . . **NOTHING, then, REDEEMS US FROM THIS WORLD**.*"

d) Greek changes

Matthew 26:28
BYZ AC > KJV-- "*For this is my blood, of the **NEW** testament*"
SB) WH NV > NASV NIV ESV-- **omit 'new'**

Mark 14:24
BYZ A > KJV-- "*This is my blood, of the **NEW** testament*"
SBC> UK NV:> NASV NIV ESV-- **omit 'new'**

Luke 22:19-20
BYZ > KJV; NU*) NASV NIV ESV-- "*This do* **IN REMEMBRANCE OF ME. LIKEWISE ALSO THE CUP AFTER SUPPER, SAYING, THIS CUP IS THE NEW TESTAMENT IN MY BLOOD, WHICH IS SHED FOR YOU**."
D-- "*This do.*" (**the rest is omitted**)

1 Corinthians 11:24
BYZ > KJV-- "*body. which **BROKEN** for you:*"
ORIGEN > SEA) WH NV > NASV NIV ESV-- **omit 'broken'**

Colossians 1:14
BYZ > KJV-- "*in whom we have redemption **THROUGH HIS BLOOD**.*"
BYZ SBA > WH NV > NASV NIV ESV-- **omit 'through His blood'**

Colossians 1:20
BYZ SAC) KJV; (WH) (NU) NASV-- "*having made peace through the blood of His cross, **BY HIM** . . .*"
ORIGEN > BYZ 8 > NIV ESV-- **omit 'by Him'**

Revelation 5:9
BYZ S > KJV-- "*Thou wast slain, and hast redeemed **US** to God by thy blood . . .*"
A > WH NU > NASV NIV ESV-- **omit "us"**

3)   Man is saved/perfected through asceticism (extreme self-denial and self-mortification)

a) Rejected truth

Matthew 15:10-11-- "*And He called the multitude, and said unto them, Hear, and understand: not that which goeth into the mouth defileth a man; but that which cometh out of the mouth, this defileth a man.*"

Colossians 2:20-22-- "*Wherefore if ye be dead with Christ from the rudiments of the world, why, as though living in the world, are ye subject to ordinances, (touch not; taste not; handle not; which are all to perish with the using;) after the commandments and doctrines of men?*"

I Timothy 6:17-- "*Charge them that are rich in this world, that they be not highminded, nor trust in uncertain riches, but in the living God, **WHO GIVETH US RICHLY ALL THINGS TO ENJOY**;*"

b) Gnostic doctrine

c) Gnostic scriptures

THE TESTIMONY OF TRUTH (Book #12, p. 453)
*"No one knows the God of truth except solely the man who will **FORSAKE ALL THE THINGS OF THE WORLD**, having renounced the whole place . . . . He has set himself up as a power; he has subdued desire in every way within himself."*
d) Greek changes

4) man is not saved just by words

a) Rejected truth

John 20:31-- *"But these are written, that ye might believe that Jesus is the Christ, the Son of God; and that believing ye might have life through His name."*

I Peter 1:23-25-- *"Being born again, not of corruptible seed, but of incorruptible, **BY THE WORD OF GOD**, which liveth and abideth for ever . . . And this is the word which by the gospel is preached unto you."*

b) Gnostic doctrine

c) Gnostic scriptures

THE TESTIMONY OF TRUTH (Book #12, p. 450)
*"For if **ONLY WORDS WHICH BEAR TESTIMONY WERE EFFECTING SALVATION**, the whole world would endure this thing and would be saved."*

d) Greek changes

Acts 5:42
BYZ > KJV NASV NIV-- *"teach and preach **JESUS CHRIST**."*
BYZ SBA) WH NU-- **omit "Jesus Christ"**

Romans 1:16
BYZ > KJV-- *"For I am not ashamed of the gospel **OF CHRIST**: for it is the power of God unto salvation to everyone that believeth:"*
BSAC) WH NU > NASV NIV-- **omit of the Christ**

II Thessalonians1:8
BYZ SA > KJV-- *"taking vengeance on them that know not God, and that obey not the gospel of our Lord Jesus **CHRIST**:"*
BYZ B) WH NU > NASV NIV ESV-- **omit Christ**

Romans 10:17
BYZ A) KJV-- *"So then faith cometh by hearing, and hearing by the word of **GOD**."*
ORIGEN > SBC > WH NU) NASV NIV ESV– *". . . by the word of **CHRIST**"*

5) Man is saved by following the example of the Redeemer in obedience

a) Rejected truth

Titus 3:5-- *"**NOT BY WORKS OF RIGHTEOUSNESS** which we have done, but according to His mercy He saved us,"*

b) Gnostic doctrine
*". . . in Gnosticism, the ultimate object is individual salvation, the assurance of a fortunate destiny for the soul after death . . . . the central object of worship is a redeemer-deity who has already trodden **THE DIFFICULT WAY WHICH THE FAITHFUL HAVE TO FOLLOW**."* (Book #3, p. 153)

ORIGEN
*". . . the only-begotten Son of God . . . emptied himself, and taking the form of a servant became **OBEDIENT** even unto death **IN ORDER TO TEACH THEM OBEDIENCE WHO COULD IN NO OTHER WAY OBTAIN SALVATION EXCEPT THROUGH OBEDIENCE**; . . . "* (Book #21, p. 242)

c) Gnostic scriptures

d) Greek changes

6) Man is saved through sacraments

a) Rejected truth

Ephesians 2:8-9-- *"For by grace are ye saved through faith; and that not of yourselves: it is the gift of God: **NOT OF WORKS**, lest any man should boast."*

Titus 3:5-- *"**NOT BY WORKS OF RIGHTEOUSNESS WHICH WE HAVE DONE**, but according to His mercy He saved us, . . .*

b) Gnostic doctrine
*"And finally, as in all mystical religions . . . **THOSE THINGS WHICH WE CALL SACRAMENTS**, play a very prominent part. The Gnostic religion is full of such sacraments. . . Everywhere we are met with the most varied forms of holy rites--the **VARIOUS BAPTISMS, BY WATER, BY FIRE, BY THE SPIRIT, THE BAPTISM FOR THE PROTECTION AGAINST DEMONS, ANOINTING WITH OIL . . . PARTAKING OF HOLY FOOD AND DRINK**."* (Book #3, p. 153)

HORT– *"**Baptism assures us that WE ARE CHILDREN OF GOD, MEMBERS OF**

CHRIST AND HIS BODY, AND HEIRS OF THE HEAVENLY KINGDOM." (Book #10, Vol.2, p. 81)

"*While yet an infant you were claimed for God by being made in Baptism an UNCONSCIOUS MEMBER of His Church . . . you have as your BIRTHRIGHT a share in the kingdom of heaven . . .* " (Book #10, Vol.2,. p. 273) - See Acts 8:37 below

"*We dare not forsake the Sacraments, or God will forsake us.*" (Book #10, Vol.1, p. 77)

WESTCOTT-- "*I do think we have no right to exclaim against the idea of the COMMENCEMENT OF A SPIRITUAL LIFE, CONDITIONALLY FROM BAPTISM.*" (Book #23, Vol.1, p. 160)

I John 5:6-- "*. . . and by His BAPTISM Christ fulfilled for the humanity which He took to Himself, though not for Himself, THE CONDITION OF REGENERATION.*" (Book #16, p. 14)

c) Gnostic scriptures

d) Greek changes

Acts 8:37 (Critical text removes doctrine of believer's baptism)
BYZ) KJV (NASV)-- "*AND PHILIP SAID, IF THOU BELIEVEST WITH ALL THINE HEART, THOU MAYEST. AND HE ANSWERED AND SAID, I BELIEVE THAT JESUS CHRIST IS THE SON OF GOD.*"
BYZ SBAC > WH NU > NIV ESV-- **omit**

7) Man is saved through sacred formulas and names

a) Rejected truth

b) Gnostic doctrine

"*Finally, SACRED FORMULAS, NAMES and symbols are of the highest importance among the Gnostic sects. We constantly meet with the idea that the soul on leaving the body, finds its path to the highest heaven opposed by the deities and demons of the lower realms of heaven, and that only when it is in possession of the names of these demons, and can repeat the proper HOLY FORMULA, or is prepared with the right symbol, or has been anointed with the holy oil, finds its way unhindered to the heavenly home. Hence the Gnostic must learn the NAMES OF THE DEMONS, and equip himself with the SACRED FORMULAS and symbols in order to be certain of a good destiny after death.*" (Book #3, p. 153)

c) Gnostic scriptures

PISTIS SOPHIA

ACTS OF THOMAS
COPTIC IEU *"The two books unfold an immense system of names and symbols. This system again was simplified, and as the supreme secret was taught in a single NAME or a single **FORMULA**, by means of which the happy possessor was able to penetrate through all the spaces of heaven . . . It was taught that even the redeemer-god, when he once descended on to this earth, to rise from it again, availed himself of these **NAMES AND FORMULAS** on his descent and ascent through the world of demons."* (Book #3, p. 153)

d) Greek changes

John 17:12
BYZ A > KJV— *"I kept them in thy name: **THOSE** that thou gavest me I have kept,"*
BC) WH NU) NASV NIV ESV-- *"I was keeping them in Your name **WHICH** You have given me, and I guarded,"*

8) Man is saved by initiation rites (the baptism is done in the nude at night, and the bridal chamber is a homosexual act whereby the transcendental Self/the Twin/the Guardian angel/daemon spirit is attached to the initiate - aka. demon possession. These initiations will be the occasion of receiving the "mark of the beast" in Revelation 13:16-18)

a) Rejected truth

Leviticus 18:22-24-- *"**Thou shalt not lie with mankind, as with womankind: it is abomination**. . . Defile not ye yourselves in any of these things: for in all these the nations are defiled which I cast out before you:"*

b) Gnostic doctrines

*"And finally, as in all mystical religions, so here too, **HOLY RITES**. . . ACTS OF INITIATION AND CONSECRATION . . . .play a very prominent part. Everywhere we are met with the most varied forms of holy rites--the various baptisms. . . .anointing with oil, sealing and STIGMATIZING, piercing the ears, **LEADING INTO THE BRIDAL CHAMBER** . . ."* (Book #3, p. 153)

CLEMENT OF ALEXANDRIA *"The letter is addressed to a certain Theodore . . . Apparently Theodore has come into contact with a group of Carpocratians from whom he has learned of a Secret Gospel of Mark containing teachings not found in the more public version known to Theodore . . . The Alexandrian church did in fact have two versions of Mark in Clements' day, a 'public Mark,' thought to have been written in Rome, with a more general audience in mind, and 'a revised version, a 'Secret Mark,' allegedly written in Alexandria for a narrow circle of initiates. Clement goes on to say that not all of what Theodore has related to him concerning the book shown to him by the Carpocratians actually comes from the Secret Mark used in Clements church . . . Clement cites two of the added passages from the 'real' Secret Gospel of Mark so that Theodore can compare them . . . According to Clement, the story was added to Mark between verses 10:34 and 10:35."* (Book #27, p. 409)

(See THE SECRET GOSPEL OF MARK below)

JESUS SEMINAR (on the Secret Mark) – *"The most striking similarity concerns the mysterious figure of a young man who appears in canonical Mark in the scene of Jesus' arrest in the Garden of Gethsemane, dressed only in a linen cloth draped about his naked body. . . he is dressed in exactly the same way as the young man* **PREPARED FOR INITIATION** *in the Secret Mark fragments."* (Book #27, p. 410)

c) Gnostic scriptures

SECRET GOSPEL OF MARK (Book #27, p. 411)
"And they come into Bethany, and this woman was there whose brother had died. She knelt down in front of Jesus and says to him, Son of David, have mercy on me. But the disciples rebuked her. And Jesus got angry and went with her into the garden where the tomb was. Just then a loud voice was heard from inside the tomb. Then Jesus went up and rolled the stone away from the entrance to the tomb. He went right in where the young man was, stuck out his hand, grabbed him by the hand and raised him up. The young man looked at Jesus, **LOVED HIM, AND BEGAN TO BEG TO BE WITH HIM**. *Then they left the tomb and went into the young man's house. (Incidently he was rich.) Six days later Jesus gave him an . . order and* **WHEN EVENING HAD COME**, *the young man went to him* **DRESSED. . . ONLY IN A LINEN CLOTH. HE SPENT THAT NIGHT WITH HIM, BECAUSE . . . JESUS TAUGHT HIM THE MYSTERY OF GOD'S DOMAIN**. . . . . *From there Jesus got up and returned to the other side of the Jordan."*

THE GOSPEL OF THOMAS
"Then they said to him, Shall we then, as children, enter the kingdom? Jesus said to them, When you **MAKE THE TWO ONE** *when you* **MAKE . . . THE MALE AND THE FEMALE ONE AND THE SAME, SO THAT THE MALE NOT BE MALE NOR THE FEMALE FEMALE** *then you will enter the kingdom . . . His disciples said, When will you become* **REVEALED TO US** *and* **WHEN SHALL WE SEE YOU**? *Jesus said,* **WHEN YOU DISROBE WITHOUT BEING ASHAMED** *and take up your garments and place them . . . under your feet like little children and tread on them, then will you see the son of the living one, and you will not be afraid."* (Book #12, p. 129)

Jesus said., When you **MAKE THE TWO ONE**, *you will become the sons of man."* (Book #12, p. 129)

"Simon Peter said to them, Let Mary leave us, for women are not worthy of life. Jesus said, I myself shall lead her in order to **MAKE HER MALE, SO THAT SHE TOO MAY BECOME A LIVING SPIRIT RESEMBLING YOU MALES. FOR EVERY WOMAN WHO WILL MAKE HERSELF MALE WILL ENTER THE KINGDOM OF HEAVEN**."

THE GOSPEL OF PHILIP
"The holy of the holies is the bridal chamber. Baptism includes the resurrection and the redemption; **THE REDEMPTION (TAKES PLACE) IN THE BRIDAL CHAMBER**. *"* (Book #12, p. 151)

"He who has been anointed possesses everything. He possesses the resurrection, the light,

*the cross, the holy spirit. The father gave him this **IN THE BRIDAL CHAMBER**; he merely accepted the gift."* (Book #12, p. 153)

d) Greek changes (An attempt has been made to coordinate Secret Mark with the following verses, alluding to the fact that the young man was following Jesus in order to be initiated)

Mark 14:51
BYZ A > KJV NASV-- *"And there followed him a **CERTAIN** young man,"*
SB > WH NU > NIV ESV-- *"And **SOME** young man"*

Mark 14:51 (already a disciple vs. wanting to become a disciple)
BYZ A > KJV-- *"and there **FOLLOWED** him a certain young man, having a linen cloth cast about his naked body: and **THE YOUNG MEN** laid hold on him."*
SBC > WH NU > NASV NIV-- *"young man **WAS FOLLOWING** him having cast a linen cloth about (his) naked (body), and THEY seize him."*

Mark 14:52
BYZ A > KJV-- *"and he left the linen cloth, and fled **FROM THEM** naked."*
SBC > WH NU > NASV NIV ESV-- *"but he, leaving behind the linen cloth, naked fled."*

9) Man is saved through faith in his own works, not that of Christ's

a) Rejected truth

Psalm 37:40– *"And the Lord shall help them, and deliver them: he shall deliver them from the wicked, **AND SAVE THEM, BECAUSE THEY TRUST IN HIM.**"*

II Corinthians 1:9-- *"But we had the sentence of death in ourselves, **THAT WE SHOULD NOT TRUST IN OURSELVES**, but in God . . ."*

Luke 18:9-- *"And he spake this parable unto certain **WHICH TRUSTED IN THEMSELVES** . . ."*

Proverbs 28:26– *". . . he that **TRUSTETH** in his own heart is a fool:"*

Jeremiah 17:9-- *"The heart is deceitful above all things, and desperately wicked: who can know it?"*

b) Gnostic doctrine

HORT-- *"O that Coleridge, while showing how the notion of a fictitious **SUBSTITUTED RIGHTEOUSNESS, OR A TRANSFERABLE STOCK OF GOOD ACTIONS**, obscured the truth of man's restoration in the Man who perfectly acted out the idea of man, had expounded the truth (for such, I am sure, there must be) that underlies **THE CORRESPONDING HERESY (AS IT APPEARS TO ME) OF A FICTICIOUS SUBSTITUTED PENALTY**!"* (Book #10 Vol.1, p. 120)

WESTCOTT– *"I do think we have no right to exclaim against the idea of the commencement of a spiritual life, conditionally from baptism, any more than we have to* **DENY THE COMMENCEMENT OF A MORAL LIFE FROM BIRTH***.*" (Book #23, Vol.1, p. 160)

John 14:1-- "*(believe also in me) The* **BELIEF is 'IN CHRIST,'** *and* **NOT IN ANY PROPOSITIONS ABOUT CHRIST.**" (Book #16, p. 33)

I John 2:20-- "**CHRISTIANS ARE THEMSELVES IN A TRUE SENSE CHRISTS**, *anointed ones. . .* (Book #16, p. 11)

c) Gnostic scriptures

PISTIS SOPHIA (Book #20, p. 52)
"*You see, O child, through how many bodies (elements?), how many ranks of demons, how many concatenations and revolutions of stars,* **WE HAVE TO WORK OUR WAY. . .** *to the one and only God*."

THE APOCRYPHON OF JAMES
"**KEEP HIS WILL** *that you may be saved; accept reproof from me and* **SAVE YOURSELVES**." (Book #12, p. 34)

"*Or do you perhaps think that the Father is a lover of mankind, or that he is won over without prayers, or that* **HE GRANTS REMISSION TO ONE ON ANOTHER'S BEHALF** *. . .*" (Book #12, p. 34 - **This rejects subsitutionary atonement**)

THE TESTIMONY OF TRUTH (Book #12, p. 451)
"**If the Father were to desire a human sacrifice, he would become vainglorious.**"

d) Greek changes

These verses change that works cannot save
Acts 15:24
BYZ C) KJV-- "**SAYING, YE MUST BE CIRCUMCISED, AND KEEP THE LAW.**"
ORIGEN > SBA > WH NU > NASV NIV ESV-- **omit**

Romans 9:32
BYZ > KJV-- "*Because they sought it not by faith, but as it were by the works* **OF THE LAW**."
ORIGEN) SBA > WH NU > NASV NIV ESV-- **omit "of the law"**

Romans 11:6
BYZ > KJV-- "**BUT IF IT BE OF WORKS, THEN IT IS NO MORE GRACE: OTHERWISE WORK IS NO MORE WORK.**"
ORIGEN) SAC > WH NU) NASV NIV-- **omit**

These verses reject the doctrine of substitutionary righteousness
Romans 3:22
BYZ > KJV-- "*even the righteousness of God which is by faith of Jesus Christ unto all* **AND UPON ALL**

them that believe:"
ORIGEN) SBA > WH NU > NASV NIV ESV-- <u>omit "and upon all"</u>

Hebrews 10:38
BYZ > KJV-- *"Now the just shall live by faith:"*
AS > (WH) NU > NASV NIV-- *"But the just **ONE OF ME** by faith shall live"*

<u>These verses omit that we must put our faith in the works of Christ.</u>
Mark 9:42
BYZ AB > KJV; (NU) NIV-- *"one of these little ones that believe **IN ME**,"*
SC > WH > NASV-- <u>omit "in Me"</u>

John 6:47
BYZ A) KJV– *"he that believeth **ON ME** hath everlasting life."*
SBC) WH NU) NASV NIV ESV-- *omit on Me"*

John 9:35
BYZ A > KJV-- *"Dost thou believe on the Son of **GOD**?"*
SBC > WH NU) NASV NIV ESV– *". . . Son of **MAN**?"*

Acts 8:37
BYZ > KJV (NASV)– *"**AND PHILIP SAID, IF THOU BELIEVEST WITH ALL THINE HEART, THOU MAYEST. AND HE ANSWERED AND SAID, I BELIEVE THAT JESUS CHRIST IS THE SON OF GOD.**"*
BYZ SBAC > WH NU > NIV ESV– <u>omit</u>

10) Man is saved (born again) when he recognizes that he has the mystical Christ in him and is therefore divine or God ("I AM")

   a) Rejected truth

   b) Gnostic doctrine

*"The discovery of the Mystic **Christ in you is being 'born from above**.'"* (Book #25, p. 45)

   WESTCOTT
   John 11:25— *"The resurrection is not a doctrine but a fact: not future but present: not multitudinous, but belonging to the unbroken continuity of each separate life. . . **I AM — NOT I SHALL BE HEREAFTER — I AM**, . . ."* (Book #16, p. 32)

   0 Gnostic scriptures

   d) Greek changes

11) Man is saved through invisible, secret SYMBOLS

a) Rejected truth

b) Gnostic doctrine
"*Finally, sacred formulas, names and **SYMBOLS** are of the highest importance among the Gnostic sects. We constantly meet with the idea that the soul on leaving the body, finds its path to the highest heaven opposed by the deities and demons of the lower realms of heaven, and that only when it is in possession of the names of these demons, and can repeat the proper holy formula, or is prepared with the right **SYMBOL** . . . finds its way unhindered to the heavenly home. Hence the Gnostic must learn the. . . **SYMBOLS** in order to be certain of a good destiny after death.*" (Book #3, p. 153)

c) Gnostic scriptures
THE GOSPEL OF THE EGYPTIANS (Book #12, p. 216)
"*. . . the baptism through a Logos-begotten body which the great Seth prepared for himself, secretly through the virgin, in order that **the saints MAY BE BEGOTTEN by the holy spirit, THROUGH INVISIBLE, SECRET SYMBOLS** . . .*"

PISTIS SOPHIA, ACTS OF THOMAS, COPTIC IEU– "*. . . unfold an immense system of names and **symbols** . . .*" (Book #3, p. 153)

d) Greek changes

12) Man must be 'born again' twice

a) Rejected truth

b) Gnostic doctrine

c) Gnostic scriptures

GOSPEL OF PHILIP (Book #26, p. 341)
"***REBIRTH*** *exists along with an **IMAGE OF REBIRTH**: by means of this image one must be **TRULY REBORN**. Which image? Resurrection. And image must arise by means of image. . . **This person is no longer a Christian but rather is Christ** (anointed).*"

d) Greek changes

c. Objects of salvation

1) Redemption includes all the angels including Satan and his angels

a) Rejected truth

Matthew 25:41-- "*Then shall he say also unto them on the left hand, Depart from me, ye cursed, into **EVERLASTING FIRE, PREPARED FOR THE DEVIL AND HIS ANGELS**:*"

Revelation 20:10-- *"And the **DEVIL** that deceived them was cast into the lake of fire and brimstone, . . . and shall be **tormented day and night FOR EVER AND EVER**."*

b) Gnostic doctrine

ORIGEN-- *"According to the 'First Principles' Origen did assert that **THE DEVIL WOULD AT LAST BE SAVED**. It is indeed an essential part of his system of thought. Again and again he returns to his favourite text, 'that God may be all in all."* (Book #21, p. xxxix)

c) Gnostic "scriptures"
THE TRIPARTITE TRACTATE (Book #12, p. 97-98)
*"Not only do humans need redemption, but also THE ANGELS, too, need redemption along with the image and the rest of the Pleromas of the aeons and the wondrous powers of illumination. . . . Therefore, he is called 'the **REDEMPTION OF THE ANGELS** of the Father,' he who comforted those who were laboring under the Totality for his knowledge, because he was given the grace before anyone else . . ."*

d) Greek changes

2) Redemption Includes Jesus Christ (the Primal Man)

a) Rejected truth

I1 Corinthians 5:21-- *"For He hath made Him to be sin for us, **WHO KNEW NO SIN**; . . ."*

Hebrews 4:15-- *"For we have not an high priest which cannot be touched with the feeling of our infirmities; but was in all points tempted like as we are, yet **WITHOUT SIN**."*

Hebrews 7:26-- *"For such an high priest became us, who is holy, harmless, **UNDEFILED, SEPARATE FROM SINNERS**, . . ."*

Hebrews 13:8-- *"Jesus Christ the same, yesterday, and today, and for ever."*

b) Gnostic doctrine

*"In Gnosticism salvation always lies at the **ROOT OF ALL EXISTENCE** and history. The fundamental conception varies greatly."* (Book #3, p. 157)

POIMANDRES– "At one time the Primal Man, who sank down into matter has **FREED HIMSELF** and risen out of it again, and like him his members will rise out of darkness into the light . . ." (Book #3, p. 157)

MANI– "*. . . the **PRIMAL MAN WHO HAS BEEN CONQUERED BY THE POWERS OF DARKNESS HAS BEEN SAVED BY THE POWERS OF LIGHT**, and thus too all his race will be saved."* (Book #3, p. 157)

WESTCOTT

John 1:51-- "***ALL that TRULY BELONGS TO HUMANITY, ALL therefore that TRULY BELONGS TO EVERY INDIVIDUAL IN THE WHOLE RACE, BELONGS ALSO TO HIM***." (Book #16, p. 27)

Hebrews 2:10-- "*The conception of teleiosai (to make perfect) is that of **bringing Christ to the FULL MORAL PERFECTION OF HIS HUMANITY**—which carries with it the completeness of power and dignity . . . **THIS 'PERFECTION' WAS NOT REACHED TILL AFTER DEATH**:. . .* " (Book #16, p. 30)

Hebrews 5:7-- "*The question has been asked for what did Christ pray? . . . Perhaps it is best to answer, generally, **FOR THE VICTORY OVER DEATH THE FRUIT OF SIN**.*" (Book #16, p. 30)

c) Gnostic scriptures

THE TRIPARTITE TRACTATE (Book #12, p. 97)
"*So that we might not be in doubt in regard to the others, **EVEN THE SON HIMSELF**, who has the position of redeemer of the Totality, **NEEDED REDEMPTION AS WELL**-- he who had become man,--since he gave himself for each thing which we need, we in the flesh, who are his Church.*"

d) Greek changes
Matthew 19:16
BYZ > KJV-- "***GOOD** Master,*"
ORIGEN > SB > WH NU > NASV NIV ESV-- "***Master***"

Matthew 19:17
BYZ > KJV-- "*Why **CALLEST THOU ME** good?* "
ORIGEN > SB > WH HU > NASV NIV ESV-- "*Why **ASK ME CONCERNING THE good**.*"

Matthew 27:24
BYZ > KJV-- "*I am innocent of the blood **OF THIS JUST PERSON**: *"
ORIGEN > B > WH NU > NASV NIV ESV– "*. . . **of this person**.*"

Luke 20:23
BYZ AC > KJV-- "***WHY TEMPT YE ME***?"
SB) WH NU > NASV NIV ESV-- **omit**

Philemon 6   (**Gnostic doctrine sees the Christ and Jesus as 2 separate persons**)
BYZ > KJV-- "*every good thing which is in you in Christ **JESUS**.*"
SAC > WH NU > NASV NIV ESV-- **omit "Jesus"**

I John 3:5 (**Critical text could teach that He was manifested to take away His own sin - the doctrine of reincarnation**)

BYZ SC > KJV NIV-- *"he was manifested to take away **OUR** sins;"*
BA > WH NU > NASV ESV-- **omit 'our'**

Revelation 16:5
BYZ > KJV-- *"Thou art righteous, **O LORD, which art,** and wast, and shalt be,"*
SAC > WH NU > NASV NIV ESV-- **omits "O Lord"**

3) Redemption includes the whole world (universal salvation)

a) Rejected truth

Hebrews 9:26– *". . . but now once in the end of the world hath he appeared **TO PUT AWAY SIN** by the sacrifice of himself.*

John 17:2– *". . . that He should give eternal life to **AS MANY AS THOU HAST GIVEN HIM**."*
Christ did not die to make possible the salvation of all mankind, but to make certain the salvation of all that the Father had given Him."
(Book #32, p. 56)

Isaiah 53:8– *". . . for the transgression of **MY PEOPLE** was He stricken."*

Isaiah 53:11–*"He shall see the travail of his soul, and shall be satisfied: by his knowledge shall My righteous servant **JUSTIFY MANY**; for he shall **bear THEIR iniquities**."*

Matthew 1:21-- *"Thou shalt call His name Jesus: for He shall **SAVE HIS PEOPLE FROM THEIR SINS**."*

Matthew 20:28-- *"The Son of Man came . . . not to be ministered unto, but to minister and to give his life a ransom for **MANY**.*

b) Gnostic doctrine

HORT– *". . . the Epistles are almost free. . . from allusions to everlasting torments . . . And little as I like to rest on isolated texts, I cannot get over the words, As in Adam all die, even so in Christ shall **ALL BE MADE ALIVE**. St. Paul cannot mean **MERELY THE UNIVERSAL REDEMPTION**, for he uses the future tense."* (Book #10, Vol.1, p. 117)

WESTCOTT
Hebrews 2:8-9-- *"The fruit of His work is **UNIVERSAL**. . . "* (Book #16, p. 18)

Hebrews 2:9-- *"The glory which followed the death marked its **UNIVERSAL EFFICACY**. Thus Christ was made lower than angels that He might accomplish this **COMPLETE REDEMPTION**."* (Book #16, p. 18)

I John 1:1-- *"That which we understand by the eternal purpose of God (Ephesians I.4), the relation of the Father to the Son. . . **THE ACCEPTANCE OF MAN IN THE BELOVED** (Ephesians I.6) was already, . . ."* (Book #16, p. 19)

I John 1:7– ". . . in Him **ALL MEN FIND THEIR TRUE LIFE**." (Book #16, p. 19)

I John 2:2-- *"Christ's **ADVOCACY OF MAN** is addressed to God in that relation of **FATHERHOOD** which has been fully revealed in the Son who **HAS TAKEN MANHOOD TO HIMSELF**. . . "* (Book #16, p. 19)

I John 2:18-- *"The teaching of Antichrist leaves **GOD AND THE WORLD STILL UNUNITED**. The proclamation of the **UNION IS THE MESSAGE OF THE GOSPEL**."* (Book #16, p. 19)

I John 4:2-3-- *"The Incarnate Savior is the **PLEDGE OF THE COMPLETE REDEMPTION AND PERFECTION OF MAN**, . . ."* (Book #16, p. 19) .

SCHAFF-- *"Never doubting in a moment that Christianity is the true religion and the Christian God the only true God, Schaff yet believed, broadminded as always, that **in the Heavenly Father's house there are many mansions, not only for each of the historic Christian denominations but also FOR EACH OF THE WORLD'S GREAT RELIGIONS**. However imperfectly these religions might represent their share of the truth, they do, nevertheless, all share in that truth."* (Book #19, p. 292)

*"**UNIVERSALISM** may be condemned as a doctrine; but **it has a right to protest against a gross materialistic theory of hell with all of its Dantesque horrors, and against the once widely spread popular belief that the overwhelming majority of the human race, including countless millions of innocent infants will forever perish**. **NOR SHOULD WE FORGET THAT SOME OF THE GREATEST DIVINES, FROM ORIGEN** and Gregory of Nyssa down to Bengel and Schleiermacher **BELIEVED IN, OR HOPED FOR, THE ULTIMATE RETURN OF ALL RATIONAL CREATURES TO THE GOD OF LOVE** who created them in his own image and for his own glory."* (Book #19, p. 292)

*"In 1846, 1 was threatened with a second heresy trial on the subject of the **MIDDLE STATE BETWEEN DEATH AND THE RESURRECTION AND THE HOPE OF THE SALVATION OF ALL CHILDREN DYING IN INFANCY AND OF SUCH HEATHEN AS WOULD HAVE ACCEPTED THE GOSPEL** if it had been offered to them in this world."* (Book #19, p. 7)

c) Gnostic scriptures

THE SENTENCES OF SEXTUS (Book #12, p. 507)
". . . it is the business of the pious man to **beseech God to SAVE EVERYONE**."

THE TRIPARTITE TRACTATE (Book #12, p. 103)
". . . *(at) the sound of a trumpet he will **proclaim the GREAT COMPLETE AMNESTY** from the beauteous east, in the bridal chamber which is the love of God the Father—according to the power. . . of the Lord the Savior, the Redeemer of all those belonging to the one filled with Love, through his Holy Spirit **FROM NOW THROUGHOUT ALL GENERATIONS FOREVER AND EVER**."* Amen.

THE APOCRYPHON OF JOHN (Book #12, p.121) "(*He says not all are saved, but some are saved after death by acquiring gnosis) But those on whom the counterfeit spirit descends are drawn by him and they go astray. And said, Lord where will the souls of these go when they have come out of their flesh?. . . The soul in which the power will become stronger than the counterfeit spirit, is strong and it flees from evil, and, through the intervention of the incorruptible one, **IT IS SAVED** and it is taken up to the rest of the aeons. And I said Lord, those, however, who have not known to whom they belong, where will their souls be? And he said to me, In those the despicable spirit has gained strength when they went astray. And he burdens the soul and draws it to the works of evil, and he casts it down into forgetfulness. And after it comes out of the body, it is handed over to the authorities. . . and they bind it with chains and cast it into prison and consort with it **UNTIL IT IS LIBERATED** from the forgetfulness and acquires knowledge. **AND IF THUS IT BECOMES PERFECT, IT IS SAVED**.*"

ASCLEPIUS (Book #12, p. 337)
"*For unbelievers are impious and commit sin. Afterwards **THEY WILL BE COMPELLED TO BELIEVE**, and they will not hear by word of mouth only, but will experience the reality itself.*"

d) Greek changes

Matthew 8:25
BYZ > KJV-- "*Lord, save **US**.*"
SB > WH NU > NASV-- **omit "us"**

Matthew 20:16
BYZ C > KJV-- "***FOR MANY BE CALLED, BUT FEW CHOSEN***"
SB > WH NU > NASV NIV ESV– **omit above**

John 6:47
BYZ A > KJV-- "He that believeth **ON ME** hath everlasting life."
SBC > WH NU > NASV NIV ESV **omits "on me"**

John 17:12
BYZ A > KJV– "While I was with them in the world, I kept them in **THY NAME**: those that thou gavest me I have kept,"
BC) WH NU > NASV NIV ESV-- "***NAME WHICH** you have given me I guarded.*"

Revelation 21:24
BYZ > KJV-- "*the nations **OF THEM WHICH ARE SAVED** shall walk in the light of it:*"
BYZ SA > WH NU NASV NIV ESV-- **omit "of them which are saved"**

4) Only the good are saved

a) Rejected truth

Romans 3:10-- *"As it is written, There is none righteous, no not one:"*

Romans 3:12– *". . . there is none that doeth good, no, not one."*

    b) Gnostic doctrine

    SATORNINOS (according to Irenaeus) (Book #26, p. 162)
*"Indeed, there are--he says--two human races which were modeled by the angels, one wicked and the other good . . . the savior came for the destruction of bad human beings and demons **AND FOR THE SALVATION OF GOOD ONES**."*

    c) Gnostic scriptures

    d) Greek changes

The souls of men are saved, not their bodies (no bodily resurrection)

    a) Rejected truth

II Timothy 2:17-18-- *"And their word will eat as doth a canker: of whom is Hymenaeus and Philetus; who concerning the truth have erred, saying that **THE RESURRECTION IS PAST ALREADY**; and overthrow the faith of some."*

Ephesians 5:23– *". . . Christ is the head of the church: and he is the **SAVIOUR OF THE BODY**."*

    b) Gnostic doctrine

*"Gnosticism recognizes . . . the separation of the spiritual man **FROM THE CORPOREAL BEING AS THE OBJECT OF SALVATION**."* (Book #3, p. 154)

"The conception of a resurrection of the body, of a further existence for the body after death, was unattainable by almost all of the Gnostics." (Book #3, p. 157)

WESTCOTT'
John 2:19-- *"(Destroy this temple, and in three days I will raise it up) On the other hand the **RESURRECTION OF CHRIST** was the raising again of the Temple, the complete **RESTORATION OF THE TABERNACLE OF GOD'S PRESENCE TO MEN**, perpetuated **IN THE CHURCH WHICH IS CHRIST'S BODY**."* (Book #16, p. 33)

John 11:25-- *"The **RESURRECTION** is not a doctrine but a fact: **NOT FUTURE BUT PRESENT**: not multitudinous, but belonging to the **UNBROKEN CONTINUITY OF EACH SEPARATE LIFE** . . . **I AM--NOT I SHALL BE HEREAFTER--I AM**, . . ."* (Book #16, p. 32)

I Peter 1:3-- *"(by the resurrection of Jesus Christ from the dead) ". . . It was by the faith in the Resurrection that **MANKIND WAS ENABLED** (note past tense) **TO RENEW ITS***

YOUTH.”
(Book #16, p. 33)

c) Gnostic scriptures

d) Greek changes

1 Corinthians 15:55
BYZ AS > KJV-- “*O GRAVE, where is thy victory?*”
ORIGEN > BS > WH NU) NASV NIV ESV– “*O DEATH* . . .”

Hebrews 10:34
BYZ > KJV– “*ye have **IN HEAVEN** a better and enduring substance.*”
SA > WH NU > NASV NIV ESV-- **omit “IN HEAVEN.”**

d. The process of salvation

1) Man is saved/perfected in stages

a) Rejected truth

John 6:47-- *“Verily, verily, I say unto you, He that believeth on Me **HATH EVERLASTING LIFE**.”*

Hebrews 10:14-- *“For by one offering **HE HATH PERFECTED FOR EVER** them that are sanctified.”*

b) Gnostic doctrine

FREEMASONS-- *“Step by step men must advance toward **PERFECTION**; and each Masonic Degree is meant to be one of those steps. Each is a development of a particular duty. . .”*   (Book #6, p. 136)

c) Gnostic scripture

THE DISCOURSE ON THE EIGHTH AND NINTH
*“This is what you call the beauty of the soul, the edification that came to you **IN STAGES**.”*
(Book #12, p. 323)

*“Rather, **BY STAGES HE ADVANCES AND ENTERS ‘INTO THE WAY OF IMMORTALITY**.’”* (Book #12, p. 326)

d) Greek changes

I Thessalonians 5:27
BYZ > KJV-- *“I charge you by the Lord that this epistle be read unto all the **HOLY** brethren.”*
SB) WH > NASV NIV ESV-- **omit “holy”**

Jude I
BYZ > KJV-- "*to them that ARE SANCTIFIED by God the Father and preserved,*"
BSAC > WH NU > NASV ESV-- **add HAVING BEEN LOVED**"

e. Event of salvation

1) Salvation is a myth and not an historical event

a) Rejected truth

b) Gnostic doctrine

WESTCOTT
John 1:29-- (*which taketh away the sin of the world*) "*The parallel passage in the Epistle. . . shews that the REDEMPTIVE EFFICACY OF CHRIST'S WORK IS TO BE FOUND IN HIS WHOLE LIFE.*" (Book #16, p. 34)

John 13:31-- (glorified) "*The thought THROUGHOUT THESE LAST DISCOURSES is of the decisive act by which the Passion had been embraced. THE REDEMPTIVE WORK OF CHRIST ESSENTIALLY WAS COMPLETED. . .*" (Book #16, p. 35)

Hebrews 10:10-- (*through the offering of the body of Jesus Christ once for all*) "*Through the offering of the body divinely prepared, WHICH OFFERING, SLOWLY MATURED THROUGH LIFE.*" (Book #16, p. 36)

Hebrews 10:10-- "*He requires REDEMPTION, FORGIVENESS, ATONEMENT AND RECONCILIATION. ALL these blessings Christ has brought to humanity BY HIS INCARNATION, HIS LIFE, HIS PASSION, HIS ASCENSION.*" (Book #16, p. 36)

c) Gnostic scriptures

d) Greek changes

f. The proof of salvation

1) The believer will shine/be luminous

a) Rejected truth

II Corinthians 11:14– ". . . .*Satan himself is transformed into an angel of LIGHT.*"

Matthew 6:22-23-- "*THE LIGHT OF THE BODY IS THE EYE: if therefore thine eye be single, thy whole body shall be full of light. But if thine eye be evil, thy whole body shall be full of darkness. IF THEREFORE THE LIGHT THAT IS IN THEE BE DARKNESS, HOW GREAT IS THAT DARKNESS.*"

b) Gnostic doctrine

c) Gnostic scriptures

> THE GOSPEL OF THOMAS (Book #12, p. 129)
> "*. . . There is light within a man of light, and he lights up the whole world. If he does not SHINE, he is darkness.*"

d) Greek changes

Ephesians 5:9
BYZ > KJV-- "*for the fruit of the **SPIRIT** (is) in all goodness and righteousness and truth;*"
ORIGEN) SBA) WH NU > NASV NIV ESV-- "*for the fruit of the **LIGHT** . . .*"

2) He will enter the kingdom laughing (Charismatic's 'holy laughter')

a) Rejected truth

Luke 13:3-- "*I tell you . . . except ye repent, ye shall all likewise perish.*"

Acts 17:30– "*. . . God . . . commendeth all men everywhere to repent.*"

b) Gnostic doctrine

c) Gnostic scripture

> THE GOSPEL OF PHILIP (Book #12, p. 154)
> "*The lord said it well: Some have entered the kingdom of heaven **LAUGHING** . . .*"

d) Greek changes

Matthew 9:13
BYZ > KJV-- "*for I am not come to call the righteous, but sinners **TO REPENTANCE***"
BS) WH NU) NASV NIV ESV-- **omit "to repentance"**

Mark 2:17
BYZ) KJV-- "*I came not to call the righteous, but sinners **TO REPENTANCE**.*"
SBA > WH NU > NASV NIV ESV--**omit "to repentance"**

3) He will have visions of God, and the Savior

a) Rejected truth

Exodus 33:20-- "*And He said, Thou canst not see MY face: for there shall **NO MAN** see Me, and live.*"

John 1:18-- "***NO MAN** hath seen God at any time; . . .*"

John 5:37– "*. . . the Father, which hath borne witness of me. Ye have neither heard His voice <u>AT ANY</u> <u>TIME, NOR SEEN HIS SHAPE</u>.*"

     b) Gnostic doctrine

     c) Gnostic scripture

THE GOSPEL OF THE EGYPTIANS (Book #12, p. 218)
"*This great name of thine is upon me, O self-begotten Perfect one, who art not outside me.* <u>*I SEE THEE, O THOU WHO ART VISIBLE TO EVERYONE*</u>."

APOCALYPSE OF PETER (Book #12, p. 374)
"*And there came in me fear with joy, for* <u>*I SAW A NEW LIGHT GREATER THAN THE*</u> <u>*LIGHT OF DAY. THEN IT CAME DOWN UPON THE SAVIOR*</u>. *And l told him about those things which I saw.*"

     d) Greek changes

Colossians 2:18
BYZ C > KJV-- "*intruding into those things which he hath <u>NOT</u> seen,*"

MARCION ORIGEN) WH NU > NASV NIV ESV-- <u>**omit "not"**</u>

     4) He will speak in tongues

        a) Rejected truth

1 Corinthians12:30– "*. . . do all speak with tongues? . . .*"

        b) Gnostic doctrine

        c) Gnostic scriptures

THE GOSPEL OF THE EGYPTIANS (Book #12, p. 217-218)
"*O Living water, O child of the child, O glorious name, really truly, really truly, O existing one who sees the aeons! Really truly, who is eternally eternal, really truly in the heart, who exists, forever, Thou art what Thou art, Thou art who Thou art! This great name of thine is upon me, O self-begotten Perfect one, who art not outside me. I see thee, O thou who art visible to everyone. For who will be able to comprehend thee <u>IN</u> another tongue? <u>NOW THAT I HAVE KNOWN THEE</u>, I have mixed myself with the immutable.*"

        d) Greek changes

1 Corinthians 14:39
BYZ) KJV-- "*speak <u>WITH</u> tongues*"
B > NU > NASV NIV ESV-- "*speak <u>IN</u> tongues*"

5) He will lift up his hands in praise

a) Rejected truth

b) Gnostic doctrine

c) Gnostic scriptures

APOCALYPSE. OF PETER (Book #12, p. 374)
*"And I told him (the Savior) about those things which I saw. And he said to me, **LIFT UP YOUR HANDS** and listen . . .   And I listened again. As You sit they are praising You.".*

d) Greek changes:

6) He will have out of body experiences

a) Rejected truth

b) Gnostic doctrine

c) Gnostic scriptures

THE PARAPHRASE OF SHEM   (Book #12, p. 34I)
*"My thought which was in **MY** body snatched me away from my race. It took me up to the top of the world, which is close to the light that shone upon the whole area there. I saw no earthly likeness, but there was light. And **MY THOUGHT SEPARATED FROM THE BODY** of darkness as though in sleep."*

d) Greek changes

7) He will experience new revelation (hear God speaking in his mind)

a) Rejected truth

John 5:37– *". . . the Father . . . hath borne witness of Me. Ye have **neither HEARD HIS VOICE AT ANY TIME**, nor seen his shape."*

Revelation 22:18-- *"For I testify unto every man that heareth the words of the prophecy of this book, If any man shall **ADD UNTO THESE THINGS**, God shall add unto him the plagues that are written in this book:"*

b) Gnostic doctrine

c) Gnostic scriptures

THE TESTIMONY OF TRUTH (Book #12, p. 449)

*"I will speak to those who know to hear **NOT WITH THE EARS OF THE BODY BUT WITH THE EARS OF THE MIND**."*

d) Greek changes

Matthew 13:9, 13:43
BY) KJV-- *"Who hath ears **TO HEAR**, let him hear."*
SB > WH NU > NASV NIV ESV-- <u>omit "to hear"</u>

g. Meaning of redemption

1) Redemption is the returning of man to his pre-existent state of deity before his fall in eternity past

a) Rejected truth

Ephesians 1:7-- *"In whom we have redemption **THROUGH HIS BLOOD**, the forgiveness of sins, . . ."*

b) Gnostic doctrine

c) Gnostic scriptures

THE TRIPARTITE TRACTATE (Book #12, p. 94)
*"Now the promise possessed the instruction and the **RETURN TO WHAT THEY ARE FROM THE FIRST**, from which they possess the drop **SO AS TO RETURN TO HIM**, which is that which is called 'the redemption.' And it is the release from the captivity and the acceptance of freedom."*

THE TREATISE ON THE RESURRECTION (Book #12, p. 55) *"**NOTHING, then, REDEEMS US FROM THIS WORLD**."*

d) Greek changes

Luke 19:45
BYZ KJV-- *"them that sold **THEREIN, AND THEM THAT BOUGHT**."*
SBA WH NU NASV NIV ESV   <u>omit "THEREIN, AND THEM THAT BOUGHT."</u>

Colossians 1:14
BYZ) KJV-- *"in whom we have redemption **THROUGH HIS BLOOD**,"*
BYZ SBA > WH NU > NASV NIV ESV-- <u>omit "through his blood"</u>

Revelation 5:9
BYZ S > KJV-- "thou wast slain, and hast redeemed <u>US</u> to God by thy blood . . ."
A > WH NU > NASV NIV ESV-- <u>omit "us"</u>

h. Purpose and results of salvation

1) To know that man himself is the Son of Man

a) Rejected truth

Acts 7:55-56-- *"But he, being full of the Holy Ghost, looked up steadfastly into heaven, and saw the glory of God, and **JESUS STANDING ON THE RIGHT HAND OF GOD**, And said, Behold, I see the heavens opened, and the **SON OF MAN STANDING ON THE RIGHT HAND OF GOD.**"*

b) Gnostic doctrine

c) Gnostic scriptures

THE TESTIMONY OF TRUTH (Book #12, p. 451)
*"These Christ will transfer to the heights since they have advanced to knowledge. And those who have knowledge . . . has come to know the Son of Man, that is, **HE HAS COME TO KNOW HIMSELF.**"*

d) Greek changes

Matthew 16:13
BYZ) KJV-- *"Whom do men say that **I** the Son of Man am?"*
ORIGEN > B) WH--NU) NASV NIV ESV--**omit 'I'**

Matthew 18:11
BYZ > KJV (NASV)– **"FOR THE SON OF MAN IS COME TO SAVE THAT WHICH WAS LOST."**
ORIGEN > BS > WH NU > NIV ESV-- **omit**

Matthew 25:13
BYZ) KJV-- *"for ye know neither the day nor the hour **WHEREIN THE SON OF MAN COMETH.**"*
SBAC > WH NU > NASV NIV ESV-- **omit 'WHEREIN THE SON OF MAN COMETH'**

Luke 9:56
BYZ > KJV (NASV)-- **"*FOR THE SON OF MAN IS NOT COME TO DESTROY MEN'S LIVES, BUT TO SAVE THEM.*"**
BYZ SBA) WH NU > NIV ESV-- **omit**

John 3: 13
BYZ > KJV-- *"the Son of Man **WHICH IS IN HEAVEN**"*
ORIGEN > SB > WH NU) NASV* NIV ESV-- **omit 'which is in heaven'**

2) To reunite the Gnostic with the Savior

a) Rejected truth

I1 Corinthians 5:18-- *"And all things are of **GOD WHO HATH RECONCILED US TO HIMSELF** by Jesus Christ,"*

Ephesians 2:16-- *"And that He might **RECONCILE BOTH UNTO GOD** in one body by the cross, having slain the enmity thereby;"*

    b) Gnostic doctrine

"The Gnostic Saviour does not come to reconcile humankind with God, but to reunite the Gnostic with himself . . . In the opening scenes of Pistis Sophia the Apostles surrounding Jesus find themselves in a special relationship with him. Jesus has come to save them. But how? And why? The reply is given by Jesus himself: because they are a part of his own strength." (Book #28, p. 106)

    c) Gnostic scriptures
    PISTIS SOPHIA (Book #28, p. 107)
"All men who are in the world have received souls from the strength of the archons of the aeons, but the strength which is in you comes from me (Jesus)."

    d) Greek changes

Philippian 4:13 (**Christ is different than Jesus**)
BYZ) KJV-- *"I can do all things through **CHRIST** which strengtheneth me."*
SBA > WH NU > NASV NIV ESV--**omit "Christ"**

I1 Corinthians 5:18
BYZ > KJV-- *"reconciled us to himself by **JESUS** Christ,"*
SBAC > WH NU > NASV NIV ESV-- **omit 'Jesus'**

3) To be wedded to the angels (Bridal chamber)

    a) Rejected truth

Matthew 22:30-- *"For in the resurrection they neither marry, nor are given in marriage, but are like the **ANGELS** of God in heaven."*

    b) Gnostic doctrine

VALENTINUS– *". . . all the souls of the Gnostics who still languish in matter will become **THE BRIDES OF THE ANGELS OF THE SOTER** (Saviour)."* (Book #3, p. 157)

    c) Gnostic scriptures

    d) Greek changes

4) He will no longer sin but will be perfect

a) Rejected truth

I John 1:8– *"If we say that we have no sin, we deceive ourselves, and the truth is not in us."*

I John 1:10-- *"If we say that we have not sinned, we make him a liar, and His word is not in us."*

b) Gnostic doctrine

c) Gnostic scripture

THE GOSPEL OF PHILIP (Book #12, p. 155)
*"He who has knowledge of the truth is a free man, **BUT THE FREE MAN DOES NOT SIN**, for 'he who sins is the slave of sin' (John 8:34). Truth is the mother, knowledge the father. Those who think that sinning does not apply to them are called 'free' by the world."*

d) Greek changes

5) Man attains Christhood and becomes divine through gnosis

a) Rejected truth

I Timothy 2:5-- *"For there is **ONE GOD**, and **ONE** mediator between God and men, the man **CHRIST Jesus**;"*

b) Gnostic doctrine

ORIGEN-- *"We are . . . almost completely dependent upon Rufinus for our knowledge of what actually it was that Origen said . . . For instance, in Ch. IV, on the Holy Spirit, Rufinus writes as follows: 'But for us there is one God the Father, from whom are all things. There is therefore one true God who as I said is the fount **OF DEITY, AND ONE CHRIST THE MAKER OF CHRISTS**, and one Holy Spirit who makes the Holy Spirit in the soul of every saint."* (Book #21, p. xxxv)

WESTCOTT
I John 2:20-- *"**CHRISTIANS ARE THEMSELVES IN A TRUE SENSE CHRISTS**, anointed ones."*   (Book #16, p. 11)

HORT
I Peter 1:11-- *"Touch not mine anointed ones . . . and do **MY** prophets no harm,"* where the **DIVINE ANOINTING OR CHRISTHOOD** *and prophethood are set in parallelism as kindred **ATTRIBUTES OF THE CHILDREN OF ISRAEL** . . . The prophet, the people to whom he belongs and to whom he speaks, and the dimly seen Head and King of the people **ALL** pass insensibly one into the other in the language of prophecy; **THEY ALL ARE PARTAKERS OF THE DIVINE ANOINTING AND THE MESSIAHSHIP WHICH IS CONFERRED BY IT**."* (Book #16, p. 28)

c) Gnostic scriptures

GOSPEL OF PHILIP (Book #26, p. 341)
"*Rebirth exists along with an image of rebirth: by means of this image one must be truly reborn . . . For this person is **NO LONGER A CHRISTIAN BUT RATHER IS CHRIST** (anointed).*"

THE APOCRYPHON OF JAMES (Book #26, p. 32)
"*The Lord answered . . . the Father . . . will love you, and **MAKE YOU EQUAL WITH ME**.*"

THE PRAYER OF THANKSGIVING (Book #121 p. 329)
"*You have made us **DIVINE** through Your knowledge.*"

EUGNOSTOS (Book #12, p. 229)
"*Through Immortal Man appeared the first designation, namely **DIVINITY** and kingdom, for the Father, who is called Self- Father Man, revealed this . . . Now through that Man originated **DIVINITY** and kingdom. Therefore he was called **GOD OF GODS**, King of Kings.*"

d) Greek changes

6) To be absorbed back into the godhead (become god)

a) Rejected truth

Genesis 3:4-5-- "*And the **SERPENT SAID** . . . **YE SHALL BE AS GODS**, knowing good and evil.*"

Isaiah 45:21-22– "*. . . **THERE IS NO GOD ELSE BESIDE ME**; a just God and a Saviour; **THERE IS NONE BESIDE ME**. Look unto me, and be ye saved, all the ends of the earth: for I am God, and **THERE IS NONE ELSE**.*"

b) Gnostic doctrine

"*The goal of gnostic striving is the release of the 'inner man' from the bonds of the world and his **RETURN TO HIS NATIVE REALM OF LIGHT**.*" (Book #20, p. 44)

". . . it (Gnosis) is more particularly 'knowledge of the way,' namely, of the soul's way out of the world, comprising the sacramental, and magical preparations for its future ascent and the secret names and formulas that force the passage through each sphere. Equipped with this gnosis, the soul after death travels upward, leaving behind at each sphere the psychical 'vestment' contributed by it: thus the spirit stripped of all foreign accretions reaches the God beyond the world and becomes **REUNITED WITH THE DIVINE SUBSTANCE**. On the scale of the total divine drama, this process is part of the **RESTORATION OF THE DEITY'S OWN WHOLENESS**." (Book #20 p. 45)

ORIGEN– "*. . . there are the real Gnostics, the real Christians who behold the mysteries of God. To these Christ appeared as a priest to open the depth of knowledge and to make them participants of His divine life,* **SO THAT THEY MIGHT BECOME GODS THEMSELVES**." (Book #7, p. 89)

and The **DEIFICATION OF THE HUMAN NATURE**.*Logos* (Book #7, p. 91)

WESTCOTT
John 3:12-- "*Such was the full revelation of the Son, involving the redemption of the world and the* **REUNION OF MAN WITH GOD** *. . .*" (Book #16, p. 18)

John 10:16-- (bring) "*This could only be by His death,* **WHICH REUNITES MAN WITH GOD** *. . .*" (Book #16, p. 18)

I John 2:18-- "*The teaching of Antichrist leaves* **GOD AND THE WORLD STILL UNUNITED**. *The proclamation of the* **UNION** *is the* **MESSAGE OF THE GOSPEL**." (Book #16, p. 19)

c) Gnostic scriptures

THE GOSPEL OF THOMAS (Book #12, p. 132)
"*Jesus said, Blessed are the solitary and elect, for you will find the kingdom. For you are from it,* **AND TO IT YOU WILL RETURN**."

d) Greek changes

9. ECCLESIOLOGY (Church, Israel)

a. Organization of the church

1) There is an upper class of the elect

a) Rejected truth

I Peter 5:2-3-- "*Feed the flock of God which is among YOU, taking the oversight (thereof), . . . neither as* **BEING LORDS OVER** *(God's) heritage, but being ensamples to the flock.*"

b) Gnostic doctrine

MANI-- "*Influenced by encratitic asceticism of the Aramaic Christians of Asia, Mani rejected marriage and the consumption of alcohol and meat, and he designated among his followers an* **UPPER CLASS OF THE ELECT WHO LIVED ACCORDING TO THE SERMON ON THE MOUNT**, *and a* **LOWER CLASS** *of auditors who were allowed to have wives or concubines and to practice birth control.*" (Book #2, p. 573)

VALENTINIANS-- *"There being thus **THREE KINDS OF SUBSTANCES** . . . **MATERIAL** that must of necessity perish . . . . ANIMAL . . . is a mean between the SPIRITUAL and the material . . . SPIRITUAL MEN . . . have attained to the perfect knowledge of God (Gnostics), and been initiated into these mysteries by Achamoth. And they represent themselves to be these persons. **ANIMAL MEN**, again, are instructed in animal things; such men . . . **HAVE NOT PERFECT KNOWLEDGE. WE OF THE CHURCH, THEY SAY, ARE THESE MEN**."* (Book #33, V.1, p. 324-325/ Irenaeus 'Against Heresies', 1.6.1-2)

(This teaching will be used to show that the Church is the 7-headed beast in Revelation 13:1 based on 7 churches of Revelation 1:20)

c) Gnostic scriptures

d) Greek changes

Acts 20:32 BYZ > KJV-- *"God, and to the word . . . which is able to build YOU up, and to give **YOU AN INHERITANCE** among all them which are sanctified."*
SBA > WH NU > NASV– *". . . and to give **THE INHERITANCE** . . ."*

Hebrews 13:21
BYZ > KJV-- *"working in **YOU** that which is well pleasing in his sight,"*
BYZ SA > WH NU > NASV NIV ESV-- *"doing in **US** . . ."*

I Peter 5:5
BYZ > KJV-- *"all of you **BE SUBJECT** one to another,"*
SBAC > WH NU > NASV NIV-- **omit 'be subject'**

II Peter 3:9
BYZ > KJV-- *"the Lord . . . is longsuffering to **US-WARD**, not willing that any should perish,"*
B> WH NU > NASV NIV ESV– *". . . towards **YOU** . . ."*

b. Works of the church

1) Don't pray, fast, or give alms

a) Rejected truth

Matthew 6:3-- *"But when thou doest alms, let not thy left hand know what thy right hand doeth:"*

Matthew 6:6-- *"But thou, when thou prayest, enter into thy closet, and when thou hast shut thy door, pray to thy Father which is in secret,"*

Matthew 6:17-- *"But thou, when thou fastest, anoint thine head, and wash thy face:"*

b) Gnostic doctrine

c) Gnostic scriptures

THE GOSPEL OF THOMAS
"*His disciples questioned him . . . Do you want us to **FAST**? How shall we **PRAY**? Shall we give alms? What diet shall we observe? Jesus said . . . do not do what you hate . . .*" (Book #12, p. 126-127)

"*Jesus said to them, If you **FAST**, you will give rise to sin for yourselves; and if you **PRAY**, you will be condemned; and if you give alms, you will do harm to your spirits.*"

d) Greek changes

Matthew 17:21
BYZ C > KJV (SV)-- "***HOWBEIT THIS KIND GOETH NOT OUT BUT BY PRAYER AND FASTING.***"
SB > WH NU > NIV ESV-- **omit**

Mark 9:29
BYZ SAC > KJV-- "*This kind can come forth by nothing, but by prayer **AND FASTING**.*"
CLEMENT) 85 > WH NU > NASV NIV ESV-- **omit 'and fasting'**

Mark 11:23
BYZ > KJV-- "*he shall have **WHATEVER HE SAITH**.*"
SS > WH NU) F41SV NIV-- **omit 'whatever he saith'**

Mark 13:33
BYZ S(AC) > KJV-- "*Watch **AND PRAY**:*"
B > WH NU > NASV NIV ESV-- **omit 'and pray'**

Luke 22:44
BYZ > KJV; (WH) NU* NASV* NIV* - *AND BEING IN AN AGONY HE PRAYED MORE EARNESTLY: AND HIS SWEAT WAS AS IT WERE GREAT DROPS OF BLOOD FALLING DOWN TO THE GROUND*
SBA   -   **Omit**

Acts 10:30
BYZ A > KJV -- "*I was **FASTING** . . .*"
BSA > WH NU > NASV NIV   **omit**

Acts 16:16
BYZ > KJV-- "*as we went to **PRAYER***"
SBAC >WH NU > NASV NIV--"to **THE PLACE OF PRAYER**"

1 Corinthians 7:5
BYZ S > KJV– "*give yourselves to **FASTING AND** prayer*"
(CLEMENT)) ORIGEN > WH NU >NASV NIV -- omit "***FASTING AND***"

2) Don't witness to unbelievers or large crowds especially if you have sinned.

a) Rejected truth

Acts 2:41 – *"Then they that gladly received his word were baptized : and the same day there were added unto them about **THREE THOUSAND SOULS**."*

Acts 4:4 -- *"howbeit many of them which heard the word believed ; and the number of the men was about **FIVE THOUSAND**."*

b) Gnostic doctrine

c) Gnostic scriptures

THE SENTENCES OF SEXTUS (#12, pp. 506-507)
*"Do not speak with a godless person about God; if you are polluted on account of impure works, do not speak about God . . . **DO NOT SPEAK WITH A CROWD ABOUT GOD**."*

d) Greek changes

Matthew 8:18, 12:15
BYZ C > KJV–*"**GREAT MULTITUDES**"*
SB >WH NU > NASV NIV– "**a crowd**"

Matthew 14:14
BYZ C > KJV NIV *"And **JESUS** went forth, and saw a great multitude"*
SB > WH NU > NASV– **omit "JESUS"**

Mark 6:34
BYZ > KJV NIV– *"And **JESUS**, when he came out, saw much people"*
SB > WH NU > NASV– **omit "Jesus"**

c. Members of the Church

1) The Church consists of many pre-extant souls

a) Rejected truth

Matthew 7:13-14-- *"Enter ye in at the strait gate: for wide is the gate, and broad is the way, that leadeth to destruction, **AND MANY** there be which go in thereat : Because strait is the gate, and narrow is the way, which leadeth unto life, and **FEW THERE BE THAT FIND IT**."*

b) Gnostic doctrine

c) Gnostic scriptures

THE TRIPARTITE TRACTATE (Book #12, pp. 63-64)
"Not only did the Son exist from the beginning, but the Church too, existed from the beginning. . . . This is to say, it is the Church consisting of many __MEN__ that __EXISTED BEFORE THE AEONS__ . . ."

d) Greek changes

d. Worship of God by the church

1) You must observe the Sabbath

a) Rejected truth

Galatians 4:9-11-- *". . . how turn ye again to the weak and beggarly elements, whereunto ye desire again to be in bondage ? Ye observe days, and months, and times, and years. 11 I am afraid of you, lest I have bestowed upon you labour in vain."*

b) Gnostic doctrine

c) Gnostic scriptures

THE GOSPEL OF THOMAS (Book #12, p. 129)
"Jesus said, If you do not fast as regards the world, you will not find the kingdom. If you do not __OBSERVE THE SABBATH__ as a Sabbath, you will not see the father."

d) Greek changes

Romans 14:6
BYZ > KJV – "__AND HE THAT REGARDS NOT THE DAY, TO (THE) LORD REGARDS (IT) NOT__."
SBAC > WH NU > NASV NIV– __omit__

e. Ordinances of the church

1) The Eucharist is Jesus

a) Rejected truth

1 Corinthians 11:24 *"And when he had given thanks, he brake it, and said, Take, eat: this is my body, which is broken for you: __THIS DO IN REMEMBRANCE OF ME__."*

b) Gnostic doctrine

c) Gnostic scriptures

THE GOSPEL OF PHILIP (Book #12, p. 148)
"***THE EUCHARIST IS JESUS***. *For he is called in Syriac 'Pharisatha,' which is 'the one spread out,' for Jesus came to crucify the world.*"

d) Greek changes

Luke 22:19-20–
BYZ > KJV; NU* > NASV NIV--" . . . *This is my body which is given for you: this do **IN REMEMBRANCE OF ME. LIKEWISE ALSO THE CUP AFTER SUPPER, SAYING , THIS CUP IS THE NEW TESTAMENT IN MY BLOOD WHICH IS SHED FOR YOU***."
D > " . . . *This is my body which for you is given: this do.*"

1 Corinthians 11:24
BYZ > KJV– " . . . *Take, eat: this is my body, which **IS BROKEN** for you: . . .*"
ORIGEN > BSA > WH NU > NASV NIV– <u>omit "IS BROKEN"</u>

f. Place and headquarters of the true church and God's temple

1) Is in Alexandria, Egypt

a) Rejected truth

Acts 7:46-47– "*Howbeit the most High dwelleth **NOT** in temples made with hands; as saith the prophet, **HEAVEN IS MY THRONE**, and earth is my footstool: what house will ye build me? saith the Lord: or what is the place of my rest?*"

Acts 11:26–" . . . *And the disciples were called Christians first in Antioch.*"

b) Gnostic doctrine

c) Gnostic scriptures

ASCLEPIUS (Book #12, pp. 334-335)
"*Or are you ignorant, Asclepius, that **EGYPT IS THE IMAGE OF HEAVEN**? Moreover, it is the **DWELLING PLACE OF HEAVEN** and all the forces that are in heaven. If it is proper for us to speak the truth, **OUR LAND IS THE TEMPLE OF THE WORLD** . . . **EGYPT** lover of God, and **THE DWELLING PLACE OF THE GODS, SCHOOL OF RELIGION** . . .*"

d) Greek changes

Matthew 21:12–
BYZ C > KJV–"*And Jesus went into the temple **OF GOD**, . . .*"

ORIGEN > SB > WH NU > NASV NIV **omit "OF GOD"**

Luke 11:2–
BYZ > KJV–"... **OUR** Father **WHICH ART IN HEAVEN**, ..."
MARCION ORIGEN > SB > WH NU > NASV NIV "**Father**"

Revelation 16:17–
BYZ KJV–"... *and there came a great voice out of the temple* **OF HEAVEN**, ..."
A > WH NU > NASV NIV **omit "OF HEAVEN"**

Revelation 20:9–
BYZ KJV "... *and fire came down* **FROM GOD** *out of heaven, and devoured them.*"
BYZ A > WH NU > NASV NIV **omit "FROM GOD"**

10. ESCHATOLOGY (Future things)

a. Resurrection/rapture

I) There Is no bodily resurrection or rapture

a) Rejected truth

II Timothy 2:17-18--"... *of whom is Hymenaeus and Philetus; who concerning the truth have erred, saying that* **THE RESURRECTION IS PAST ALREADY**; *and overthrow the faith of some.*"

b) Gnostic doctrine

"*The conception of a resurrection of the body, of a further existence for the body after death,* **WAS UNATTAINABLE** *by almost all of the Gnostics.*" (Book #3, p. 157)

ORIGEN-- "*Origen regarded as credible neither the millenarian hope of Christ's return to this earth* **NOR THE EXPECTATION OF A LITERAL RESUSCITATION OF THIS BODY**." (Book #8, p. 78-79)

WESTCOTT
John 11:25-- "*The* **RESURRECTION** *is not a doctrine but a fact:* **NOT FUTURE BUT PRESENT**: *not multitudinous, but belonging to the unbroken continuity of each separate life...* **I AM--NOT I SHALL BE HEREAFTER--I AM**,..." (Book #16, p. 32)

I Peter I:3-- "(*by the resurrection of Jesus Christ from the dead) was by the faith in the Resurrection that mankind* **WAS ENABLED** *(past tense)* **TO RENEW ITS YOUTH**." (Book #16, p. 33)

c) Gnostic scriptures

*"This view, that the Christian's resurrection has already taken place as a spiritual reality, is advocated in **THE TREATISE ON THE RESURRECTION, THE EXEGESIS ON THE SOUL, and THE GOSPEL OF PHILIP**. . ."* (Book #12, p. 4)

GOSPEL OF PHILIP (Book #26, p. 340)
*"While, we exist in this world we. . . must **acquire resurrection** . . ."*

*"Those who say they will die first and then rise are in error. If they do not **FIRST RECEIVE THE RESURRECTION WHILE THEY LIVE**, when they die they will receive nothing."* (Book #12, p. 153)

THE TREATISE ON THE RESURRECTION (Book #10, p. 56)
*". . . it is more fitting to say that the world is an illusion, rather than the **RESURRECTION WHICH HAS COME INTO BEING** through our Lord the Saviour, Jesus Christ."*

THE TESTIMONY OF TRUTH (Book #12, p. 45I)
*"Do not expect, therefore, the **CARNAL RESURRECTION**, which is destruction, and they are not stripped of it (the flesh) who err in expecting a resurrection that is empty."*

d) Greek changes

Acts 24:15
BYZ > KJV-- *"that there shall be a resurrection **OF THE DEAD**, both of the just and unjust."*
SBA > WH NU > NASV NIV ESV– **omit 'of the dead'**

I Corinthians 15:55
BYZ AS > KJV-- *"**O GRAVE**, where is thy victory?"*
ORIGEN) BS) WH NU > NASV NIV ESV-- *"**O DEATH** . . ."*

Philippians 3:11
BYZ > KJV-- *"If by any means I might attain unto the resurrection **OF** the dead"*
55:.) WH NV.> NASV NIV ESV-- *". . . resurrection **FROM AMONG** the dead"*

II Timothy 2:18.
BYZ AC > KJV; (Nil) NASV NIV-- *"saying that **THE** resurrection is past already;"*
S > WH-- *"**A** resurrection . . ."*

Hebrews 10:34
BYZ > KJV-- *"knowing **IN** yourselves that ye have **IN HEAVEN** a better and an enduring substance."*
SA > L4H NV > NASV ESV–*"knowing to have **FOR** yourselves a better possession"*
NIV-- *"knowing to have yourselves a better possession"*

b. Second coming of Christ

1) Second coming is figurative and present, not literal and future

a) Rejected truth

11 Thessalonians 2:2-3-- "*. . . be not soon shaken in mind, or be troubled, . . . as that the **DAY OF CHRIST IS AT HAND**. Let no man deceive you by any means: . . . .*"

II Peter 3:3-4-- "*Knowing this first, that there shall come in the last days scoffers, walking after their own lusts and saying **WHERE IS THE PROMISE OF HIS COMING**?*"

Titus 2:13– "*Looking for the blessed hope, and the glorious appearing of the great God and our Saviour Jesus Christ;*"

Revelation 22:20-- "*Surely I come quickly.*"

b) Gnostic doctrine HORT

I Peter1:7-- (at the revelation of Jesus Christ) "*to show There is nothing in either this passage OR OTHERS ON THE SAME SUBJECT, apart from the **FIGURATIVE LANGUAGE OF** Thessalonians, to show that the revelation--here spoken of is to be **LIMITED TO A SUDDEN "PRETERNATURAL THEOPHANY. IT MAY BE A LONG AND VARYING PROCESS**, though ending in a climax.*" (Book #16, p. 17)

Revelation 1:8-- (I am the Alpha and Omega, the beginning and the ending, saith the Lord (God), which is, and which was, and which is to come, the Almighty) "*This verse must stand alone. **THE SPEAKER CANNOT BE OUR LORD**, when we consider 1:4,. . . and **ALL SCRIPTURAL ANALOGY IS AGAINST THE ATTRIBUTION OF 'THE LORD GOD' WITH OR WITHOUT 'ALMIGHTY' TO CHRIST**.*" (Book #16, p. 26)

WESTCOTT -- "*Westcott repeats similar errors concerning the Second Coming of the Lord Jesus Christ throughout his works. He refers the Second Coming to the coming of the Holy Spirit (. . . John 14:16. . .); He speaks of 'several comings of Christ' (I John 2:18 . . .); He refers to the expression, 'as often as Christ comes' (I John 2:18. . .) He says that 'He is still coming' in the 'flesh' (. . . I John 4:2 . . .); and he refers to a 'continuous **spiritual coming' of Christ** (. . . I John 5:6. . .).*" (Book #16, p. 34)

John 14:3 - (. . . I will come again, and receive you unto myself) "*But though the words refer to the last coming of Christ, the promise **MUST NOT BE LIMITED TO THAT ONE 'COMING'** which is the consummation of **ALL 'COMINGS'**. Nor again must it be confined to the 'coming' to the church on the day of Pentecost, or the 'coming' to the individual either at conversion or at death, though **THESE 'COMINGS' ARE INCLUDED IN THE THOUGHT**. Christ is in fact from the moment of His Resurrection **EVER COMING TO THE WORLD AND TO THE CHURCH, AND TO MEN** as the risen Lord (Comp. I.9). This thought is expressed by the use of the present I come as distinguished from the future I will come, as of one isolated future act. The 'coming' is regarded in its **CONTINUAL***

**PRESENT** . . . _Side by side with this **CONSTANT COMING**, . . ."_ (Book #16, p. 34)

c) Gnostic scriptures

d) Greek changes

Matthew 25:13
BYZ > KJV-- "_**WHEREIN THE SON OF MAN COMETH**_."
SBAC > WH NU) NASV NIV ESV-- **omit**

I Thessalonians 2:19
BYZ > KJV-- "_in the presence of our Lord Jesus **CHRIST** at His coming?_"
BYZ SBA > WH NU > NASV NIV ESV-- **omit "Christ"**

I Thessalonians 3:13
BYZ > KJV-- "_the coming of our Lord Jesus **CHRIST** with all His saints._"
BYZ SBA > WH NU > NASV NIV ESV-- **omit 'Christ'**

Revelation 1:8
BYZ KJV-- "_saith the **LORD**, which is, and which was, and which is to come, the Almighty._"
BYZ SAC > WH NU > NASV NIV ESV-- "_says the **LORD GOD** who is . . ._"

Revelation 11:17
BYZ > KJV-- "_**AND ART TO COME**;_ "
A > WH NU > NASV NIV-- **omit**

c. Heaven

1) Heaven is not a literal place, but is figurative

a) Rejected truth

b) Gnostic doctrine

WESTCOTT
John 1:18-- "_The 'bosom of the Father' (**LIKE HEAVEN) IS A STATE AND NOT A PLACE**._" (Book #16, p. 16)

John 3:13-- "_hath ascended up (gone up) to heaven . . . No man hath **RISEN INTO THE REGION OF ABSOLUTE AND ETERNAL TRUTH**, so as to look upon it **FACE TO FACE**, and in the possession of that knowledge declare it to men; . . ._" (Book #16, p. 16)

John 14:2-- (In my Father's house) "_. . . so it is to be conceived of the heavenly, so far as earthly figures can **SYMBOLIZE** that which is spiritual, . . . But it is impossible to define_ *further what is thus **SHADOWED OUT. HEAVEN** is where God is seen as our Father. We dare **NOT ADD ANY LOCAL LIMITATION**, even in thought, to this final conception.*" (Book #16, p. 46)

I Peter1:5-- (reserved in heaven) "It is hardly necessary to say that this WHOLE LOCAL LANGUAGE IS FIGURATIVE ONLY: . . . ." (Book #16, p. 16)

I John 3:3-- (And every one that hath this hope in Him) *"The practical conclusion from the great Christian **HOPE OF THE ASSIMILATION OF THE BELIEVER TO HIS LORD** is given as a coordinate thought."* (Book #16, p. 16)

c) Gnostic scriptures

d) Greek changes

Matthew 5:48
BYZ > KJV-- *"even as your Father **WHICH IS IN HEAVEN**"*
SB > WH NU > NASV NIV ESV-- *". . . your **HEAVENLY** Father"*

Matthew 16:2-3
BYZ > KJV; (WH) NU* NASV* NIV*--**"WHEN IT IS EVENING, YE SAY, IT WILL BE FAIR WEATHER: FOR THE SKY IS RED, AND IN THE MORNING, IT WILL BE FOUL WEATHER TO DAY: FOR THE SKY IS RED AND LOWRING. O YE HYPOCRITES, YE CAN DISCERN THE FACE OF THE SKY; BUT CAN YE NOT DISCERN THE SIGNS OF THE TIMES?"**
ORIGEN > SB-- <u>omit</u>

Matthew 23:9
BYZ > KJV NASV NIV-- *"**one is your Father, WHICH IS IN HEAVEN.** "*
 SB > WH NU-- *"one is your **HEAVENLY** Father"*

Mark 11:26
BYZ A > KJV (NASV)-- *"**BUT IF YE DO NOT FORGIVE, NEITHER WILL YOUR FATHER WHICH IS IN HEAVEN FORGIVE YOUR TRESPASSES**."*
SB > WH NU) NIV ESV ESV-- <u>omit</u>

Luke 11:2
BYZ AC > KJV-- *"**OUR Father WHICH ART IN HEAVEN,** ."*
MARCION ORIGEN > SB > WH NU > NASV NIV ESV-- <u>omit</u>

Luke 11:2
BYZ SAC .> KJV-- *"**THY WILL BE DONE, AS IN HEAVEN, SO IN EARTH.** ."*
MARCION ORIGEN > B > WH NU > NASV NIV ESV– <u>omit</u>

Luke 22:43

8Y2 > KJV; (WH) NU* NASV* NIV* ESV-- "*AND THERE APPEARED AN ANGEL UNTO HIM FROM HEAVEN, STRENGTHENING HIM.*"
SBA-- **omit**

Luke 24:51
BYZ SBA > KJV; (WH) NU* NIV ESV-- "*AND CARRIED UP INTO HEAVEN.*"
S > NASV-- **omit**

John 3:13
BYZ A > KJV-- "*no man hath ascended up to heaven, but he that came down from heaven, even the Son of man WHICH IS IN HEAVEN.*"
ORIGEN > SB > WH NU > NASV* NIV* ESV-- **omit 'which is in heaven'**

Hebrews 10:34
BYZ > KJV-- "*knowing in yourselves that ye have IN HEAVEN a better and an enduring substance. .*"
SA) WH NU) NASV NIV ESV– **omits 'in heaven'**

I John 5:7-8
BYZ > KJV-- "*For there are three that bear record IN HEAVEN, THE FATHER, THE WORD, AND THE HOLY GHOST: AND THESE THREE ARE ONE. AND THERE ARE THREE THAT BEAR WITNESS IN EARTH, the Spirit, and the water, and the blood: and these three agree in one.*"
CLEMENT) BYZ SBAC > WH Nil) NASV* NIV* ESV– "*three there are who bear record, the Spirit, and the water, and the blood.*"

Revelation 16:17
BYZ > KJV-- "*temple OF HEAVEN*"
A > WH NO) NASV NIV ESV-- **omit "of heaven"**

d. Hell

1) Hell is not a literal place but figurative, and is in fact a type of purgatory

a) Rejected truth

b) Gnostic doctrine

ORIGEN-- "*The place for the rejected is hell. There they experience the fire of judgment which Origen understood to be the individual's conscience tortured by the sense of its sinfulness. But this is a PURIFYING FIRE, and even the wicked, including the devil, will finally reach the intended goal, although it be only after infinite ages.*" (Book #7, p. 91)

HORT
Revelation 2:11 - (the second death) "*Then as to the order of promises, the SECOND DEATH stands between the Garden of Eden and the Manna. It might thus be EITHER THE*"

*DELUGE as Bishop Temple implies, called the second death in contrast to the expulsion from the Garden. It probably is a **COMBINATION OF THE DELUGE AND SODOM**, The Water-flood and the Fire-flood.*" (Book #16, p. 17)

c) Gnostic scriptures

d) Greek changes

Mark 9:44
BYZ A > KJV (NASV)-- "***WHERE THEIR WORM DIETH NOT, AND THE FIRE IS NOT QUENCHED.***"
SBC.> WH NU > NIV ESV-- **omit**

Mark 9:45
BYZ A > KJV-- "***INTO THE FIRE THAT NEVER SHALL BE QUENCHED:***"
BSC > WH NU .> NASV-- **omit**

e) Translation changes

NASV, NIV-- **change all references to 'hell' in the O.T. to either 'Sheol' or 'the grave.'**

2) There is no everlasting judgment

a) Rejected truth

b) Gnostic doctrine

HORT-- "*. . . the Epistles (are) almost free (as far as I can recollect) from allusions to **EVERLASTING TORMENTS** . . . And little as I like to rest on isolated texts, I cannot get over the words, As in Adam all die, even so in Christ shall all be made alive. St. Paul cannot mean merely the universal redemption, for he uses the future tense . . . and is, moreover, speaking of the resurrection; further, the same universality is given to the one clause as to the other . . . . Nor did I see how to dissent from the equally common Universalist objection, that **FINITE SINS CANNOT DESERVE AN INFINITE PUNISHMENT**.*" (Book #10, Vol.1, p. 117-118)

"*I agree with you in thinking it a pity that Maurice verbally repudiates purgatory, but I fully and unwaveringly agree with him in the 3 cardinal points of the controversy; 1) that eternity is independent of duration; 2) **THAT THE POWER OF REPENTANCE IS NOT LIMITED TO THIS LIFE**; 3) that it is not revealed whether or not all will ultimately repent.*" Book #10, Vol.1, p. 275)

"*. . . Purgatory is not a word that I should myself adopt, because it is associated with Roman theories about the future state for which I see no foundation. But the idea of purgation, of cleansing as by fire, seems to me inseparable from what the Bible teaches us of the Divine* *chastisements; and though little is directly said **RESPECTING THE FUTURE STATE, IT SEEMS TO ME INCREDIBLE THAT THE DIVINE CHASTISEMENTS SHOULD IN THIS RESPECT CHANGE THEIR CHARACTER WHEN THIS VISIBLE LIFE IS ENDED**.*" (Book #10, Vol. 2, p. 336)

c) Gnostic scriptures

d) Greek changes

e. New heavens and earth

1) Will come about when a portion of mankind has redeemed itself

a) Rejected truth

Revelation 12:3-4,9-- "*And there appeared another wonder in heaven; and behold a great red dragon, having seven heads and ten horns, and seven crowns upon his heads. And his tail drew the **THIRD PART** of the stars of heaven, and did cast them to the earth: And the great dragon was cast out, that old serpent, called the Devil, and Satan, which deceiveth the whole world: he was cast out into the earth, **AND HIS ANGELS WERE CAST OUT WITH HIM**.*"

b) Gnostic doctrine

"*When the entire **THIRD SONSHIP** has redeemed itself, God will take pity on the world, and he will allow the descent of 'the great unconsciousness' upon the rest of mankind. Thereafter no one will have even an inkling that there was ever anything like the Spirit.*" (Book #3, p. 571)

c) Gnostic scriptures

d) Greek changes

2) There will be a godless and classless society.

a) Rejected truth

Revelation 21:1, 3-- "*And I saw a new heaven and a new earth: for the first heaven and the first earth were passed away . . . And I heard a great voice out of heaven saying, Behold, the tabernacle of **GOD** is with men, and **HE WILL DWELL WITH THEM**, and they shall be His people, and **GOD HIMSELF SHALL BE WITH THEM** and be their God.*"

Revelation 22:3-- "*And there shall be no more curse: but the throne **OF GOD** and of the Lamb shall be in it; and His servants shall serve Him:*"

b) Gnostic doctrine "*BASILIDES foresees a godless and classless society.*" (Book #3, p. 571)

c) Gnostic scriptures

d) Greek changes

SECTION III

Index Of Words, Phrases, And Scriptures

Bibliography

1. Besant, Annie: ESOTERIC CHRISTIANITY The Theosophical Publishing House, 1901

2. ENCYCLOPEDIA OF RELIGION: Gnosticism

3. ENCYCLOPEDIA BRITTANICA: Gnosticism (by Tullock) 1910

4. Gromacki, Robert G: TRANSLATIONS ON TRIAL: IS YOUR BIBLE THE WORD OF GOD? What We Believe (Cedarville College)

5. Waite, Revelation D. A: DEFENDING THE KING JAMES BIBLE, Bible For Today, 1992

6. Pike, Albert: MORALS AND DOGMA OF THE ANCIENT AND ACCEPTED SCOTTISH RITE OF FREEMASONRY, Jenkins, L. H., Inc. f 1871

7. Neve, J. L: A HISTORY OF CHRISTIAN THOUGHT, Vol.1 Muhlenberg Press,

8. Chadwick, Henry: EARLY CHRISTIAN THOUGHT AND THE CLASSICAL TRADITION Oxford University Press, 1966

9. Lightfoot, J.8: THE APOSTOLIC FATHERS Baker Books, 1989

10. Hort, Arthur Fenton: LIFE AND LETTER& OF FENTON JOHN ANTHONY HORT MacMillan and Co. Ltd, 1.896

11. Scrivener, George H: PHILIP SCHAFF', CHRISTIAN SCHOLAR AND ECUMENICAL PROPHET Mercer Press (Ecumenical publication)

12. Robinson, James M: THE NAG HAMMADI LIBRARY Harper Collins, 1978

13. Richardson, Jabez, THE GREAT MESSAGE The Great School of Natural Science, 1927

14. Nichols, James Hastings: ROMANTICISM IN AMERICAN THEOLOGY - Nevin and Schaff at Mercersberg, The University of Chicago Press, 1961

15. Mead, G. R. S: FRAGMENTS OF A FAITH FORGOTTEN University Books, Inc.

16. Waite, D. A: HERESIES OF WESTCOTT AND HORT The Bible for Today, Inc., 1979
Printed by Plains Baptist Challenger Lubbock, Texas

17. Richardson, J. E. RICHARDSON'S MONITOR OF FREE-MASONRY Barnes & Noble Books, 1993

18. Funk, Hoover and The Jesus Seminar: THE FIVE GOSPELS MacMillan Pub. Co., 1993

19. Penzel, Klaus: PHILIP SCHAFF - Historian and Ambassador of the Universal Church Mercer Press, 1991

20. Jonas, Hans: THE GNOSTIC RELIGION Beacon Press, 1958

21. Origen: ON FIRST PRINCIPLES Peter Smith, 1973

22. Barnstone, Willis: THE OTHER BIBLE Harper Collins, 1984,

23. Westcott, Arthur: LIFE AND 'LETTER OF 'BROOKE FOSS WESTCOTT Macmillan and Co., Limited, 1903

24. Newberry, Thomas: THE ENGLISHMANS GREEK NEW TESTAMENT Zondervan Publishing House, 1970

25. Kingsland, William: AN ANTHOLOGY OF MYSTICISM AND MYSTICAL PHILOSOPHY Methuen and Co., Ltd., 1927

26. Layton, Bentley: THE GNOSTIC SCRIPTURES (Ancient Wisdom for the New Age) Doubleday, 1987

27. Miller, Robert Jr THE COMPLETE-GOSPELS Harper Collins, 1992

28, Filoramo,- Giovanni: A-HISTORY OF GNOSTICISM Blackwell, 1990-

29. Prophet, Elizabeth Clare: FORBIDDEN MYSTERIES OF ENOCH Summit University Press, 1983

30. Vermes, Geza: THE DEAD SEA SCROLLS IN ENGLISH JSOT (Sheffield Academic Press, Ltd.), 1962

31. Marrs, Texe: DARK SECRETS OF THE NEW AGE Crossway Books, 1987

32. Pink, Arthur: THE SOVEREIGNTY OF GOD The Banner of Truth Trust, 1928

33. Roberts, Alexander and Donaldson, James: ANTE-NICEAN FATHERS Hendrickson Publishers, 1994

34. Riplinger, G. A. NEW AGE BIBLE VERSIONS A.V.,Publications, 1993

35. Bauer, Walter: ORTHODOXY AND HERESY IN EARLIEST CHRISTIANITY Fortress Press, 1971

About the Editor

The editor of this book, Dr. D. A. Waite, received a B.A. (Bachelor of Arts) in classical Greek and Latin from the University of Michigan in 1948, a Th.M. (Master of Theology), with high honors, in New Testament Greek Literature and Exegesis from Dallas Theological Seminary in 1952, an M.A. (Master of Arts) in Speech from Southern Methodist University in 1953, a Th.D. (Doctor of Theology), with honors, in Bible Exposition from Dallas Theological Seminary in 1955, and a Ph.D. in Speech from Purdue University in 1961. He holds both New Jersey and Pennsylvania teacher certificates in Greek and Language Arts.

He has been a teacher in the areas of Greek, Hebrew, Bible, Speech, and English for over thirty-five years in ten schools, including one junior high, one senior high, four Bible institutes, two colleges, two universities, and one seminary. He served his country as a Navy Chaplain for five years on active duty; pastored three churches; was Chairman and Director of the Radio and Audio-Film Commission of the American Council of Christian Churches; since 1969, has been Founder, President, and Director of THE BIBLE FOR TODAY; since 1978, has been President of the DEAN BURGON SOCIETY; has produced over 800 other studies, books, audio cassettes, CD's, VCR's, or DVD's on various topics; and is heard on a thirty-minute weekly program, IN DEFENSE OF TRADITIONAL BIBLE TEXTS, on radio, and streaming on the Internet at <u>BibleForToday.org</u>, 24/7/365.

Dr. and Mrs. Waite have been married since 1948; they have four sons, one daughter, and, at present, eight grand-children, and eleven great-grandchildren. Since October 4, 1998, he has been the Pastor of the Bible For Today Baptist Church in Collingswood, New Jersey.

Order Blank (p. 1)

Name:_____

Address:_____

City & State:_____Zip:_____

Credit Card #:_____Expires:_____

Latest Books

[ ] Send *Gnosticism: The Doctrinal Foundation of the New Bible Versions* (213 pp. Perfect Bound ($20.00 + $8.00 S&H)

[ ] Send *Biblical Separation* By Dr. D. A. Waite (132 pp., Perfect Bound $14.00 + $7.00 S&H)

[ ] Send *Modern Version Failures* By Charles Kriessman (152 pp., Perfect bound $14.00 + $7.00 S&H)

[ ] Send *The Sixth 200 Questions Answered* By Dr. D. A. Waite (188 pp. perfect bound $15.00 + $7.00 S&H)

[ ] Send *The Fifth 200 Questions Answered* By Dr. D. A. Waite (150 pp. perfect bound $15.00 + $7.00 S&H)

[ ] Send *The Fourth 200 Questions Answered* By Dr. D. A. Waite (168 pp. perfect bound $15.00 + $7.00 S&H)

[ ] Send *The Third 200 Questions Answered* By Dr. D. A. Waite (180 pp. perfect bound $15.00 + $7.00 S&H)

[ ] Send *The Second 200 Questions Answered* By Dr. D. A. Waite (178 pp. perfect bound $15.00 + $7.00 S&H)

[ ] Send *The First 200 Questions Answered By Dr. D. A. Waite* (184 pp. perfect bound $12.00 + $7.00 S&H)

[ ] Send *A Critical Answer to James Price's King James Only-ism* By Pastor D. A. Waite, 184pp, perfect bound ($11+$7 S&H)

[ ] Send *The KJB's Superior Hebrew & Greek Words* by Pastor D. A. Waite, 104 pp., perfect bound ($10+$7 S&H)

[ ] Send *Soulwinning's Versions-Perversions* by Pastor D. A. Waite, booklet, 28 pp. ($6+$5 S&H) fully indexed

[ ] Send *2 Timothy--Preaching Verse by Verse*, by Pastor D. A. Waite, 250 pages, perfect bound ($11+$7 S&H) fully indexed.

[ ] Send *A Critical Answer to God's Word Preserved* by Pastor D. A. Waite, 192 pp. perfect bound ($11.00+$7.00 S&H)

[ ] Send *Daily Bible Blessings* By Yvonne Waite ($20.00+$8 S&H

[ ] Send *Revelation–Preaching Verse By Verse* By Dr. D. A. Waite ($50+$10 S&H--1030 pages.

Send or Call Orders to:
THE BIBLE FOR TODAY
900 Park Ave., Collingswood, NJ 08108
Phone: 856-854-4452; FAX:--2464; Orders: 1-800 JOHN 10:9
E-Mail Orders: BFT@BibleForToday.org; Credit Cards OK

Order Blank (p. 2)

Name:_____

Address:_____

City & State:_____Zip:_____

Credit Card #:_____Expires:_____

[ ] Send *The Occult Connections of Gail Riplinger* by Dr. Phil
    Stringer ($12.00 + $7.00 S&H).

[ ] Send *A WARNING!! On Gail Riplinger's KJB & Multiple
    Inspiration HERESY*,133 pp. by Pastor DAW ($12+$7S&H)

[ ] Send *Who Is Gail Riplinger?* 146 pp. by Aleithia O'Brien
    ($12.00 + $7.00)

[ ] *The Messianic Claims Of Gail A. Riplinger*, By Dr. Phil
    Stringer, 108 pp., perfect bound ($12.00 + $7.00 S&H)

[ ] Send Husband-Loving Lessons, by Yvonne S. Waite; $25 +
    $7.00 S&H A very valuable marriage manual

[ ] Send *8,000 Differences Between Textus Receptus & Critical
    Text* by Dr.J.A. Moorman, 544 pp., hd.back ($20+$7 S&H)

[ ] *Early Manuscripts, Church Fathers, & the Authorized
    Version* by Dr. Jack Moorman, $20+$7 S&H. Hardback

[ ] Send *The LIE That Changed the Modern World* by Dr.
    H. D. Williams ($16+$7 S&H) Hardback book

[ ] Send *With Tears in My Heart* by Gertrude G. Sanborn.
    Hardback 414 pp. ($25+$7 S&H) 400 Christian Poems

Preaching Verse by Verse Books

[ ] Send *2 Timothy--Preaching Verse by Verse*, by Pastor D. A.
    Waite, 250 pages, hardback ($11+$7 S&H) fully indexed.

[ ] Send *1 Timothy--Preaching Verse by Verse*, by Pastor D.
    A.Waite, 288 pages, hardback ($14+$7 S&H) fully indexed.

More Preaching Verse by Verse Books

[ ] Send *Romans--Preaching Verse by Verse* by Pastor D. A.
    Waite 736 pp. Hardback ($25+$7 S&H) fully indexed

Send or Call Orders to:
THE BIBLE FOR TODAY
900 Park Ave., Collingswood, NJ 08108

Phone: 856-854-4452; FAX:--2464; Orders: 1-800 JOHN 10:9
E-Mail Orders: BFT@BibleForToday.org; Credit Cards OK

Order Blank (p. 7)

Name:_____

Address:_____

City & State:_____Zip:_____

Credit Card #:_____Expires:_____

Miscellaneous Authors (Continued)

[ ] Send *Why Not the King James Bible?--An Answer to James White's KJVO Book* by Dr. K. D. DiVietro, $10+$7 S&H

[ ] Send Brochure #1: "Over *1000 Titles Defending the KJB/TR*" Compiled by Dr. D. A. Waite. No Charge

Send or Call Orders to:
THE BIBLE FOR TODAY
900 Park Ave., Collingswood, NJ 08108
Phone: 856-854-4452; FAX:--2464; Orders: 1-800 JOHN 10:9
E-Mail Orders: BFT@BibleForToday.org; Credit Cards OK

**Pastor D. A. Waite, Th.D., Ph.D., Director
The Bible For Today, Incorporated
Editor**

This study was made by Mrs. Janet Moser who lived in Southfield, Michigan, who has passed on to her reward in Heaven. She was first introduced to the truths about the superiority of the King James Bible and the Masoretic Hebrew, Aramaic, and Greek Textus Receptus that underlies it by listening to this writer on a radio broadcast. The program was hosted by Miss Barbara Egan. It was called "LET'S GO VISITING." Barbara interviewed me on that broadcast about my book, *DEFENDING THE KING JAMES BIBLE*. Upon hearing the broadcast, Mrs. Moser contacted me. Later on, she came fr a visit with her husband and another couple to the home of Mrs. Waite and me. They purchased many books and materials from our BIBLE FOR TODAY and returned to their home in Michigan.

When she began looking into the heresies of Westcott and Hort, she became interested in some of their views relating to Gnosticism. From this interest, she began a search which has resulted in this study. I persuaded her to let us have it as it is so that others might begin to see what she has found out through her intensive study. Because Mrs. Moser suffered from a severe allergic condition, she remained in a sympathetic environment such as her home. Her home was the best place for her to be. This allowed her the time to do research, to study, and to write. We admire such a person who fills her time with important spiritual pursuits.

I have added page numbers to her study and made a TABLE OF CONTENTS so that it might be easier to see all that is contained within it. I have also added an exhaustive INDEX OF WORDS, PHRASES, AND SCRIPTURES which will enable the reader easily to look up the many details about Gnosticism that are found in this book.

The author, Mrs. Janet Moser, is now with the Lord. I appreciate all the good research she had done in this book. It is hoped that many will profit greatly by it.

Sincerely for God's Words,
Pastor D. A. Waite, Th.D., Ph.D.
Director, THE BIBLE FOR TODAY, INC.

B.F.T. #2732   ISBN #978-1-56848-099-2

CPSIA information can be obtained
at www.ICGtesting.com
Printed in the USA
BVHW051543060222
628059BV00007B/133